# AKRON'S DAILY
# MIRACLE

Series on Ohio History and Culture

**Series on Ohio History and Culture**
  Kevin Kern, Editor

Kathleen Endres, *Akron's "Better Half": Women's Clubs and the Humanization of a City, 1825–1925*

Russ Musarra and Chuck Ayers, *Walks Around Akron: Rediscovering a City in Transition*

Heinz Poll, edited by Barbara Schubert, *A Time to Dance: The Life of Heinz Poll*

Mark D. Bowles, *Chains of Opportunity: The University of Akron and the Emergence of the Polymer Age, 1909–2007*

Russ Vernon, *West Point Market Cookbook*

Stan Purdum, *Pedaling to Lunch: Bike Rides and Bites in Northeastern Ohio*

Joyce Dyer, *Goosetown: Reconstructing an Akron Neighborhood*

Robert J. Roman, *Ohio State Football: The Forgotten Dawn*

Timothy H. H. Thoresen, *River, Reaper, Rail: Agriculture and Identity in Ohio's Mad River Valley, 1795–1885*

Brian G. Redmond, Bret J. Ruby, and Jarrod Burks, eds., *Encountering Hopewell in the Twenty-first Century, Ohio and Beyond. Volume 1: Monuments and Ceremony*

Brian G. Redmond, Bret J. Ruby, and Jarrod Burks, eds., *Encountering Hopewell in the Twenty-first Century, Ohio and Beyond. Volume 2: Settlements, Foodways, and Interaction*

Jen Hirt, *Hear Me Ohio*

Ray Greene, *Coach of a Different Color: One Man's Story of Breaking Barriers in Football*

Mark Auburn, editor, *Hail We Akron!: The Third Fifty Years of The University of Akron, 1970 to 2020*

Deb Van Tassel Warner and Stuart Warner, eds., *Akron's Daily Miracle: Reporting the News in the Rubber City*

Titles published since 2006.
For a complete listing of titles published in the series,
  go to www.uakron.edu/uapress

# AKRON'S DAILY
# MIRACLE

## Reporting the News in the Rubber City

*Edited by*

*Deb Van Tassel Warner and Stuart Warner*

The University of Akron Press
Akron, Ohio

ISBN: 978-1-629221-94-6 (paper)
ISBN: 978-1-629222-01-1 (ePDF)
ISBN:978-1-629222-02-8 (ePub)

A catalog record for this title is available from the Library of Congress.

∞The paper used in this publication meets the minimum requirements of ANSI/NISO
z39.48–1992 (Permanence of Paper).

Cover: Cover illustration by Chuck Ayers. Cover design by Amy Freels.

*Akron's Daily Miracle* was designed and typeset in Minion Pro with Myriad display by
Thea Ledendecker and Amy Freels and printed on sixty-pound white and bound by
Bookmasters of Ashland, Ohio.

*We dedicate this book to Dale and to all absent friends.*

# Contents

## The Competition

## Dealing with Change

# Acknowledgments

In addition to the 28 Akron journalists and former journalists who wrote chapters for this book, several former Beacon Journal staff members volunteered to copy edit and fact check. We are grateful for the editing assistance from Carla Davis, Kathy Fraze, John Greenman, Jim Kavanagh, Ann Sheldon Mezger, Roger Mezger, Charles Montague, Marcia Myers, Olga Reswow, Lynne Sherwin and Sarah Vradenburg. For believing in the worthiness of this project and supporting it without reservation, we also thank Director Jon Miller, Marketing Manager Julie Gammons, Editorial & Design Coordinator Amy Freels and Print Manufacturing & Digital Production Coordinator Thea Ledendecker of The University of Akron Press. We also want to thank the Special Collections staff at the Akron-Summit County Public Library for helping us locate photographs and Kim Anderson, executive assistant to the publisher at the Beacon Journal, for obtaining permission to use the photos. And finally, a thank you to Kendall Allen Rockwell for sharing Dale Allen's unpublished memoir with us.

*Deb Van Tassel Warner and Stuart Warner*

# Introduction

This book is not a history of media in Akron. It begins with the death of the heir to John S. and James L. Knight's newspaper empire and ends with the demise of Knight Ridder Newspapers, with a coda about how the Knight spirit lives on. In between is a collection of essays from those who produced the news in the Rubber City, written in the hope it will reinforce the value of excellent local journalism.

From the time we began work on this book, we lost four Beacon Journal newsroom leaders from the era memorialized on these pages: former Editor Dale Allen, former Managing Editor Larry Williams, former Editorial Page Editor David Cooper, and Bonnie Bolden, who was copy desk chief, features editor, and metro editor. The title comes from an essay in Dale's unpublished memoir. An excerpt:

> We called our newspaper "the daily miracle," and there was good reason for that description, even if some of our readers thought otherwise. They had other names for what we produced. Some used generic terms, such as "rag" or "yellow sheet" or "scandal sheet" or "lining for the bird cage." Others gave special names to papers serving their communities. In my hometown of Joplin, Mo., folks called the morning newspaper "the morning liar" and the evening paper "the evening apology." In Raleigh, N.C., readers called the News & Observer "the News & Disturber." In Cleveland, when readers wrote about their Plain Dealer they labeled it "the Pee Dee." In Kent, Ohio, The Record Courier became "the Wretched Courier." And in Akron folks had another name for the Beacon Journal: "The Leaking Urinal."
>
> But, in my view "daily miracle" still seems an apt description. Name another business in which a brand new product is put on the assembly line every day, pumped out during our peak years by the hundreds of thousands, then delivered to customers. And not just Monday through Friday, but every day of the week, 365 days a year. Even after witnessing

the miracle firsthand for 40-plus years, my mind still boggles at what we did, in part because of the myriad tasks required to put that newspaper on a subscriber's porch or in their newspaper box each day. And to do it for a minimal charge of 10 cents or a quarter a copy back a few years ago. Even with all the new technology we brought to the table in the latter years of the 20th century, the work to produce the daily newspaper remains a wonder to behold.

# Chapter 1

## The Death of the Heir to the Knight Empire

Mary Ethridge

John S. Knight has loomed large in my life from its beginning. Sometimes literally.

In my early childhood, I knew Mr. Knight as my dad's boss, a towering, reserved man whose visits to our home required my patent leather shoes and best manners.

As an adult, JSK's presence haunted me as I drove past the John S. Knight Convention Center to work as a reporter at the Beacon Journal years after both Mr. Knight and Dad had died.

At the paper, I'd meet with colleagues in the JSK room where larger-than-life photographs of the man peered over my shoulder, ordering me to, "Get the truth and print it!" Readers who objected to something I'd written would tell me, "John S. Knight would be rolling in his grave." After leaving the Beacon Journal, I did some freelance work for the John S. and James L. Knight Foundation. His life and legacy have surrounded me for decades.

But in December of 1975, together in a Boston hospital room, we were just two people linked by loss — an old man and a teenager stunned by violence and grief. This moment marked what I consider the "before" and "after" segments of my life, a clear line of demarcation between innocence and experience, the time between when life made sense and when it didn't.

Let me first go back to the "before." During Mr. Knight's visits to our home when I was young, he was often accompanied by his adult grandson, John S. Knight III, or "Johnny," who worked as an editorial writer at the Detroit Free Press under my dad's tutelage. Both my dad and I adored Johnny. Dashing, hip and as warm as his grandfather was reserved, Johnny charmed me completely. Although he was 14 years my senior, he'd break away from

John S. Knight (left) looks over the Beacon Journal in 1955 with Knight Newspapers executives Lee Hills (center) and Knight's brother, James. JSK was grooming his grandson, John S. Knight III, to take over the company until the younger Knight was murdered. (Beacon Journal file photo)

adult conversation to talk to me earnestly. His questions went well beyond the favorite-subject variety that adults usually pose to kids. We discussed the Vietnam War, music, saving the planet.

I can still see him sitting in my parents' living room, a vision of cool in hip huggers and platforms. When I told him I'd just started Spanish classes, he taught me how to roll the "r"s in *ferrocarril*. It means railroad, something I've never forgotten. And Johnny was ever one for showing affection through extravagant gestures. When I told him I was teaching myself to play Led Zeppelin on a plastic toy guitar, he whipped out $300 and told me to buy a real one. I did. A Yamaha FG 200. I used the leftover money to buy tickets to an Elton John concert at the Richfield Coliseum.

I've tried to remember the last time I saw Johnny, and I think it was likely at the party to celebrate the creation of Knight Ridder, Inc., in the summer of 1974. At the time, Knight Newspapers, Inc., had 16 daily newspapers in seven states, including papers in Detroit and Philadelphia as well as Akron. Ridder Publications, Inc., had 18 dailies in 10 states from the Midwest to the West Coast, plus The New York Journal of Commerce.

The merger was one of the most significant events in 20th-century American journalism. Together Knight Ridder had a circulation of more than eight million, making it the largest newspaper chain in the nation.

The celebration was held at my parents' house in West Akron. My father, Mark Ethridge Jr., was then executive editor and vice president of the Beacon Journal. It was a position he would abandon two years later, chased by tragedy.

My job at the party was to answer the door and welcome guests. They were a who's who of newspaper journalism and Akron society. Edwin J. "E.J." Thomas, chairman of the Goodyear Tire and Rubber Co., was there, along with Lee Hills, the first chairman of Knight Ridder. So were Beacon Journal lifestyle writers Betty Jaycox and Polly Paffilas. Former editor Ben Maidenburg came. So, of course, did Bernard, "Bernie" Ridder, head of Ridder Publications. He brought along his son, P. Anthony "Tony" Ridder, the man who would one day blow the whole thing up.

Spirits were upbeat. Everyone seemed well aware of the importance of the moment. My dad told me that if a bomb were to be dropped on our house that night, American journalism would never be the same.

That particular bomb never dropped, of course. But an entirely different sort did fall 17 months later.

In December of 1975, I was a junior at prep school in New Hampshire. I'd called my parents on a Sunday, giddy, to tell them a senior — a handsome boy from Houston named Arthur Seeligson III — had asked me to the winter formal. My dad answered the phone, which was unusual. He believed the phone should only be used for business or urgent matters. I heard him cover the mouthpiece and say to my mom, "Should we tell her?" My mom must have signaled yes, because the next thing out of his mouth rocked my world.

"I have some bad news," he said. "Johnny Knight was murdered." Completely freaked out, I just hung up on him.

I've never been one for public displays of emotion, but I stood up in the dorm phone booth, my legs shaking, and screamed. Really screamed. I can still I see my dorm mates running toward me and embracing me as I sobbed. I've gotten bad news several times since then, of course, but never have I reacted the way I did that day. At the time, the only person I'd ever known who'd died was my grandmother. This was some whole other horrible kind of thing.

I still have my teenage diaries. I wrote that day in the purple prose of a 16-year old: "Johnny Knight is dead. I loved him. I loved him. I loved him. I think of his smile and the long talks we had. I love you, John. I want you to know that, and when I play (guitar), I'll play for you."

We weren't allowed to watch television at my school, so I was spared the media coverage of the murder, but my father filled me in later that week.

At the time of the murder, Johnny was 30. He was special-projects editor of an afternoon tabloid, the Philadelphia Daily News. He had a $1,050-a-month apartment in Philadelphia's fashionable Rittenhouse Square, and he was the heir to the largest newspaper chain in the nation.

The details of the murder were titillating, and the media were all over it. Three men — addicts and hustlers Felix Melendez, Salvatore Soli and Steven Maleno — had talked Johnny into letting them into his apartment in the wee hours of Dec. 7, 1975. They intended to rob him for drug money. Melendez, known as a procurer of gay prostitutes, had apparently known Johnny from Philadelphia's underground gay scene.

Melendez, Soli and Maleno hog-tied Johnny and gagged him with his own neckties. Johnny had houseguests, an old college friend, Dr. John McKinnon and his wife, Rosemary. The scene was mayhem. The intruders brandished scuba spears, knives and a rifle, which, at one point, Rosemary McKinnon grabbed away from Maleno, according to her court testimony.

In the end, Melendez stabbed Johnny four times and hit him over the head with a blunt instrument. The McKinnons emerged relatively unharmed.

Maleno killed Melendez a few days later.

It was certainly a sensational story. The police found gay pornography in the apartment and reported Johnny had been a regular at the city's so-called "leather" gay bars. Johnny had never come out as gay or bisexual. He was almost always accompanied by a beautiful woman when I saw him. His gay lifestyle was certainly a shock to his grandfather.

When I asked Dad how JSK was taking it, he said he'd retreated to Boston's Massachusetts General Hospital, suffering from stress and grief. My dad asked me to visit Mr. Knight in the hospital. Boston was just an hour-long bus ride from my school. The bus for the city left campus every Wednesday and Saturday.

Part of me didn't want to go. Would I be welcome? What would I say to him? But part of me needed to share my grief, to offer comfort where I could and get some in return.

So I took the bus to Boston. I still remember what I was wearing — a green-and-white checked skirt, a green sweater and knee socks. It was cold and raining when I arrived at the hospital.

I was ushered into a room that looked more like a gracious living room than a hospital. It's where they put wealthy patrons. Heavy damask swags draped the windows, and the carpet was soft underfoot. Artwork in elaborate gold frames graced the walls. But there in the middle of the room was an old man wearing a robe, in bed, and looking especially thin, gray, bereft. John S. Knight had known his share of grief already. He'd lost two sons and two wives. He was tired.

I held his hands in mine, kissed his cheek and told him how very sorry I was and how much I loved Johnny.

"Do you know what they're saying about him?" he asked, on the verge of tears. "They're saying bad things about him. But he was a good boy. A good boy."

I assured him I believed Johnny was a good boy. I can't remember what else we said, but after a minute or two, he took his hands from mine and buried his face in them. "He was a good boy," he said between sobs. "Why did this happen? What am I going to do without him?"

I can't remember making my exit. The visit lasted less than 10 minutes, but I still think of it today. It was one of the hardest things I've ever done.

After the murder, my dad went back to work at the Beacon Journal with a heavy heart. He chafed under the blunt editorial hand of JSK. They butted heads continually. My dad wanted to apply sophisticated standards of noninvolvement to a paper that always been entwined with the community. JSK sometimes killed stories that found fault with prominent people or companies in town, over my father's objections. It vexed Dad. For his part, JSK felt my father wasn't listening to his advice or guidance.

My dad tried to hang on. He had been waiting for the day JSK would step down and let Johnny take over, but that hope was gone. He spiraled into a depression. My parents' marriage suffered under the pressure. And in July of 1976, Dad quit the Beacon Journal after three tumultuous years there. He quit my mother after 27 years of marriage. I felt he quit me. He moved south. I saw him only twice after that, the last time when he was dying of lung cancer in North Carolina in 1985. It took me years of therapy to understand and forgive.

In 2006, when my bosses at the Beacon Journal gathered the newsroom staff to tell us Knight Ridder was being dissolved and the papers sold, it felt personal to me. I'd been there at the beginning of the company in 1974, and felt its promise. I couldn't bear to watch its undoing. It felt too much like the breakup of my family years before.

The bosses handed out coffee mugs that read, "Knight Ridder 1974-2006" in funereal black lettering as a souvenir, which I found a ridiculous gesture. A coffee mug that looks like a tombstone? Really?

I loved being a reporter. It allowed me to have a career consistent with the values I learned from JSK, Johnny, my dad and others. I thought I'd work there until I died. But I took a voluntary layoff, leaving as the sale of the Beacon Journal was being finalized.

Oddly, I keep that pathetic coffee mug on my desk now to remind me I once worked for a journalism powerhouse in its heyday and that loss is part of life, no matter how much we wish it weren't.

# Who We Were

# Chapter 2
## A Mystical, Magical Place...

Regina Brett

Brigadoon.

For a time, the Beacon Journal was our Brigadoon.

It was a mystical, mythical, idyllic place that opened, and for a time, was magical.

Pure magic.

I started there in 1986 and left in 2000. It was the best place I ever worked at in my entire life. It gave me friendships for life and a best friend who introduced me to the love of my life.

Many of us spent the best years in journalism there, those magical years between Watergate and Twitter, as our colleague Bob Paynter once said. Together we committed journalism. We saw it as our sacred duty, not just our bread and butter. Back then, the management told us to ignore the business side of the newspaper and just focus on the story. Just get the story.

Back then, we didn't have customers, we had readers. We didn't write content, we wrote stories. We didn't care about clicks and comments or angry calls to the editor or the cancellation of subscriptions or whether some big business threatened to pull their ads. There was a solid, sacred wall between us and circulation/marketing/distribution and we were never to scale it. What a blessing that was. It gave us permission and freedom to take on any subject.

We never set out to get anyone, we simply set out to get the facts and tell them in the best way possible in words, photos and graphics. That solid wall between the newsroom and the business of news gave us the ability to tell powerful stories and to fulfill our greatest mission: To comfort the disturbed and to disturb the comfortable.

Most stories were generated from the bottom up. They came from the writers and reporters who knew their beats, not from editors sitting in glass offices. Knight Ridder editors were encouraged to trust the writers to find and generate the best stories. Those editors gave us free rein. When big news broke, we spontaneously gathered in the newsroom and brainstormed openly who would cover what, then we ran off to do our jobs. We didn't just go back to make calls from a cubicle. We hit the streets.

We were a Knight Ridder paper when it meant something. Actually, back then it meant everything. It meant a mid-sized paper in Akron, Ohio, could send reporters all over the world to cover the Cleveland Orchestra or the Olympics or a little girl falling down a well in Texas. The paper sent me to Northern Ireland to write about kids who came to Akron for the summer to escape the Troubles. It also sent me to El Salvador to write about a boy who lost his leg to a land mine who got a prosthetic leg at a hospital in Canton. The paper let me write magazine stories and I got to fly — not just fly in, but fly — The Goodyear Blimp.

It was the little paper that could, and did, cover big stories. We didn't have to talk about teamwork. No one needed to give us phony pep talks or incentives to work together. We were more than a team. We were a family. We worked well together because we cared deeply about each other and about telling the truth, and about giving people not just stories they wanted to read, but stories they *needed* to read.

Readers trusted us. They let us in their homes and hospital rooms hours after their kids were gunned down and trusted us to tell the world the truth about what happened.

The John S. Knight Room was like a chapel. His typewriter sat in a glass case and the walls around it were covered in his quotes. We were a Knight paper where great writing mattered. To see that steel instrument where he hammered out editorials made me appreciate the great foundation he laid for us all.

The Knight DNA in the Akron Beacon Journal made us feel invincible. On both triple homicides I covered and on the endless shootings I covered, I went door to door interviewing people where it happened without a clue as to who committed the crimes. I had no fear. That reporter's notebook and that First Amendment were my shield and my sword. I felt immortal, even the day some guy chased me off his property with a shotgun, the day a homeless man slugged the photographer next to me (Lew Stamp) and the day an angry mom nearly decked the reporter with me (Bob Hoiles). They were just more good stories to tell back in the newsroom.

If I had to pick one best memory, it was standing with my daughter — for whom most days were Take Your Daughter To Work Day — the day Firestone Tire and Rubber Co. announced it was relocating its headquarters from Akron to Chicago. The news to Akron was like Art Modell moving the Browns to Baltimore. Firestone was one of the pillars of Akron and CEO John Nevin had just kicked it down.

I was a single parent, so I ran home, picked up my daughter, brought her back to the newsroom where my colleagues fed her vending-machine food from the Blue Room until we all finished writing. There's nothing like seeing the truth fly by on wet newsprint and feeling the quake of the floor under your feet with your daughter standing next to you watching the presses roll.

We had the finest colleagues. Everyone raised the bar and set it so high, you wanted to be better. But it didn't feel competitive. There was a rare organic camaraderie. Everyone cheered for you when you hit one out of the ballpark. They weren't competitors; they were your cheerleaders. And your catalysts. They inspired you and rooted for you and made you better. Write a good story and you were greeted by a barrage of emails offering congratulations for a smart lead or boffo ending.

Bill O'Connor used his pen like a paintbrush. He was my first mentor, and he actually gave me his pen. That silver sword sits on my writing shelf with his initials on it. He always cautioned, "Don't set out to tell a great story. Just tell the story. Release it like Michelangelo released the figures from the marble."

Thrity Umrigar wrote pure poetry. Bob Hoiles taught me more than any reporting class ever did about how to cover crime stories. Steve Love made places and scenes come to life so clearly a blind person could see them. Stuart Warner was that rare editor who climbed into your skin when he edited your work so your voice still shaped every word, even the ones he added.

And the photo staff — what gems they all were. Ed Suba Jr., Robin Witek, Susan Kirkman, Paul Tople, all of them worked with you to tell the story. We were partners telling the same story. Back in the newsroom, I'd give them what I had written and they showed me what they shot and together we'd edit both the words and the photos to tell the best story. Our choices were never based on ego, just what was best for the story.

The Beacon Journal made me a journalist. I started in December of 1986 as a business reporter just six months out of college. Then I became a general assignment reporter, social services, magazine writer, region page writer (yes, I was stuck on that page, too). Then I became a columnist in 1994.

My start was rocky. In 1986 Goodyear Tire and Rubber Co. was in the midst of a takeover attempt and the paper needed a business writer to cover the nonessentials, which back then included health care. The interview went well until Editor Dale Allen and Managing Editor Larry Williams asked how I'd write a profile of Martin Marietta. I gave a detailed account of how I would gather background on Mr. Marietta. Dale cringed. Larry looked ready to deliver a kidney stone as he broke the news that Marietta was a major defense corporation.

They hired me anyway.

They didn't just hire me. I was a single parent with an 8-year-old, so in a way they hired her, too. She spent many hours in the newsroom. My co-workers taught her how to type and to make photocopies of her fingers, and bought her candy when she got tired of hearing the lie we all told our kids, "Just a few more minutes and we can leave."

They raised us both. They gave me advice when it was time to teach her to drive, allow her to date and send her off to college. They taught me how to string words together, to knock on the doors of grieving families, to get out of the way and let the story tell itself.

When my colleagues won Pulitzer Prizes for the Goodyear takeover attempt and the Question of Color race project, they were gracious enough to make all of us feel like we were part of it, too. We kept putting out the paper while they worked on the big story. We were The Little Paper That Could and did tackle and take down the giants.

Together we celebrated victories and made the bad times bearable. When I got cancer and announced it in a memo on the staff bulletin board, I was instantly wrapped in love, especially by Jim Carney. When I lost my hair to chemo, the first reporter to see me complimented me on my nice scalp.

I am forever grateful to the Beacon Journal and my colleagues for giving me my best years in journalism and to Dale Allen, who trusted me enough to make me a columnist.

There are so many magic moments and memories that we share. Here are a few that I treasure:

The S.O.B. Bake Sale, short for Save Our Beacon. After the Ridder family took over the parent corporation, we got nickel-and-dimed to increase the profit margin. The final straw came when we had to ask to get new notebooks. We held a mock bake sale smack in the middle of the newsroom to let management know how we felt, then we donated the money to a food bank.

We were tired of yet another upcoming "reorganization" and all the rumors of who was moving to which new beat, so one night after the mind-numbing routine of calling 825 cities asking every bored cop who answered, "Anything happen today?" Kim McMahon and I created The Rumor Control Board. We cut up an employee directory and posted every person's name under a push pin on a big map with fictitious beats. Every day people moved names around, even the editor.

We held tailgate parties on the parking deck, chili-cook offs on the copy desk and had our own baking contests with Olga Reswow winning every time.

A memo from the copy desk reminding us to list events in the order of Time, Date, Place sent a few of us over the edge. The Avengers (whose identities were revealed only after Managing Editor Jim Crutchfield summoned the entire newsroom into the Knight Room) sent out their own memo called TDP: Too Damn Petty with a few harsh words. (Yes, we did apologize to the copy desk cop, but I'll never toss out the scarlet letter A that I, Sheryl Harris and Kim McMahon wore to the meeting.)

We all suffered at least one near miss on the parking deck, which allowed traffic to go up and down in the same lanes. And who didn't encounter Fran Murphey slumped over in her car? I mistook her for dead. Nope, just napping. She also slept in the women's restroom. Yes, we had a couch. The lady under the newspapers was Fran, whose office looked like a newspaper recycling center.

Who can forget Craig Wilson's karate-chop sneezes or Pat Englehart setting the phone on fire while smoking at his desk? Yes, people used to smoke in the newsroom. And do a few other things. When a K-9 drug sniffing dog came to visit one day for a photo op, the dog made a bee line to a certain reporter's desk and was quickly shooed away.

The Blue Room was the closest we had to a cafeteria, full of vending machines offering non-food options and tables where we played euchre, edited each other's stories and griped about what rotten play they got.

When John Greenman decorated his office with a fancy stuffed chair, someone on the business desk brought in the tackiest chair he could find and propped it up under our giant blow-up dinosaur. That was back when HR ignored all the wind-up toys and irreverent cubicle art and art department décor that looked more fun than Pee Wee's playhouse.

Who can forget the smell of cherry tobacco wafting up the front staircase? The security guard's pipe was the sweet smell of home to me.

Every Election Day was a party with pizzas and mystery memos from past employees posted the next morning. The Annual Guild party skits got better every year along with the infamous reading of The Ann Hill Letter by Ted Schneider, who performed it in various costumes, including an orange mini-skirt, braids and lederhosen.

Cupid ran out of arrows, as couples abounded: Katie & Jim, Ann & Roger; Stuart & Debbie, Char & Art, Dave & Beth and Sheryl & Derf.

The Beacon Journal churned out authors: Andrea Louie. Terry Pluto. Bob Dyer. Thrity Umrigar. Stuart Warner. John Backderf. Steve Love. Dick Feagler. Mark Dawidziak. Chuck Klosterman. Kathy Fraze. Bill O'Connor. Michael Weinreb. Regina Brett. David Giffels. Roger Snell. Jane Snow. Many of us earned national and international acclaim, and we didn't have to leave Northeast Ohio to do it.

We were always proud of working in Akron, a quirky town full of quirky people, places and things, including being the birthplace of Alcoholics Anonymous, home to LeBron James, Cadillac Hill, the Akron Aeros, the Soap Box Derby, Skyway and Luigi's, whose phone number never leaves the memory: 330-253-2999.

In time, our Brigadoon slowly faded away. Barely a glimmer is left. Even the big rotating BJ sign that stood high atop 44 E. Exhange St. for decades is gone. And so is the newspaper as we knew and loved it.

That giant BJ on the clock tower used to make some people smirk, but it made us smile.

It was our Big Joy and remains so, if only in our memories.

# Chapter 3
## . . . And We Were All Pirates

Bill O'Connor

We were pretty much an average bunch of citizens, my colleagues and I. We were men and women, married and single, straight and gay, Black and white and all the shades in between. We mostly stayed out of trouble, went to church or synagogue, or ignored that aspect. An observer might decide, looking at our home lives, that we were nice folks, albeit mildly boring.

Ah, but there was more to us. One hell of a lot more. When we went to work, we didn't go to a job. We climbed onto a pirate ship. If that talented graphic artist Derf (a fellow pirate) were to put us into one of his novels, we'd have eye patches and a wooden leg here and there, and John S. Knight at the wheel with a parrot on his shoulder. When the pirate ship Akron Beacon Journal sailed into your port, the common folks cheered and the powerful started hiding files.

It's a fanciful conceit, but one not without substance. I know it to be true of everyone I worked with in that wonderful crazy house, the newsroom of the Akron Beacon Journal. There is so much of them in this sketch. This task is trying to tell you about 20 years among a band of men and women who filled the atmosphere with energy and intelligence, with laughter and sparring and, most of all, with the dedication of true believers.

When asked about his newspapers, Knight often echoed a Quaker phrase. "Our job," he said, "is to speak truth to power." I soon realized that was the guiding force in that newsroom, was in the very DNA of the place. Whatever your beat, tell it like it is. If you're writing straight news, your opinion is pollution. Even when opinion was allowed — columns or reviews — give your honest opinion, whether it pleases anyone or not.

At its peak, there were 187 of us in that newsroom. We could not know it then, but our pirate ship would soon become a ghost ship. The fully loaded newsroom has largely disappeared. Oh, The New York Times or The Washington Post have ample newsrooms, but they're not what I'm talking about. There was a time when smaller cities supported aggressive and fiercely independent newspapers. Their strength and influence have been sapped, and we all know why. News doesn't arrive on your doorstep. It slithers into your ear. Constantly.

There still is an Akron Beacon Journal, but it doesn't have the wealth of yesteryear. To survive, the Beacon has had to shapeshift. Much of the work — printing, some editing — is done elsewhere. The newsroom is barely a fifth of its size at its peak. But you know what? The idea, the DNA has not evaporated. Surprisingly often, the Beacon punches above its weight. I suspect that's a lot harder to do than once-upon-a-time. Time wears down mountains.

But there was a once-upon-a-time on our pirate ship. The story began — every day. The world was a ball of tangled wires, some of them live. You were too busy getting from day to day, so we unraveled it for you, best we could. We told our readers who wore a mask and robbed the convenience store, or who wore a suit and robbed your bank account. Our reporters covered five counties, and if you lived in Akron or Millersburg, we told you how much the school board paid for the new buses. If you were a local politician gorging at the taxpayers' table, or hustling a Ponzi scheme, the sound of the Beacon hitting your doorstep was not unlike the castanet of a rattlesnake.

If you dined at a restaurant or saw a movie or play, watched a TV show, or attended a symphony concert, you looked for critics like Jane Snow, Dick Shippy, David Bianculli, Mark Dawidziak, Don Rosenberg, Mark Faris or Elaine Guregian, and then a few of you set the record straight that he/she didn't know the first thing about that movie, play, TV show, concert. But Snow was right, the fries there were soggy. It was bad form to argue with food writer Snow. She carried a couple of James Beard awards in her holsters.

The newspaper won four Pulitzer Prizes, two while I was there. (I had a minor role in one.) What most stays with me, however, was not any prize. I cherish most how everything was a story. I never heard an editor ask a reporter how the article was going. "How's your story coming?" Stories are about people. Day after day, stories, real stories, were our heart and soul, the wind in our sails.

A newsroom before deadline is a storm of puzzle pieces and everyone is tossing a piece of the puzzle into the air, or snatching it out to see where it best fit. We writers sometimes preened. Our names were out there. But our role was just a part of the daily puzzle. A good newspaper, and we were damn good, is an ensemble effort.

I wrote for the paper and so am somewhat myopic about what I so often depended upon. The photographers hid out in a corner cave with the mysterious darkroom. They were a raucous clique. Ott Gangl, a blond bear of a man, had a contagious laugh. When I heard it, I started laughing, even though I had no idea what he was laughing at. A dozen or so of them, they were photojournalists, officially. They really were artists. Ott, Ed Suba Jr., Ted Walls — ah, so many I slight those not mentioned. They gave life, substance, to the paper. Once a year, the Beacon would publish each shooter's favorite photos from the past year. They could have hung in an art gallery.

The illustrator/artists had another hideaway. Again, I fail by omission in mentioning only a few. Susan Mango Curtis, Terence Oliver, Art Krummel, Kathy Hagedorn, Derf, Denny Balogh and others. The paper published a Sunday magazine. When Balogh did the art for a story of mine, it would win awards. For the art.

There were line drawers, layout people, who fit the puzzle pieces together. Tom Moore, a gentleman, wore a tie as he mapped. Ted Schneider, a pipe sticking out of his beard, would stare intently at his easel, then suddenly spring up and quickstep to the back shop, where the printers prowled.

Copy editors, eight or more of them, sat in a square horseshoe, the unflappable copy desk chief, Kathy Fraze in the center, Capt. Kirk in command. "(Don) Fermoyle, I put 'court case' in your file. Make it quick." Once, I was complaining those barbarians had mutilated my golden prose. Larry Froelich looked up from his work. "Yeah, yeah," he said. "We threw a rock through a Rembrandt. Go grab a cup of coffee. We're on deadline."

The copy desk saved us from looking silly or being sued. Year after year, it won the award among Knight Ridder newspapers for fewest mistakes. Our copy editors were better than those at the behemoths, such as The Philadelphia Inquirer. Copy editors wrote the headlines. Mickey Porter, as a copy editor, wrote a head for a Snow story about edible flowers. "If It Smells Good, Eat It." It soon was on college dormitory walls across the state.

Imagine the newsroom before deadline, all those different skills, competing for space in that daily puzzle. There were, every day, marvelous battles, with everybody scrambling, clawing, fighting. For what? Excellence. To tell it right, to show it right.

What I knew best is the writing and editing part of the puzzle. For the last third of my time, Bonnie Bolden was my editor. I wrote some good stuff, now and then, working with Bonnie. That's because she expected it to be good.

Tim Smith was my first editor. He had hired me. He and his assistant, Pat Englehart, were the two-cylinder engine running the planning, tracking down, and reporting local news.

Tim seemed almost always happy, and when he wasn't, when things weren't going well, he seemed perplexed that anyone would panic. Tim was so happy because he was metro editor, a job akin to the guy who pounds the wooden hammers for the rowers on a slave ship.

Tim was steady-as-she-goes. Pat spun through the newsroom, a Tasmanian devil flinging story ideas, sources, while roaring encouragement. He smoked those little De Nobili stogies, in the days we were allowed to poison ourselves at work. Once Pat, excited and on the phone, lost his cigar while hopping up and down. He had flung it into a waste basket and a few minutes later, as dozens of people tap-tapped the news into existence — whoosh! — a waste basket belched flames and ash.

He had been the driving force behind the Beacon's Pulitzer for coverage of the shootings at Kent State University. I saw a guy who got just as excited when he read a police report of a serious accident when one driver, cited for running a stop sign, said there was no stop sign. There was a stop sign, but it was the wrong height and partially obscured by a hedge. The readers, and the court, learned that because Pat handed the cop reporter a tape measure and offered gentle guidance. "Get the hell out there and measure the goddamn stop sign. And keep the tape with you in the future."

The first big story I worked on concerned negotiations between the tire companies and the United Rubber Workers union. I interviewed and wrote about the head negotiator for B.F. Goodrich. In those days, the union would deal first with one of the big three — Goodyear, Firestone, Goodrich. Once that one was settled, the others would pretty much make the same contract. The story came out on Sunday, page one. That was a big deal. Sunday circulation was about 220,000.

Monday morning Pat, who had not worked on the story, walked over to my desk. (No cubicles then.) He told me I made the company guy look like a stereotypical union negotiator. I took umbrage. I was still pouting at noon, deadline, for we were a P.M. paper then. Pat walked over again — loafers, slacks, white shirt, bow tie. His face was all eyebrows and sideburns and moustache, topped by two of the damnedest eyes you ever saw, the dancing lasers of a raving maniac, or a raving saint.

"We're getting together for lunch at the Printers' Club. Come on over." I had just received entrance to one of the magical places of my life. The Printers' Club was across the street, a narrow, windowless cave owned, indeed, by the printers' union. It had opened a month before I arrived. Printers tended bar on off days, and their wives cooked for the lunch menu. The favorite was mac and cheese. The place was packed for lunch. Mostly Beacon people — printers, delivery-truck drivers, bean counters, secretaries.

A round table opposite the door was the largest in the room. It was unofficially but unassailably reserved for reporters. Ten or so of us would squeeze in at the round table and eat our mac and cheese, or tomato soup and grilled-cheese sandwich, or mashed potatoes and meat loaf. Large pitchers of beer would pass among us and lunch might last two hours. And during all that time, we talked, about how to approach a complicated story, how to handle this or that judge, prosecutor. We couldn't stop.

The focal point of that table was Englehart. I could feel the respect they all had for this wild-eyed, gesturing man. In spite of his effusiveness, there was a strength, even a grace, about him, the aura of a man who gives everything he is for something bigger than himself. He swept them up in his enthusiasm, in the pure joy of finding and telling a good story. By the end of that first lunch, he had me.

I want to tell you about the writers of those stories. When you read these few examples, be advised that I am reaching into a bucket of jewels. Each one I take out glows, radiates the beauty of a true tale lovingly told. Yet the ones I had no time to retrieve are just as impressive. Jewels all of them.

Early in my time as a pirate, I was sent out to do stories some distance away. This was before cell phones, before portable or hand-held computers. If the story was for that day's paper, I would not have time to return to the newsroom and write it. I would find a public phone and call the rewrite desk, call Don Bandy or Jim Dettling, among others. I would feed them raw notes, in no particular order. By the time I'd return to the newsroom, Bandy or Dettling would have transformed those notes into a flowing narrative that told all, and more, than I had dictated. They had taken those raw notes and fashioned a story.

We had hot-shot columnists — Mickey Porter, Regina Brett, Carl Chancellor, Stuart Warner, Jewel Cardwell, Abe Zaidan, and more. Columnists tended to be prima donnas. Porter covered the cocktail party at the Firestone Country Club for the opening of the World Series of Golf, a tournament just a notch below the majors. All the big shots, golfers and money bags, were there. Porter wore coveralls with a company logo — Acme Gorilla Removal. Warner never needed an umbrella. His hat brim kept him dry. And, of course, there was the legendary Fran Murphey, who wore farmer overalls every day, as did many of the hundreds of admirers and big shots who showed up at the Akron Civic Theater for her retirement send-off. She had come on board during the Second World War and sailed for half a century, tossing the confetti of thousands of glimpses into how the common folk lived. Shortly after I arrived, she came over and took my picture. I asked her why. "Go to hell, O'Connor," she said. It was her way of welcoming me aboard. Nobody out prima-donnaed Frances B. Murphey.

Quiet, solid talent fashioned the stories in our newsroom, the little stories and the big ones. The NFL Hall of Fame induction in Canton was a big deal. Reporters and fans from around the country arrived to watch the ceremonies. The night before the official festivities, local people held a party on the streets where they lived. Who told their story? Jim Quinn did — Quinn a solid, often unheralded writer — unheralded because he did it all the time. "Ann Gordon of Canton sat on her porch and eyed the massive crowd milling about on her street. 'You know, it never rains on this night,' she said, shaking her head." Read it carefully, Quinn's story, and you get a sense of what Hall of Fame Day meant to the people who still would be there when the visitors left.

The Beacon was good at investigative pieces, following a trail doggedly until what was really going on was cornered. What surprised me, because I was not good at it, was how many reporters who had routine beats had another gear, instantly, when signed onto an investigative effort.

Certain reporters, though, were the master sleuths. None was better than Bob Paynter. He'd disappear from the newsroom for days, and when he turned in his stories, a Ponzi scheme was exposed, or we learned of obstacles deliberately placed in the paths of Black leaders taking the reins in a bigoted society, or labor shenanigans. Always, though, Bob and any team he headed told what was important about such matters — how it affected people.

He did a study of liquor stores and found they were heavily concentrated in poor neighborhoods, especially poor Black neighborhoods. He wrote a series of stories, titled "Cluster of Despair." He found eight liquor stores in one small area. Those were statistics. Bob's talent was to show what they meant. He told about John Leeks, who said by the time he was 13, he was getting drunk every weekend. "If children learn what they live, then the textbooks for John Leeks' youth were the street-corner ways of a shared pint in a brown paper bag."

Charlene Nevada was the most versatile reporter on our pirate ship. Over the years, she covered about every important beat — education, medicine, labor, politics — and did so at a consistently high level, did it all with the easy competence of the talented pro, and the mischievous delight of a kid. Covering politics, she entered the Ocasek building, a government office complex, and was sternly told she had to sign in every time she arrived. Day after day, she complied. She signed in as Minnie Mouse, Blondie Bumstead, Nancy Drew, Candy Kane, Becky Thatcher. Writing a column advising (and sometimes cautioning) shoppers, she told of the difficulty of finding a Christmas present for a teenage son. He wanted a lock-picking kit.

Sports writer Sheldon Ocker covered the Cleveland Cavaliers and all manner of professional and amateur sports. His longest span was covering the Cleveland Indians. Our sports writers never were in awe of the posing people they covered. A TV station tried to get the Indians to hire their guy, Bruce Drennan, to announce games. Sheldon wrote that "the desire of the station to foist Drennan on the Tribe" was "relying on impulse rather than thoughtful consideration and a voice that makes a chain saw seem soothing."

His coverage of the baseball team? You can check that out in Cooperstown, N.Y. That's where the Baseball Hall of Fame enshrines the great ones. After he retired, they invited Sheldon to join them.

Tom Melody held several positions in the sports department. I still admire his columns. His writing style reminded me of a wrought-iron fence. Delicately crafted iron. He covered just about every major sporting event — Super Bowls, World Series, major golf tournaments — everything.

At the end of his career, he wrote: "Curiously, though, all this seems to run together, a great modern painting of a sort. Collisions, calamities, champions and an occasional chump.... Sport is, after all, not much more than an exercise in trivial pursuit.... You can take it or leave it — and it doesn't matter."

He then told of his favorite column, how he went hunting for a column and ended up watching a footrace. They were boys in a Special Olympics preliminary. The racers toed the line, Tom wrote. The starting gun went off.

After a few steps, one kid fell down. "Then, as if grabbed by a great, unseen hand, they (all) go back to the child who had fallen. They dust him off and smooth his uniform, they pat his skinned knees, they look at one another, they smile and they're off again toward the finish line. The lump in my throat threatens to strangle me and I think...that this is what sport ought to be about."

I spent my first career studying literature. I spend my second watching its creation.

John Olesky, who wore several editing hats during a long career, runs a blog for former pirates. At the top is a list of those who have died. John S. Knight left us in 1981. His spirit never did. I look at that list and realize a part of each one of them is part of who I am. And each of them had a part of me. I understand now that my life, like our beloved newsroom, is a flying puzzle and now there are empty spaces to my puzzle, more and more of them.

Ah, but it was a magical once-upon-a-time, sailing on a pirate ship.

# The Stories We Had to Cover

Stuart Warner douses Managing Editor Larry Williams with champagne, delighting Assistant Managing Editor/Metro John Greenman, as Beacon Journal staffers celebrate winning a Pulitzer Prize in 1987 for coverage of the raid on Goodyear Tire and Rubber Co. (Beacon Journal file photo)

# Chapter 4

## 'A Bringer of Change' for Akron and the Newsroom

Stuart Warner

Change was on the way to the Beacon Journal and Akron in 1986.

On Sunday, March 30, Executive Editor Dale Allen headed south on I-77 to the Akron-Canton Airport on a summons to meet his boss, Knight Ridder Vice President Larry Jinks.

"A dozen possibilities passed through my brain, most of them making no sense at all," Dale wrote in his unpublished memoir. Was he being moved out of the newsroom? To another paper? Maybe they were going to fire him.

But there was one possibility he hadn't considered: He was offered the job as editor of the paper. Corporate had been unhappy with the bickering between Editor Paul Poorman and General Manager Jim Gels and was replacing both of them. Gels was shipped to the company's paper in Duluth, Minn., to replace publisher John McMillion. McMillion was coming to Akron as the paper's first publisher since Ben Maidenburg retired in 1975. Poorman was offered another job at the Beacon, but decided to resign. The job was Dale's if he wanted it. He did.

Tim Smith, who had been elevated to the managing editor's position by Poorman, also left to teach at Kent State University as Dale ascended to the top spot.

"When Smith and Poorman left, Dale was free to reframe the newsroom to take advantage of the people he'd hired and promoted and, as importantly, to reorient (or relieve) veterans from the Kent State coverage, who'd become smug and lacked intensity," recalled John Greenman, then the Beacon's executive news editor.

At his former paper, the Philadelphia Inquirer, Dale found just the right person to deliver that intensity.

Larry Williams was a rising star in Knight Ridder. His degree was in engineering, but his passion was journalism. He joined the Inquirer in 1971, advancing to business editor, where he supervised two Pulitzer Prize-winning projects, including the coverage of the near-disaster at the Three Mile Island nuclear plant.

Smith had supervised only metro news and the copy desk as managing editor. "Dale...delegated vast authority" to Larry, Greenman said. "Larry would not have come to Akron without it. Indeed, he turned down the job of Sunday Business Editor of the New York Times to come to the Beacon Journal."

I was the Beacon's local columnist, writing Warner's Corner, when Larry arrived. I was known mostly for wearing a hat and writing about Stowbillies, Kenmorons and empty storefronts in Akron's downtown. Not Larry's kind of journalism. And, oh, yes, I constantly took pokes at "Muffy" and "Buffy" and everyone else who lived in the affluent suburb of Hudson, where Larry and his family bought a rambling colonial-style home. Often, my Hudson humor was not appreciated by the village's newest resident. And more than once he killed a column with questionable taste, like the time a politician in Columbus proposed hiring prostitutes to tell people about the danger of AIDS. I innocently wondered how they would fill out a job application, including the question, "Position Desired?"

I had no idea at first of the impact Larry would have on me and all of us at the paper and, perhaps, on the city of Akron.

Within weeks after Larry joined the paper, British financier Sir James Goldsmith bought his first shares of stock in the Goodyear Tire and Rubber Co. This was a man who described himself as "a bringer of change." In Larry Williams, he met his match.

### The new ME takes charge

Larry Williams arrived in Akron that summer like a stumpy Mr. Rogers on speed. He changed into a rumpled blue cardigan after arriving at the office each day, his reading glasses defying gravity from their perch on his forehead. He motivated the newsroom by demanding hard work, Philadelphia-style. Good enough was never good enough. But his hard edges were softened by a gracious smile and an infectious cackle that reverberated around the third floor of 44 E. Exchange St.

The timing was auspicious. On Monday afternoon, Oct. 7, 1986, Business Editor Doug Oplinger noted a sharp rise in Goodyear's stock. Oplinger grew up in nearby Springfield Township and started with the Beacon Journal as a stringer in 1970, returning as a full-time reporter after completing graduate school at Northwestern University. He joined the business desk when it consisted of only three people and had been promoted to business editor just a few months before Larry was hired. Oplinger stayed at the paper for 46 years, retiring as managing editor in 2017.

His institutional knowledge told him something was up when the stock closed at a 15-year high of almost $37 at the end of the trading day.

"In Akron, just about everybody had a relationship with a tire company," Oplinger said in an interview with Bowling Green State University years later. "We were the Rubber Capital of the World. We had four major companies here and Goodyear, by far, was the largest employer. It was tens of thousands of people who had a direct connection to the company."

Oplinger assigned reporters Rick Reiff and Larry Pantages to write a brief story for the Tuesday paper about the uptick and the rumor that a New Jersey chemical company, GAF Corp., was making a play for Goodyear.

"The activity created enough concern at Goodyear for Chairman Robert E. Mercer to send a letter to all employees saying that the company is closely watching the stock market," they wrote.

There was reason for concern but it originated far from the Jersey shore.

On Friday, Oct. 17, someone purchased 2.1 million shares of Goodyear stock. By that time, the Beacon's business department was at full throttle, sometimes updating stories and changing headlines every few hours. Larry Williams became a driving force behind the coverage.

"The story could not have been made more appealing to Larry," Dale wrote in his unpublished memoir. "He understood the language of finance; terms I had read a few times but had not a clue what they meant. Arbitrageurs, junk bonds, leveraged buyouts — these were the things we read about that happened on Wall Street and other financial centers, but not in little old Akron, with its folksy title as the Rubber Capital of the World."

Dale noted that Larry found a willing partner in Oplinger, a fellow Eagle Scout. "Bringing Doug together with Larry Williams was like touching a match to a gentle mixture of kerosene and enthusiasm," Allen wrote. "It seemed Doug had been waiting his whole career to find someone to light his fuse, to provide him with clarity and purpose, even if he did not really need much of a kick-start."

Together, and with the help of editors like John Greenman and Deb Van Tassel from metro news and more than 50 staffers, they produced the kind of news coverage that you'd expect to find in the Wall Street Journal, not the Akron Beacon Journal.

"Larry was modeling the Philadelphia Inquirer's coverage of Three Mile Island," recalled Greenman, who later became publisher of Knight Ridder's paper in Columbus, Ga.

Thirty-nine reporters and eight photographers in Philadelphia worked on the coverage of the near-nuclear disaster "many for weeks, and most with no days off and little sleep during and beyond the first, weeklong crisis," recalled Michael Pakenham, associate editor of The Inquirer during TMI, writing 25 years later in the Baltimore Sun.

At the end, the Inquirer wrote a novella-length reconstruction, Greenman said. Many reporters contributed. Steve Lovelady wrote through their drafts, constructing and maintaining the narrative line. One editor, Larry Williams, supervised.

Seven years later, Williams brought that blueprint to Akron.

### Key characters in the takeover bid

The coverage ratcheted up after Oct. 25, when Goldsmith was identified as the potential buyer of Goodyear.

In addition to Goldsmith, Chairman and CEO Mercer, and the other usual suspects like Akron Mayor Tom Sawyer and Congressman John Seiberling, the grandson of Goodyear's founder, readers of the Beacon were introduced to these players:

- Steve Seigfried, a Goodyear Aerospace electrician who represented the worst of Akron's fears — he had already been laid off by three other companies. Now his latest job was in jeopardy.
- Jeffrey Berenson, a lead partner in Merrill Lynch's merger and acquisition group who was identified as the primary architect of the takeover bid.
- Donald Walsh, a vice president at Akron's Merrill Lynch brokerage who was feeling the heat from local residents for the corporate parent's role in fueling the takeover attempt.

- Rufus Johnson, the janitor at the Goodyear barbershop whose exhortation, "It's Rambo time, Mr. Mercer," became the company's anthem.
- Mark Blitstein, Goodyear's director of investor relations, the company's lead defender.

The business department had only three staffers when Dale Allen arrived in 1980. He had tripled the team by 1986, but they were still working around the clock to keep pace with the Goodyear story.

Pantages, Reiff and Greg Gardner were the primary writers, with Glenn Proctor, Katie Byard, Ron Shinn and others taking readers behind the scenes of board rooms, union halls and stock exchanges. The '80s had ushered in an era of Wall Street greed unseen since the Roaring Twenties, and all of Akron understood the awful implications of a successful raid on the city's largest employer. Goodyear assets would be sold off for a quick profit. Investment in research and development as well as corporate philanthropy likely would be reduced, even halted. Workers would be laid off. The only winners would be Goldsmith, investment bankers and large shareholders with no stake in the city's wellbeing. The losers would be the community at large.

Pantages remembers the day they scored a major coup: a phone interview with Goldsmith.

"The PR person we called almost every day, Lissa Perlman, had finally come through for us in setting that up. Maybe that was the interview where Goldsmith said, 'I am a potential bringer of change,' and we realized from his own lips what the threat to the city and the employees really was. I think he also clarified himself a little by adding something like, 'I say 'potential' because nothing's happened yet.'"

They rushed back to their desks to write the story for the final afternoon edition.

"When the papers came off the press, we grabbed a bundle and jumped in the car and drove to the Dubl Tyme restaurant right across the street from the [Goodyear] HQ. We wanted to give the papers away and get reaction from workers during their lunch break. Much to our chagrin, we went into the place (I think it was me and Greg Gardner; maybe Reiff, too) and there were like three people in there. Not what we were hoping for."

Business wasn't the only angle getting coverage. The government team went full bore, with Bill Hershey reporting from Washington, Mary Grace

Poidomani from Columbus and Charlene Nevada from City Hall. Meanwhile reporters Francisco Badillo, Don Bandy, Kathleen Byland, Mark Calvey, Bill Canterbury, Jim Carney, Patrick Cole, Mark Dawidziak, Jim Dettling, Bob Dyer, Diane Paparone Evans, John Funk, Peter Geiger, Laura Haferd, Robert Hoiles, John Kostrzewa, E.L. Langer, Steve Love, Marcia Myers, Terry Oblander, Bill Osinski, Yalinda Rhoden, Eric Sandstrom and Cristal Williams produced stories that showed the impact on the community. Stories like:

A church in Akron refusing to sell its 100 shares of Goodyear stock even though it needed $150,000 to buy a new roof.

High school students starting a stock-buying campaign and writing letters to Congress and to Merrill Lynch.

Joan Lukich, whose family had more than 200 years of combined service at Goodyear, wearing a sandwich board and walking the streets of Akron, urging citizens to buy the company's stock. "United We'll Stand, Divided We'll Fall," was her message.

Gaylon White, a Goodyear public relations executive, was reading every word. The former journalist was assigned to study media coverage of takeover attempts, both previous and present. He said the Beacon Journal's coverage of the financial angles was almost as sophisticated as that of the New York Times and the Wall Street Journal. "But no major newspaper had ever covered the impact on the community like the Beacon did.... You guys ought to win a Pulitzer," he told me back then.

White had other jobs, too. He was told by Corporate Communications Director William Newkirk to "be disruptive." Goodyear wanted the media to show the public that Goldsmith wasn't like us.

To that end, White enlisted a lot of help from Warner's Corner, feeding me stories about Goldsmith's lascivious lifestyle, Rufus Johnson's fighting words to Mercer and a little item that went 'round the world: The corporate raider had a distaste for anything rubber, especially rubber bands.

The guy is buying the world's largest tiremaker and he has a rubber phobia? My readers ate it up, especially after I published his New York address and urged them to send him gobs of rubber bands.

There is no way to know exactly what dissuaded Goldsmith. By mid-November, Mercer had confided to associates that Goldsmith had won, that there was nothing the company could do to prevent the takeover. Yet a few days later, after facing a raucous crowd of Goodyear workers at a congressional hearing and taking a tongue-lashing from Seiberling ("Who the hell are you?" he bellowed), Goldsmith walked away from the deal, selling back his stock to Goodyear for a $94 million profit — not bad for 10 weeks' work.

Years later, Denis Kelly, a former Merrill Lynch executive, told me he never understood why Goldsmith settled when victory was at hand. "He was not the sort of fellow to back down."

Then he paused as he recalled the events of those days.

"You know, he really did not like all those bags and bags of rubber bands showing up. That bothered him. He said, 'Why are they sending me all those rubber bands?'"

### Assembling a team for the wrap-up report

The Goodyear siege was over on Thursday, Nov. 20, though the fallout would be felt for years to come. The next day, Larry told me I would be the lead writer on a team that would produce a narrative reconstruction of what had just happened. I wasn't sure why he chose me, given our prior disagreements over my columns. Maybe Dale told him about some of the long-form stories I had written as religion writer. Perhaps it was because of the sources I had developed as a columnist. Regardless, I immediately began clipping and reading every relevant story since the day Goodyear opened its Airdock in September to kick off that year's United Way campaign. That weekend Larry and I met at the office and put together a detailed outline. Monday morning, Nov. 24, we went to work.

By Monday evening, I was, in sports parlance, choking. The task facing us then now seems impossible. Our goal was to fill an eight-page section with 15,000 to 20,000 words, much of it new reporting. And we had less than a week to finish. The section was scheduled to hit the newsstands on Sunday, Nov. 30, three days after Thanksgiving.

I was sensitive about my role on the project. The other reporters on the team were Melissa Johnson from the metro staff, Reiff and Pantages. Williams, Oplinger and Greenman were the editors.

There was also resentment among the other business writers who had been covering the story 24/7 for several weeks that I was on the team at all. And I admit, I had no idea how to spell or pronounce *arbitrageur* before I began the assignment. I thought a raider played for Oakland.

Maybe that is why I found myself struggling to find any words at all as I began to write the first chapter that Monday afternoon on my Commodore 64 in my home office. By midnight I still had nothing. By 2 a.m. Tuesday

I had deleted blocks and blocks of copy. The green screen was still blank. My wife, Deb Van Tassel, told me to go to bed, start again in the morning. I couldn't do that. I couldn't face the rest of them with empty pages. By 5 a.m. I was fading fast. Sometime between 5:30 and 6 a.m. I fell asleep on the couch next to my desk with not a word written.

After a brief nap I awoke re-energized at 7 a.m., and started writing again. By 9 a.m. I had a full draft of the first chapter. The solution had been simple. On Saturday, Sept. 13, 1986, Goodyear had opened its Airdock to the public for the first time in more than 50 years, according to news reports. More than 300,000 turned out to watch. Traffic was so bad that even a hero like Sen. John Glenn couldn't reach the site. I placed each of the main characters at that moment in time in the drama that would play out as The Goodyear War. The story began like this:

> The sun seemed to be shining on Akron as it had few times in recent history.
>
> At a few minutes past 11 a.m., the 600-ton front doors of the Goodyear Airdock began sliding apart ever so slowly.
>
> Hearts pounded as fast as the Akron's Symphony Orchestra's timpani drums rising to the first crescendo of the theme from "2001: A Space Odyssey."
>
> Men and women cried.
>
> It was a day to remember where you were.

I showered quickly, got to work by 9:30 a.m., and no one on the team had any idea that I had pulled an all-nighter.

From there, the rest of the narrative started to flow.

I went to work on chapters two and three, which introduced our two main characters, raider Goldsmith and Goodyear's Mercer.

As they continued to report, Reiff and Pantages worked on chapters four through six, which took us into this world of finance that most of us knew little about. Yet they made it understandable for the folks in Akron. An excerpt:

> As the Goodyear rumors were circulating, another takeover battle was ending that would dramatize the new power of corporate raiders and portend bad news for Goodyear.
>
> Campeau Corp., a Canadian real estate firm, was in the process of a successful hostile takeover of the much bigger Allied Stores chain. Campeau's revolutionary weapon was an equity contribution, some $1 billion from its investment banking firm, First Boston Corp. This was

a departure from the usual takeover, in which a raider relied primarily on borrowing (often 'junk bonds') to pay the costs of a tender offer for all or some of the target company's shares. The risk arbitrageurs, financial pros who invest in stocks of targeted companies, had to decide whether the potential reward of lining up with the raider offset the risk a deal would fall through.

Six months earlier, not many of us would have had a clue what that meant. Now it was dinner conversation in Akron.

Still, there seemed an insurmountable amount of work to finish by our Saturday night deadline.

Melissa Johnson continued to interview people in the community as I wrote. Pantages and Reiff scored an interview with Mercer, who recounted the most minute details of his lunch meeting with Goldsmith at the financier's New York townhouse like these:

Several bottles of wine were nearby in buckets.

Goldsmith offered some to Mercer. He declined. "I don't like to drink at noon," Mercer told Goldsmith.

"Would you care for some water?" Goldsmith asked.

"That would be helpful," Mercer said.

"Fizzy or otherwise," Goldsmith asked.

"Otherwise," Mercer replied.

Getting that kind of detail while still writing made for long days. We were working past midnight every day but by late Wednesday we realized we'd have to work through Thanksgiving Day, even if we already had plans.

"I remember walking into the newsroom at mid-morning on Thanksgiving Day to check on the story's progress," Allen recalled in his memoir. "The first person I saw was Larry Williams, his feet propped up on a desk in the middle of the newsroom, sound asleep, a file folder crammed with notes strewn across his lap. He had been at the paper throughout the previous night. For Larry, that was probably a very exciting way to spend Thanksgiving."

Larry did give us two hours off in the afternoon to have dinner with our families. I remember swallowing some turkey and mashed potatoes with my wife and our 2-year-old, who most people knew then as Baby Corner. Then I must have crashed for a nap. Once again I was refreshed and back in the office by 5 p.m.

We continued to write until 4 o'clock Friday morning, completing all 11 chapters, some 20,000 words.

All that was left when we returned at noon on Friday was the final edit. Piece of cake, I assumed, even though I hadn't had time for any cake or pie on the holiday. I was used to my copy sailing through the desk. How long could this take? Three or four more hours and we'd be done, I thought.

I'd never experienced the kind of deep dive into a story Larry put us through for the next 20 hours. He questioned every assertion, demanded more information for every clause. It was a clinic in professional editing.

But there were seven of us working on the final draft, and I know that when everyone tries to put his or her own footprint into the text it can spoil a good story, so I sat down at the editing terminal and refused to budge through revisions of the first few chapters. I also said something else that did not endear me to my colleagues. "The first three chapters (which I had written) are in really good shape. Why don't we speed things up by starting at chapter four?"

Uh, no. Larry was not about to skip over a single word. We started with page one, line one, and worked our way meticulously through the draft, six others talking while I typed in *most* of their suggestions.

As the hours passed that night into morning, we discovered that chapter eight, which I hadn't written, was based on a false premise and had to be totally revised. I finally relinquished my seat and sacked out on a nearby couch as the six others hashed through a couple of thousand words.

By chapter nine, I was ready to go again and managed to regain control. But as we approached the finish, I realized we had no ending. Writers struggle over their opening, but often forget the significance of a great finish. I had nothing. Was I going to face another writer's block?

Then one of my colleagues noted that Goldsmith had never been to Akron throughout the ordeal.

And there was our walk-off.

"Left behind was testimony to the enormous power of Goldsmith's brand of capitalism," we wrote. "He had terrified Akron without ever once setting foot in the city."

### Putting the story to bed

We finished the final draft at 8 a.m. on Saturday, Nov. 29. Then it was time for Executive News Editor Bruce Winges, Art Director Art Krummel, Assistant Managing Editor for News Colleen Murphy and their staffs to

Steve Seigfried, shown with his wife, Betty Lou, in November 1986, feared for his job at Goodyear Aerospace during the attempted takeover after losing positions at the Loral Corporation, Sun Rubber, General Tire, and Bearfoot Company. (Akron Beacon Journal/Susan Kirkman)

On Nov. 18, 1986, U.S. Rep. John Seiberling, grandson of Goodyear's cofounder, berated Sir James Goldsmith for criticizing the company while admitting he knew nothing about the tire industry, asking: " Who the hell are you?" (Akron Beacon Journal/Ed Suba, Jr.)

take over. Copy editor Mickey Porter combed over every word with Larry, struggling to stay awake, at his side.

They had already begun some preparation earlier in the week, but they had no idea how much clay they would have to mold until they arrived much earlier than usual that morning. Typically, Saturday nights are slow, most of the pages for the Sunday paper prepared in advance. But when Deb and I stopped by 44 E. Exchange St. that evening, it was as busy as an election night, with copy editors, page designers and artists, not to mention all the folks in the composing room, scurrying to make their 11 p.m. deadline.

The final product was simply outstanding. The layout of the eight-page section was clean, bold. The photos, surrounded by a gray border, jumped off the page. Artist Dennis Balogh's Page 1 illustration captured the turmoil of the previous 10 weeks. And the headline said it all: "The Goodyear War...Hard to tell the winner from the loser."

I guess our readers appreciated it, because we reprinted thousands of copies. We also sent copies to journalists around the country. Before the internet, that was the only way to promote your own work, and we thought others might take notice.

They did.

Dale was on the Pulitzer Prize jury in March 1987, one of dozens of journalists judging the best work of the previous year in the myriad categories. Dale was among the jurors judging the photography entries, but during a break for lunch he got some unexpected news.

"Seated next to me was an editor, whose name I have forgotten, who was a member of the jury charged with selecting the winner in the local general reporting category," Dale wrote in his memoir. "It was in that category that we had submitted our coverage of the attempted takeover of Goodyear by Sir James Goldsmith.

"I had never met the juror before but, when we made our introductions, he told me that our Goodyear coverage was among the best he had seen that morning. He said something like this: 'I haven't seen all of the entries yet, but the one you guys submitted was the best I've seen so far.' Then, he added something to the effect that he had never seen a story so well reported in all his years as a journalist."

The names of the finalists are supposed to be kept secret, but back then, someone was always leaking them and Dale had a heads-up that we were on the list. The top three entries in each category are then sent to the Pulitzer's board of directors, which selects the winner.

And when the prizes were announced on April 17, 1987, Dale already knew that outcome, courtesy of his and Larry's former boss, Philadelphia Inquirer Editor Gene Roberts.

I wish Dale had given me a hint because I was out speaking to a community group and missed the initial celebration. But since Publisher John McMillion wouldn't bend his policy of no alcohol in the newsroom, I was back in time when the champagne bottles were uncorked at the Cascade Holiday Inn that evening.

At first, the festivities seemed a little subdued; I thought it should be a little more like my days in sports, where the winning teams knew how to party. So I grabbed a bottle, popped the cork, and dumped the bubbly over Larry's head.

Many congratulatory telegrams followed. Robert Mercer wrote to Dale Allen: "The Beacon Journal saved Goodyear."

Maybe. Maybe not. Because of Goldsmith, Goodyear was never the same company again. To pay for Goldsmith's retreat, Goodyear had to sell off assets, including the company's jewel, Goodyear Aerospace Corp., and lay off workers. Within the next 10 years, it lost its crown as the world's biggest tiremaker to Bridgestone of Japan. Goldsmith had changed Akron forever.

Larry Williams brought change to the Beacon Journal newsroom as well. He remained at the paper for only three years before he was promoted to Knight Ridder's Washington bureau. He died at age 74 on Dec. 9, 2019. But his legacy lives on with those who worked with him, even though not all of us appreciated the impact he had at the time.

We remained at odds over my column so I never thanked him for the lessons learned that one long week reconstructing the takeover attempt. But when I returned to editing a few years later, I hope I was able to inject some of the same kind of passion and attention to detail into the writing of my reporters, who won two more Pulitzers and were finalists three other times.

Others had a similar experience.

"I remember telling Dale that Larry put me into therapy," John Greenman recalled about his daily story meetings with the managing editor.

"'But you became a strong assigning editor,'" Dale said.

"'True enough,'" Greenman replied.

# Chapter 5
## The Real Ernest Angley

Bob Dyer

I used to think he was merely a buffoon.

When I was in college, my buddies and I would gather around the television in the lounge of our dormitory and tune in his show to get some laughs.

We'd mock Ernest Angley and roll our eyes at the incredible naivete of his flock, the people who believed that this weird little man with the awful, jet-black wig could cure their ailments with a slap to the forehead.

Why, to hear him tell it, he was God's own hand-picked link to humankind.

We weren't the only ones laughing.

Comedian Robin Williams had a field day, mimicking Angley with a character named "Rev. Earnest Angry."

Williams' 1979 comedy album "Reality…What a Concept" featured an 8-minute bit in which he parodied Angley's style, absolutely nailing the preacher's weird movements and voice inflections.

Williams also spoofed Angley in his TV comedy series "Mork & Mindy," and fileted him in a 1986 "Saturday Night Live" monologue.

*"I can heeeeeal you!"*

*"No, you can't, because you have a dead animal on your head."*

In those days, it was hilarious.

But four decades later, I discovered that this bogus faith-healer was not just a buffoon. He was also, according to stories I was told by 21 former members of his congregation, downright evil.

Those interviews, conducted in the summer and fall of 2014, led to a six-part investigative series that became the talk of the town and was picked up by media organizations throughout the nation.

Part one began this way:

Depending whom you ask, one of two things is happening at the big Cuyahoga Falls church run by legendary television evangelist Ernest Angley:

- The devil himself has infiltrated the church, and Angley, who is a prophet of God, has been working tirelessly to fight him off.
- Angley's church is a dangerous cult where pregnant women are encouraged to have abortions, childless men are encouraged to have vasectomies and Angley — who preaches vehemently against the 'sin' of homosexuality — is himself a gay man who personally examines the genitals of the male parishioners before and after their surgeries. They also say he turns a blind eye to sexual abuse by other members of his church.

By the end of part six, it was almost impossible not to believe the second scenario.

Four years later, a two-part series about a man he allegedly sexually abused further cemented that notion. And one year after that, another two-part series put the final nail in Angley's reputational coffin.

The whole thing began in the summer of 2014 when I got a call from a stranger. She said her husband had made a recording of a Sunday service on July 13 that she figured would grab my attention.

She sent me the digital recording via email, but initially I couldn't open it. The software available to Beacon Journal staffers in 2014 wasn't exactly state of the art. For instance, the primary word processing program on most of our computers was Word 2000.

It took two more tries before she could come up with a format I could open. But the wait was certainly worth it.

The recording captured a 2½-hour church service during which Angley and two others addressed widespread rumors that an assistant pastor had resigned because Angley had sexually abused him.

Angley, then 93, stood at the pulpit in front of a large crowd and pleaded his case:

"I'm not a homosexual. God wouldn't use a homosexual like he uses me. He calls me his prophet, and indeed I am....

"They called Jesus a homosexual, did you know that? And still do. Because he was with men. Oh, Mary Magdalene and a few women. But you can't stop the people's lies."

Then he addressed his history of urging the males in his congregation to submit to vasectomies:

"I've helped so many of the boys down through the years," he said in his slow, singsong cadence.

"They had their misgivings. Sure, I'd have them uncover themselves, but I did not handle them at all.

"And I would tell them how [the procedure] would work. And they'd have to watch it. I'd have some of them come back to me that I felt needed to. And I would tell them, I would look at them, their privates...so I could tell how they were swelling.

"One young man, he decided to put in a garden [doctors advise against physical exertion after a vasectomy]. And he'd like to died. If he'd just told me — ask me....

"Another one was constipated. It was awful. And he was just dying deaths.

"And another one, one of his testicles fell out, absolutely fell out. 'It's dangerous, you should have a nurse.' But I knew they wouldn't get one....

"And some of these turned against me."

They certainly did. In droves. They believed the story that was circulating about Angley and the Rev. Brock Miller, a young man raised in the church from childhood, whom Angley had named an assistant minister at the age of 18.

Yes, 18. As if a virginal 18-year-old would be qualified to counsel middle-age couples about marital problems.

Miller quit the church after telling his family that Angley sexually abused him on and off for nine years.

Rumors had flown around town for decades that something was amiss at Grace Cathedral. I was told after the series was published that the Beacon had been approached at least twice about the situation but that no one at the newspaper was intrigued enough to dive into what would surely be a tough, time-consuming investigation that may or may not pan out.

The difference this time: I had a tape recording. Which meant I had a doorway into the story.

Taking a hiatus from my normal three-columns-per-week duties was a relatively easy sell with management. Editor Bruce Winges and Managing Editor Doug Oplinger agreed to clear the decks for me — for as long as it took.

Why? Because this was no everyday preacher. Angley was an internationally known figure, a cultural icon who traveled the globe on mission trips in his own Boeing 747, and a 60-year resident of Akron.

When he first arrived in town, the North Carolina native delivered his fire-and-brimstone presentations in a huge tent in the Ellet area. Soon he moved into an old theater on West Market Street and eventually into his own building on Canton Road in Springfield Township. Later he bought the 5,000-seat Cathedral of Tomorrow from Rex Humbard, renaming it Grace Cathedral.

The church always declined to release attendance figures, but during Angley's heyday the rambling parking lot in the shadow of the 494-foot tower commonly referred to as "Rex's Erection" was consistently jammed.

My series changed that.

The key to the credibility of the series, called Falling from Grace, was the huge percentage of sources who allowed me to use their names in print.

After a couple folks said they were willing to go on the record, I used their decision to persuade others to own their stories, too.

Giving up their names to the general public was no small issue, given the subject matter. One of the named women said she was forced into an abortion, and gave a detailed account. A man whose name I used said he had been sexually abused as a 13-year-old by an Angley associate, and claimed Angley turned a blind eye to it.

The most important interview was one I didn't expect to get: a 90-minute sit-down with Angley, in his office, accompanied by photographer Phil Masturzo.

Angley brought along Associate Pastor Chris Machemer and usher Mike Kish, both of whom kept jumping in, putting words in Angley's mouth. I was there to interview Angley, not them, but they figured he needed help.

He did. Angley said far too much for his own good, and I'm quite sure he regretted giving the interview almost as soon as we were out the door.

After that day, neither Angley nor any of his assistants would ever talk to the Beacon Journal again. During the writing of the series I wanted to confirm a few details and could not get a return call. Although the details were minor, and I was able to write around them, I wanted to do everything possible to make sure I had everything nailed down.

We figured a lawsuit was a real possibility — especially after we received a lengthy, threatening letter from Angley's attorney before we had published a single word. It was sent to the Beacon's outside lawyer, Karen Lefton, by William Chris, from the prominent Akron firm Roderick Linton Belfance. He wrote:

> Grace Cathedral is concerned that the articles will be slanted in such a way as to unfairly paint the church in an unfavorable light due to the reporter's perceived biases against the church and Reverend Angley.

Over the years, Mr. Dyer has written articles mocking Reverend Ernest Angley as a charlatan and has mockingly referred to Reverend Angley as "Ernie." He has also called the church's airplane "Big Bird." (See articles from 06/04/09 and 06/11/11.) Mr. Dyer has also sarcastically referred to Reverend Angley as "the Pride of Cuyahoga Falls" and the parish members of Grace Cathedral as "a vast army of little old ladies." We would hope that your newspaper and its reporter would avoid imposing its values on others and be fair in its reporting, before belittling the good people of the Grace Cathedral family.

Yes, I had had plenty of fun at Angley's expense. But those were opinion columns carrying my photo; these would be straight news stories that carried only a byline.

Still, we bent over backward to make sure we were bulletproof. Attorney Lefton read every line of every story and showed up with a slew of questions and suggested revisions, which were reviewed closely by Winges, Oplinger and me.

We had some fights. I won a lot of them and lost a few. In the end, I was completely satisfied with all six installments.

The second day of the series focused on allegations that Angley ignored reports of sexual abuse of young church members.

The third installment took a close look at the controversy over Miller, the associate pastor who quit.

Day four detailed how Angley tore apart families by ordering his parishioners to turn their backs on those who had departed, in many cases resulting in members shunning their own spouses or children.

Installment No. 5 featured ex-followers who questioned his use of the donations that were flooding in, such as Angley paying an estimated $26 million for a Boeing 747-SP, an aircraft so large it would not fit inside any hangar at its home field, Akron-Canton Airport. Angley used it only once or twice a year for overseas mission trips. The rest of the time it was parked out on the tarmac.

Some big donors who had left the church expressed buyer's remorse, including an Akron man who gave $80,000 over a five-year period.

"I was guilted into giving," he said. "It was brainwashing. I was manipulated." He was worn down by donation pitches from the pulpit that lasted more than an hour.

My final installment drew the attention of the U.S. Department of Labor.

After I reported that his workers were underpaid or unpaid, especially in the for-profit Cathedral Buffet restaurant, inside the main church building, the Labor Department investigated and in late 2015 sued Angley for $194,254 in back wages and an equal amount for damages, for a total of $388,508.

The suit alleged violations of minimum wage, overtime, record-keeping and child-labor laws involving 238 current and former employees.

Angley appealed, saying the employees were volunteering to do "God's work," but a judge upheld the ruling in 2017 and Angley shut down the buffet a few weeks later.

In 2018, however, the U.S. Sixth Circuit Court of Appeals reversed that ruling and sent the case back to the district court for potential further action. The three-judge panel disagreed with the district court's assertion that restaurant employees were "coerced" into working for free, making a distinction between "economic coercion" and "spiritual coercion."

The 2014 series was picked up by the Washington Post, USA Today, Forbes and many others, as well as international websites.

The first installment drew 413,000 page views on Ohio.com during the first week alone, and the entire series registered 654,478 views. That total would continue to climb as other websites linked to our stories.

Bob Dyer's detailed reporting revealed a darker side of the Rev. Ernest Angley. (Phil Masturzo/Akron Beacon Journal)

After the first two installments, Cleveland Scene, an alternative weekly that had taken a couple of potshots at me over the years, praised my effort.

"First off," wrote Eric Sandy, "Bob Dyer's 'Falling from Grace' series is quickly unfolding as a touchstone of Northeast Ohio journalism. His two-month investigation has pried open a sense of secrecy surrounding Angley's Grace Cathedral in Cuyahoga Falls."

My phone and email exploded.

Dozens of the folks who contacted me said they had experienced horrors similar to the ones I had documented.

The vast majority of my emails were complimentary. The nastiest responses were voicemails that were, of course, anonymous.

Two letters to the editor nicely illustrated the extremes.

A few days after the final chapter, Akron resident Sandy Zee wrote a letter headlined "Tormenting Angley."

> Bob Dyer should have stopped and thought before shredding a 60-year-old ministry. He will never know for sure if the handful of people coming out of the fellowship at Grace Cathedral are telling the truth or not.
>
> No one, not even the Pope, can force anyone to abort a baby or get a vasectomy. It sounds like these "witnesses" made some decisions they deeply regret and need someone to blame to find some measure of validation....
>
> The Beacon Journal is asking for fewer and fewer subscribers if Dyer continues this mockery of the church....
>
> The reverend is 93 years old. Does Dyer intend to torment him all the way to his eternal rest? He better stop and think.

A couple of weeks later, the editorial page printed a letter from Marty Wendall in Kent, who took a decidedly different tone:

> Kudos to Bob Dyer, who has courageously opened up a long overdue and painful investigation. He has broken the silence, which has far-reaching opportunities for healing and, I hope, justice for all....
>
> The victims who have been encouraged to step forth and bravely reveal their stories are also to be commended and greatly supported. They have been deeply wounded. They have been living in a state of darkness, great pain and confusion.
>
> Their voices, as they begin to heal, could possibly have a ripple effect, touching others who also need to break their silence....
>
> The trauma of sexual abuse and being seriously violated deserves not only a path and opportunity for healing, but a feeling that justice

will prevail. Justice for all means that the Rev. Ernest Angley and his associates who chose to follow his sick ways need to face the consequences of the serious harm they have inflicted on so many.

Dyer's investigation is a worthy first step in a process that needs to continue in our judicial system. For it is not Angley, his associates or Grace Cathedral that deserve an "amen." The grand "amen" goes to Dyer for his persistent and sensitive reporting.

Angley was no stranger to bad press.

In 1978, a 65-year-old heart patient collapsed at an Angley rally in North Carolina but an ambulance was not called for 15 minutes because an usher said, "Leave her alone. She is in the spirit." She died.

A year later, a man who came to Cuyahoga Falls from Chicago because he thought Angley could restore his sight was mugged and had to be hospitalized. Grace Cathedral did nothing to help. After a public outcry, Angley wrote a letter to the editor complaining about the verbal "attacks" on him.

In 1984, he was arrested in Munich, Germany, on charges of fraud and practicing medicine without a license.

In 2006, officials in Guyana blasted him for claiming he could cure AIDS.

Still, Angley had been virtually untouchable despite the ongoing whispers that something was amiss at Grace Cathedral.

As time passed, my series slowly faded from my consciousness — until late 2017, when I received an email from the previously unreachable Rev. Brock Miller.

On a January weekend in 2018, Angley's former assistant minister drove all the way from his home in South Carolina to Akron solely for an interview in a conference room at the newspaper.

"It took me these [four] years to heal and be ready to talk, but thank God I'm in a good place now," he said. "I need this closure. I want others to know the truth so that they can escape and find freedom as I have."

Miller said he had been sexually abused by Angley for nine years and that he left the church in 2014 because he just couldn't take it anymore. At least a dozen times, Miller said, his boss required him to disrobe and masturbate in front of him.

Miller said he grudgingly acceded because, having grown up in the church, he believed Angley was "the man of God" and wouldn't ask him to do something that wasn't right.

Starting in 2006, Miller said, Angley would summon him to his home for what he called a "special anointing," in which Miller would be required to strip and lie on a circular bed while Angley massaged him.

The stories he told were graphic, chilling and eminently believable.

Seven months later, Miller claimed the same things in the lawsuit he filed in Summit County Common Pleas Court against Angley and Grace Cathedral. Because of Angley's conduct and the church's failure to halt it, the lawsuit said, Miller suffered "severe and permanent injuries, great pain of body and mind, mental anguish and required psychological and medical treatment."

He was seeking "full back pay, benefits and reinstatement to a position [or] front pay," plus compensatory and punitive damages.

Angley countersued. As of this writing, no trial date had been set.

Then, at the dawn of 2019, I finally got indisputable confirmation that Angley had been sexually involved with a male employee. But it wasn't Miller.

A person I had never spoken with called and offered to let me hear a tape recording of a 1996 telephone conversation in which Angley admitted to his assistant minister at the time, the Rev. Bill Davis, that he had had sexual relations with a man who was employed by their church.

The source felt called to action after reading about the exchange of lawsuits between Angley and Miller and believed releasing the tape would show that Angley had a history of sexual abuse involving his employees a history that spanned more than two decades.

On the 23-year-old tape, Davis expressed anger over Angley telling someone that Davis' wife, Regina, made a "vulgar" comment. Word got back to her, and she was distraught.

> Davis: "There's been horrible discord here ... [while Angley was on a mission trip in Africa]. It's all I could do to keep [Regina] from talking. She was so angry over that word 'vulgar.' You know what she said she was going to tell? She said, 'I'll tell you what vulgar is: Him and [name withheld] naked, laying in Angel's bed, masturbating each other and going to the bathroom to have to wash the ejaculation off his hands.'" Angel is Angley's wife, who died in 1970.
>
> Angley: "That's not true because I didn't ejaculate him. I didn't make him come."
>
> Davis: "Well, you was both naked in that bed."
>
> Angley: "Well, I didn't make him come."

Davis: "Well, he made you come then because he... described your penis."

Angley: "He didn't make me come. No, he didn't."

Davis: "Well, you was in there naked."

Angley: "Well, I didn't say I wasn't."

Davis: "That's vulgar."

At the end of the 8½-minute tape was the following exchange.

Davis: "You've inflamed people. ... It's not about your affair with [name withheld], and your sexual promiscuousness [or] impropriety, whatever you want to call it. Now, that hasn't got out. But it's got out about me leaving," which he decided to do after his relationship with Angley had deteriorated badly.

I couldn't have cared less that Angley was gay except for two factors.

First, he consistently condemned homosexuality. In a 1995 book called "Oh, God, What a Mess!," he wrote, "Homosexuality is vile, vile before God; and it will send souls to hell."

The second problem was that, in both cases, Angley had allegedly taken advantage of church employees — underlings.

As troubling as all of the accusations were, one of the most shocking aspects of his ministry, to me, was Angley's overall outlook on life. He consistently told his flock they should not reproduce because God didn't want them to. "I wouldn't want to be brought into this world now," he told me.

Even if you had strong faith?

"No, because the people of strong faith go down. And their children are in danger.... It wasn't like that when I was a kid. We could walk up and down the streets, we could play at night and we were not molested at all."

Angley and his wife never had children. When I asked why, he said: "We didn't want children. We wanted to give our lives to the work of God.... My wife really loved children, but she didn't feel like that we should have them."

Many former members of his church thought there was a strong ulterior motive to his anti-reproduction stance: If his parishioners had children, they would spend far less time in church — and donate far less money.

It was clear to me that Angley had indeed developed a dangerous cult. I would not have been totally surprised if he decided to end it and take them with him, à la James Jones in Guyana.

The most memorable part of uncovering Angley was something that happened about seven months after the 2014 series.

I was sitting on the terrace at Beau's Grille in Fairlawn, eating dinner with a friend. A woman walked over and introduced herself.

She said, "You don't know me, and I don't want to interrupt your meal, but I had to tell you how much I appreciate your stories on Ernest Angley.

"He split up our family. But as a direct result of your stories, the whole family got back together. I can't thank you enough."

That remains one of the best moments in my career.

You can't do much better in journalism than improving people's lives by introducing light to places that thrive in darkness.

# Chapter 6
## The Death of Charlie Wright

Steve Love

Charlie Wright came upon Akron like a sudden, violent storm, leaving behind pain, questions and wreckage. No one had been prepared for little Charlie's story, but journalists are expected to bear witness to the worst of humanity, to steel themselves, suppress emotion and tell the story, no matter how horrific. They do not learn this in a classroom. They learn by seeing and doing, from professional experiences and the raw material of their own lives.

I had lived through bad before, yet nothing equipped me to cope with the story of the 7-year-old with the bright eyes, big smile and endless curiosity. Not the worst I had seen. Not the worst I had endured. Charlie's story became the community's and my worst of the worst.

From the moment I graduated college, death had been visited upon me. One of my early assignments for a small newspaper in California's Mojave Desert was to write about a bus crash that resulted in multiple deaths. I was the first journalist at the accident on a desert highway near Barstow. An overturned bus, clipped by a wrong-way, drunken driver, had caught fire and burned. Its seats still held charred bodies. The sight and smell remain. If such a disaster was unusual, death in the late 1960s was not.

The Vietnam War raged. Fort Irwin and the Marine Corps Supply Depot were Barstow neighbors. Almost daily a wire-service teletype clattered out casualties from the military bases or city. Family and friends had to be interviewed, photos obtained, stories written. It was numbing.

Not as numbing, though, as the relentless loss of my closest friends, victims of an apocalypse, the Four Horsemen of modernity: war, alcohol, disease and murder. My best friend from my Oklahoma hometown was killed in Vietnam in 1968; my best friend in Sacramento, where I finished high school, the victim of a drunken driver; the best man in my wedding and my boss at the Tulsa Tribune lost to a long struggle with cancer, and my closest friend from that Tulsa time, who had become Fort Wayne Sentinel editorial page editor, murdered in the home my wife and I had recently visited. His wife and son were also killed, his 2-year-old daughter left to wander the house for two days before the bodies were discovered. I knew death too well.

I did not know Charlie. Neither did some 15 other Beacon Journal writers who told a story that wracked Akron interminably and lives on today. We learned, as did the community, that we did not have to know Charlie personally to love him, to shudder at what had happened to him, to record the lasting mark he made as Akron's transcendent face of child abuse.

First-grader Charlie liked to rise early in the East Exchange Street upstairs apartment he shared with mother Loretta, brother David, and, at times, Loretta's boyfriend, Wayne Doyle, a long-haul truck driver from Chicago. Charlie rose early to secretly call a number he kept in his heart as much as his head. He was calling home, the only real one he ever knew.

On Friday, April 24, 1987, however, no call came to Shirley and Tom Strittmatter, foster parents to the Wright brothers. Charlie lay near death from a beating at Doyle's hands two nights before. Doyle had overheard Charlie ask his mother to get rid of Doyle. The disciplinarian turned brutalizer had grabbed Charlie and shaken him, according to his mother, who intervened. Neither she nor 8-year-old David was awake to protect Charlie when Doyle hauled him out of bed at 3 a.m., took him to the basement, and struck him with such force he ruptured Charlie's small intestine in three places, according to Summit County Coroner William Cox. The bowel's contents leaked into Charlie's abdomen, slowly poisoning him.

When the story of Charlie's life and death unfolded in the newspaper and during trials of Loretta Wright and Doyle, whom she had met as a truck-stop prostitute, community response was swift, angry and directed not only at Wright and Doyle but also at the Summit County Children Services Board (CSB). It had three times taken the brothers from their mother only to return them. There was blame enough to go around: Doyle, for the beating that killed Charlie, and Loretta Wright, for failing to seek medical attention for him despite the diligent urging of his Mason Elementary School teachers and administrators. A murkier responsibility ran deeper.

State law requires that Children Services try to reunite families. So juvenile court ruled the brothers should be returned to their mother. Their father, David Wright Sr., was in prison. The paternal grandparents said they had raised nine children and could not take the boys. "Too old, you know," said Charles Wright, 59. Multiple county and state investigations of CSB's procedures and actions, as well as two verdicts in a wrongful death lawsuit brought by the grandparents who did not take in their grandchildren, found no wrongdoing. CSB's internal review concluded mistakes were made but that it could not have prevented Charlie's death.

This conclusion lent credence to justice's blindness and Doyle's guile in masking his malevolence. He could be duplicitous in spades. Loretta Wright knew him as a shapeshifter. "Wayne," she said, "could make you believe what he wanted you to believe." Doyle's father, Robert, whom the boys visited in Chicago with Wayne, thought Wayne treated Charlie and David like sons. Even skeptical foster mother Shirley Strittmatter was duped by Doyle. "I feel so bad," she said. "He had me so fooled."

When it came to Charlie and David, Shirley was not easily fooled. She knew them as if they were her own children, the ones she had wanted but had been unable to have. Instead, Shirley and Tom Strittmatter gave a loving home to two little boys who needed one as much as the Strittmatters needed them. The boys lived with the Strittmatters for more than three years of five they had spent in foster care, coming and going on failures of their mother and decisions of Children Services and courts. It took Charlie's death to change this and save his brother.

The Strittmatters had become Charlie and David's foster parents without guarantee of permanence. They risked broken hearts because of who they were. After Charlie was killed, Loretta Wright relinquished parental rights to David and by November 1987, the juvenile court had given CSB permanent custody. It, in turn, and with approval of probate court, allowed the Strittmatters to adopt David in 1988. "Our biggest regret," Shirley said, "is we cannot celebrate this beginning with two little boys named David and Charlie." They did, however, bring into the family another little boy, Chad, at the time they adopted David. Even with their pain, they had more love to give to these two new Strittmatters.

If only Loretta Wright had listened to a warning from her friend Diana Santiago, who recognized Doyle as dangerous, the ending might have included Charlie. "I warned her Wayne was going to hurt her kids," Santiago said. This insight fell on ears deafened by love and a conjurer's magic.

At the same time, many in Charlie's life, from neighbors to the concerned owner of a nearby carryout store and laundromat, attempted to help Charlie when his own fear prevented him from helping himself. He knew if he spoke up, Doyle would beat him. David tried to be Charlie's buffer, to provide a diversion and take the beatings when Doyle put them "on punishment," telephone books stacked on the backs of their hands, arms extended. Drop one and there was hell to suffer, the kind that came to Charlie after he spoke out against Doyle.

The investigation and response of Lt. Ed Duvall Jr., commander of the Akron Police Department's Juvenile Unit, into Charlie's specific hell offered, at least to me, a better understanding of the feelings Charlie's death evoked in so many others, feelings that reflected well on the Akron community but to which working journalists were supposed to be immune. I did not see every gruesome detail Duvall saw, but I did look into the eyes of grieving family and friends and hear their and the community's collective wail.

Carolyn Beck, a Cuyahoga Falls resident, focused the hurt and anger into creation of an advocacy group for children called KIDDS (Kids in Danger Deserve Safety). KIDDS vowed to work for changes to state law and got the attention of Children Services by helping defeat a CSB levy, the type that usually drew broad support. People demanded CSB change to better protect other Charlies of the community. "The second time a child is taken out of that dangerous situation," Beck suggested, "you don't put them back."

Politicians, including grandstanders, jumped into the fray with their big feet. In the end, however, good came from heightened community pressure. Summit County established a Child Mortality and Morbidity Review Committee to examine deaths of children under 18. Its goal was to reduce the likelihood there would be another Charlie Wright. Over the years this vigilance spread to neighboring counties and throughout the state. No panacea, it did prove an evidence-based countermeasure.

After the unusual CSB levy outcome, no one wanted to attribute the failure to Charlie Wright's death, even if it was surely a factor. Community response and discussion and a better telling of the Children Services story produced the funding still critical to protecting children. It also focused attention on the dilemma faced by those who perform social work on behalf of their community: Be too aggressive in protecting children and risk being accused of meddling in private affairs and threatening the sanctity of the family. Be too restrained and face accusations of shirking responsibility. Judgment exists on a razor line and can be imperfect.

Make no mistake, though, judgment was rendered in Charlie's story: In the court of public opinion. In the court of law. In the internal court that is the conscience of every person who played a part in Charlie's life and its aftermath. Journalists unless you were a columnist as I was for much of a 40-year-career — are not to make judgments or share opinions. They must strive for the impossible: objectivity. Try it. When I first wrote about Charlie Wright, it was to provide an early narrative of what I and others had learned of his life and death. I wrote with a point of view — I came down on the side of the innocent Charlie — but straitjacketed my opinionated self. I cannot do that in this essay, because it is, uh, *personal*.

Among those who make it easier to now arrive at judgments are both the guilty and the innocent victim. I most blame Loretta Wright because she ignored the first rule of parenting: Above all else, protect your children. Doyle was a danger to Charlie and David — and David knew this. After the trip with Doyle to Chicago, he never wanted to go again. Something changed; he recognized the truth about Doyle, probably without knowing of the frightening premonition that Diana Santiago had shared with his mother. I came to accept the crush of conflicting feelings verboten to journalists that telling Charlie's story pushed to the fore. Those feelings did not make us unprofessional. Ed Duvall Jr. allowed me to see this.

When Wayne Doyle first became eligible for parole in 1997, 10 years after being sentenced to prison for 15 to 40 years for involuntary manslaughter, child endangering, and two counts of felonious assault, Duvall joined the Strittmatters, the law enforcement community, Summit County Prosecutor Maureen O'Connor and others to vehemently oppose Doyle's release. Before the Ohio Parole Board, Duvall and David Strittmatter put a face on the opposition. O'Connor had called for a grassroots letter-writing campaign. The parole board received 16,000 letters, most ever regarding a parole. The only comparable community response was to villainous corporate raider Sir James Goldsmith's attempted takeover of the iconic Goodyear Tire and Rubber Co. A little boy touched as many lives as Akron's largest company.

No one had forgotten angelic Charlie. Michael Callahan, who prosecuted the case, made sure the parole board saw photographic evidence of what Doyle did to Charlie. Years later, Callahan still considered it the biggest, most affecting of his many high-profile cases.

Similarly, nothing in his career moved Duvall more than Charlie. He saw his body in the apartment, attended Charlie's autopsy and interviewed witnesses, including David Strittmatter. Duvall said: "When we were in the interview room listening to David... telling his life, what he and Charlie went through, how Doyle put them "on punishment," beat them with his fists and feet and screwdrivers, I felt tears rolling down my cheeks. I think about Charlie every day."

Cops can cry yet be professional. Duvall, as good and tough as they come, was not afraid to care. After his death from cancer at 59 in 2008, Duvall was honored by Children Services, the Akron Police Department and Akron Children's Hospital with an award bearing his name. It salutes annually "a local law enforcement officer's tenacity, commitment, and integrity while serving the families and children of Summit County." Michael Matulavich, police chief and Duvall colleague, added another Duvall quality. "Because," Matulavich explained, "you can't do what Ed Duvall did all those years with kids and not have compassion."

Duvall treated David Strittmatter with kindness. In turn, David not only opened up to Duvall with his and Charlie's story but also shared it in court, Shirley Strittmatter standing strong by his side in the witness box. David was the only person who could testify he had seen Doyle beat Charlie, the brother so close to him people mistook them for twins. Charlie thought they might be. He even quizzed Shirley Strittmatter: "Are we twins, Mom?" If they were not precisely "twins," they shared a mutual, deep-seated, if unarticulated, desire to survive Doyle.

They had too much against them. They had to counter their mother's selfish interest in saving herself. Did Loretta Wright see Wayne Doyle as her escape from a tawdry life and thus ignored the violence that infected him? By the time she recognized Doyle as a dead end and tried to evict him from her life — even changing the locks — it was too late. Doyle took the door off the hinges and walked right back in. Neighbors saw some of what was going on. For fear she could lose her sons again, Loretta threatened one woman not to take her concerns to Children Services or police. Most critical, when Charlie could have been saved by medical attention, she knew the help he needed would expose their sad lives. She saved herself instead.

So, yes, Loretta Wright deserves blame for Charlie's death. She also merits credit for providing testimony against Doyle that reinforced David's account (and helped her) and for encouraging David's adoption by the Strittmatters, something she could have done earlier. Even this was not selfless. It allowed her to walk away from the mess she had made of so many lives.

When David legally became a Strittmatter, Children Services as much as acknowledging the family had been right for the Wright brothers all along,

Summit County Juvenile Court Judge William Kannel had to swat away objections from David's biological but criminal father and his paternal grandmother, Sharon Wright. She had to settle for creating a foundation to honor the grandson she did not take into her home because she said she was ill.

Though there were bumpy times through the years, including David leaving when he was 16 before returning, Strittmatters and sons mostly prospered in one another's love. A foreshadowing of this outcome occurred the day Charlie died, David at his side. When later he walked through the door of the Strittmatter house, Shirley, overwhelmed by Charlie's death, could not immediately find the words to comfort David and reassure him. She need not have worried. David had the perfect words for them both, announcing, simply: "I'm home, Mom."

Charlie's big brother/protector demonstrated maturity beyond his years. He had a mind of his own and opinions he voiced confidently. When twice juries found Children Services not guilty in the wrongful death suit his grandparents filed, David expressed disappointment. It was not because of the money at stake. "I just didn't want another kid to die for them to open their eyes," he said. "They need to care more about what they're supposed to be doing." The fact that Joe White, the CSB's beleaguered executive director, was highly regarded in social work and had been brought in to improve the effort and outcome of the agency did not sway David, who stuck in the dagger when he said: "I had hoped there would be a lesson for them. I think they made a mistake taking me from [the Strittmatters] the first time."

David got another chance; Charlie did not. The brothers knew where their home should have been. Loretta Wright knew, too. From the time she was arrested, she said she wanted David returned to the Strittmatters. Like David, she received a second chance, but she wasted hers. After her conviction for involuntary manslaughter and child endangering for the neglect that led to Charlie's death, she was sentenced to prison for six to 25 years. She served only 18 months before receiving shock probation.

Returning to Akron, Loretta Wright found a community in an unforgiving mood. She was a pariah. She had difficulty finding work or a place to live. She began using her maiden name, Jones. She kept only one appointment with her probation officer before hitchhiking across country and hiding in plain sight in Tucson, Ariz. She claimed she ran not to avoid being sent back to prison but to give David a chance to grow up beyond her dark shadow, which he did.

After dodging the law for more than 10 years, Loretta Jones was arrested by Tucson police on a Summit County probation violation warrant; she also was wanted there for passing bad checks. Callahan, by then Summit County prosecutor, returned to the courtroom for her probation-violation hearing, again standing up for the lost Charlie. "It's a heart-wrenching case that should never have happened in the first place," he said. "So many people saw what was happening to that child. If someone would have stepped in, he'd still be alive today."

Common Pleas Judge John Adams reimposed the 6-to-25-year sentence on Charlie's mother, returning her to prison. By 2019 she no longer was in the penal system, but Wayne Doyle remained in Allen Correctional Institution in Lima, Ohio. He could receive a parole hearing in 2020. His maximum 40-year sentence will expire April 24, 2027, six days before his 75th birthday.

Meanwhile, Charlie's name still comes up each time another child in Summit County dies violently or suffers horrific abuse. It has not ended, but Charlie is not forgotten.

He lies at rest in Rose Hill Burial Park and Mausoleum in Fairlawn, where the Strittmatters often visited. What happens after death is life's final mystery. Long ago, after the loss of the friends I loved so much, I concluded what is important is not the hereafter but the here and now and what a person does with it. Shirley and Tom Strittmatter offered living examples of what could be done. Shirley died November 15, 2018. Listed among those who preceded her in death was son Charlie Wright. In her heart, Charlie always was *her* son.

I have scoffed at those "Together Again" evocations that sometimes accompany obituary photos. I am reconsidering my cynicism. Even a jaded former journalist can imagine Charlie and Shirley together again and hear a faint echo of David in what Shirley might have first said to Charlie were such a thing possible: "I'm home, Charlie. Mom's home."

## Chapter 7
## Lane School: Finding the Pulse of a Neighborhood

Laura Ofobike

The Akron Board of Education has spent the past decade and a half "right-sizing" school facilities as the city steadily loses population. Besides, many of the structures were aged and could not keep up with new demands and technologies. Across the city, sparkling new buildings have risen like phoenixes to replace the old schools. Others have undergone extensive renovation. Several have been closed and the facilities repurposed, sold off or pulled down.

School closings never have been a simple matter of reckoning with the numbers. Debates frequently ensue over which buildings need to be closed or torn down. Residents in affected neighborhoods sometimes protest and challenge board decisions. Preservationists question the wisdom of losing elements of local history. Sometimes, residents use the hammer at their disposal and threaten to vote down a school levy. School closures get emotional, and quickly so, because histories — personal as well as communal — are vested in a neighborhood school. Sometimes, the emotions raised by a closing remain raw years after a building is shuttered.

Akron has experienced school closures before, and the latest cycle of downsizing may be little different from earlier ones. The changing landscape of Akron Public Schools typically is chronicled in the news pages. On the editorial page, though, we didn't get to break news; rather, we got to feel the pulse of neighborhoods and probed beneath the surface as residents came to terms — or not — with the reality of a decommissioned school. As often happens when feelings run high, the editorial page was expected to step into the controversy to help find a path to a solution.

Such was the case with the closure of Lane Elementary School in near-west Akron, during an earlier round of downsizing long before the school district launched the current reconstruction program in 2002.

Lane School was closed in 1980 along with a handful of others in the city. The property was sold at auction in 1981 to an Akron businessman, Clyde Hughes of Akron Inner-City Construction. For more than a decade, the shuttered school stood in the Lane-Wooster neighborhood in Ward 3 as a cautionary tale on managing the aftermath of a closing.

In the summer of 2019, the school board announced that it had sold at auction several of the school buildings shuttered as a result of the reconstruction. In highlighting the prolonged tensions after Lane School was closed and sold, the hope is that, in this instance, the past will not be prologue to the future. The relevance of Lane in this context is not so much the story of a school sidelined by a city's changing demographics and projections. It is more the story of perceived abandonment and its residual bitterness; of the loss of a sense of place and community; and, eventually, a story of resurgent hope.

Lane School arguably was a casualty of circumstances, the weight of which no school board could manage effectively. Prominent among the background factors leading up to the closure was the steep fall in tire manufacturing in Akron. The city's economic base was weakening, and its glory days as the Rubber Capital of the World were fading. The school district would cite significant losses in population and subsequent decline in enrollment among the reasons for closing Lane.

In predominantly Black, working-class neighborhoods such as Lane-Wooster, the strains of economic decline were already evident in rising unemployment and poverty rates. The economic stresses were further exacerbated by racial tensions over civil rights, in particular in the 1968 riots in the neighborhood and the district's controversial busing and school desegregation efforts.

Yet, one factor stands out still among residents in the neighborhoods near downtown. To this day, the residents who lost their neighborhood school maintain that Lane School might have survived had it not been for the city government routing a new highway through the heart of the established, but hard-pressed, communities near downtown.

The construction of the Innerbelt, beginning in the 1970s, cut a wide swath through downtown, splitting previously connected neighborhoods. Homes and business properties were lost to the project. Families and many of the enterprises that had anchored the neighborhoods were displaced and had to relocate. Enrollment in Lane School further eroded as a result of the disruptions to community life.

(It is no small irony to those who lost their homes and businesses that the Innerbelt, which was never completed as planned, is partially dismantled today. City officials concede it has not lived up to the grand vision. In the neighborhoods that were torn apart, the loss of a sense of community, to which Lane School was integral, was a steep price to pay.)

When I first became acquainted with the history of Lane School in 1991, the building at 501 Howe St. had been vacant for several years, a hulking mass of crumbling concrete on 1.6 acres. What must have been a magnificent edifice at one time, and a neighborhood hub where generations of children were nurtured, was festooned with graffiti. Boarded-up doors and windows had been pried open. Three floors of empty space invited vagrants and all manner of illegal activity. Discarded clothing, empty beverage containers and needles here and there made it all too clear the kind of traffic that was passing through. Broken glass and trash littered the floors. Rain from leaks in the roof pooled in puddles on the floors. The walls were mottled with mildew and mold. What pipes and fixtures remained were too rusted to be of value to scavengers. Outside, the sidewalks were crumbled, and weeds grew tall and wild. At some point, intruders removed a transformer in the basement and deposited it in a playground nearby, where it leaked into the ground.

The decommissioned school property fetched $25,000 at auction in 1981. Whatever the owner's vision was for the building, it never materialized. The structure, which dated to 1902, required a massive investment of funds to clean up and renovate. The cost to bring it up to code in 1988 was estimated at $1.4 million. From the start, the owner was in a running battle with residents and the city about conditions at the site. He failed to secure the building and grounds against vandals and criminal activity. He could not keep up with the tax payments, and residents complained about rats and other health hazards.

The property was put on the auction block once again in 1989. R.J. Talley of the Dendi Group based in Columbus bought it for $2,000. The owner put the property on the market as is, with a $225,000 price tag. There were no takers, and no visible effort to clean up and rehabilitate the property for any other use. By 1991, the estimated cost to rehab the building for use had jumped to $3.7 million.

Frustration rose as the old school deteriorated. Long-term residents who had weathered the disruptions were struggling to maintain their property values and a sense of place. The shell of the old school seemed like adding insult to injury. They were dismayed that the building had become a haven of crime and a health hazard. They were none too happy about their children being bused to distant schools. But mostly, they were angry that neither City Hall nor the school system appeared keen to address their concerns and their pleas to tear down the building.

Lane School had become a major liability. Its neighbors were stuck with the imposing hulk, a problem for which there seemed to be no ready solution. For the school board, selling the property may have been an easy decision: It took a redundant building off its hands. But, a decade after the fact, the families that remained in the neighborhood saw the closing and the resulting decay — from the routing of the Innerbelt to the sale of the school — as the culmination of policies pursued without regard to their long-term consequences. Every year the decrepit building stood was confirmation to them of bad faith in official circles. They felt ignored by both the school district and city government. As the years rolled by with no action, the residents were convinced that theirs was a neighborhood outside the margins of official concern. Amid the boarded-up homes, rising crime and falling property values, Lane School was Exhibit A of a city averting its eyes to the plight of the neighborhood.

There was no disagreement that the building was a danger and a monumental blight in a neighborhood that had its share of rundown properties. The question was: Whose responsibility was it to get rid of it? Who would bell the cat?

A decade of inactivity had proved the inability of either owner to put up the money for demolition or renovation. It was unlikely as well that a new buyer could be enticed to take on the cost to repurpose a building chockfull of asbestos located in a low-income, inner-city neighborhood where the prospects of turning a profit were minimal. By 1993, the Dendi Group had lowered its sights and the price tag to $50,000. The property still did not sell.

For its part, the school board absolved itself of all responsibility. It had sold the building legally to a legitimate buyer as it needed to do. As the board and the superintendent argued at the time, the district had no obligation to intervene and no intention to "trespass" on private property after a valid sale.

City Hall, likewise, argued its authority was limited. City officials had sued the first owner before in an effort to force demolition and had lost the case. Without a court order, the city pointed out, it could not tear down privately owned property.

But the property owners surrounding the school quadrant on Lane, Howe, Moeller and Campbell streets and their ward representative, Marco Sommerville, were arguing more than legal obligation. After a decade of contending with drug dealers, petty criminals, vandals and vermin, they were arguing a moral responsibility. They were arguing their due as taxpayers thus: They paid taxes to the city. Should they not have an expectation to be safe in their homes from crime and other hazards? They paid school levies, yet the fallout from an action taken by the school system was destroying the value of their homes and their quality of life. Under those circumstances, would it be unreasonable to withhold support for the next school levy?

In his search for allies in the fight to raze Lane School, Sommerville was wearing out the ear of David Cooper, the Beacon Journal's editorial page editor. The councilman's hope — not unfounded — was that the weight of the editorial voice would nudge City Hall to take aggressive measures to address the situation, preferably financing a demolition.

Sommerville and Cooper took a tour of the offending site and the Lane-Wooster neighborhood on a summer afternoon in 1991. Back at the office, Cooper instructed me to call Sommerville. I took the councilman up on his offer of a guided tour of the school premises and, over the course of several visits, listened to residents who were willing to talk. Some who had called the police in earlier years about the criminal goings-on around the school had been cowed into silence by threats and intimidation. Except for a few who remained publicly critical, they had given up that anything would ever be done.

The neglect and decay were tangible. Less visible but as palpable were the anger and the sense that City Hall would never have tolerated similar conditions in a more affluent or white neighborhood. There is a tragic and enduring legacy to the national and local history of racial discrimination. People who have felt the sting of it perceive institutional conduct through the pall of racism. Motives become suspect; and inaction becomes evidence of ill will. That undercurrent was strong on the question of what to do about Lane School.

Between conversations with the neighbors, details of the closure and sale of the old elementary school and discussions in editorial meetings, it became clear that one way the editorial page could facilitate a solution was to keep the issue on the public radar. Over several months, columns and editorial pieces laid out the challenges posed by the sale and its aftermath. Among other options, we encouraged City Hall to finance a professional assessment of demolition or rehab costs and a feasibility study for nonprofit use of the property.

The editorial responsibility as we saw it was to make sure the city did right by the neighborhood on several levels. First, there was the economic argument. The crumbling building and unkempt grounds were deepening distress in an area that needed an economic stimulus. Second, there was the civic argument. For the taxes they paid, the residents deserved value in terms of protection from health hazards, crime and intimidation. Third, there was the crying need for positive action to chip away at the hard underlay of distrust from perceived racism.

City Hall did find a way, eventually, to address the problem. In 1993, the city bought back Lane School from the Dendi Group for $40,000 with funding from its federal Community Development Block Grant. For the owner, that wasn't a shabby deal at all, considering how little it had paid for the facility in 1989. Getting rid of the old school proved an expensive proposition. The city paid $248,000 more to remove asbestos and raze the building in 1994.

The footprint of Lane School is long gone. In the space created by the demolition sits Millerview, an allotment of modest, single-family homes developed in 1996. The development was named in honor of George C. Miller, the first Black principal in the Akron Public Schools who headed Lane Elementary School in 1962-65. For a neighborhood that had long endured gross neglect and, some would say, disrespect, the choice was an astute gesture of recognition. The shadow over the quadrant removed, more cleanup, renovation and housing construction followed. Optimism, long in short supply in the neighborhood, rose with visible changes.

As neighborhood campaigns go, the struggle over Lane School some 25 years ago would be easily forgettable — except that the present makes the past eminently relevant. The Akron Public Schools has divested itself in recent years of several buildings it no longer needs. There is no guarantee that all of the new owners will be any more resourceful or responsive than the buyers who started out with high ambition over the old Lane School and saw it dissipate to the detriment of an entire neighborhood.

One would hope that the experience has helped in some way to shape sensitivities in other neighborhoods and in city government regarding the transfer of former public facilities to private owners. Then as now, the district's obligation remains as it was: none, once a facility passes into private hands. City Hall, which took the financial hit with Lane, appears to have taken the cue to guard itself against similar situations in the future.

In June 2018, City Council passed the Vacant Building Registration Ordinance. It requires owners of vacant commercial and industrial buildings to register the properties and to file a plan for use, including reasonable time frames for rehabilitation, demolition or securing the property. It enables the city to keep tabs on potentially problematic properties and their owners. It sets standards and procedures for inspection, maintenance and an appeals process. The ordinance also imposes administrative and criminal fines for violations and noncompliance. The annual registration fees and the schedule of fines for repeated violations would seem also to offer a measure of assurance of a revenue source to hold owners accountable.

It is likely that more school buildings will have to be closed as the population of Akron continues to contract. The neighbors of those schools and the students who passed through those doors become custodians of memories, not simply of the brick-and-mortar edifice but of who they were. The hope is that if the ordinance functions as anticipated, no other neighborhood would have to endure the protracted hazard and blight that the old Lane School came to represent — or need to struggle as long and as hard to erase an affront to the worth of their community.

It is difficult to trace a direct line between the Beacon's editorial focus and the demolition of the old school. Yet, it is undeniable that turning editorial attention periodically to the neighborhood's dilemma kept the issue in view and exerted pressure on City Hall to persist in finding a solution. The Lane debacle was not a high-profile, citywide concern by any means. Still, it underscored the critical importance to any segment of a community, especially the marginalized, that a local newspaper keeps its ears close to the ground and tuned to matters that concern people where they live.

## Chapter 8
### Sept. 11, 2001 — 'We Had a Job...a Duty'

Ann Sheldon Mezger

*"David, look at that."*

I can still hear myself say those words, still see him glance up at the TV screen above my desk.

The time had to be about 8:50 a.m. The date was Sept. 11, 2001, a Tuesday not yet seared into memory as simply 9/11.

I was a Beacon Journal deputy metro editor then and I arrived at work shortly after 8. As usual, one of the first things I did was turn on the television that sat on a shelf bracketed to a pillar in the middle of the third-floor newsroom. The sound was off, CNN's chatter captioned.

Metro Editor David Hertz, whose desk was next to mine, showed up about 8:30. Since it was primary election day in Akron and a handful of other communities, fewer staffers than usual were in the newsroom. They would be needed in the evening to write and edit stories after election results came in.

As I began to organize the day's local news coverage, I looked up from my computer. A CNN caption said a plane had crashed into the World Trade Center in New York City. The image — a shot through a studio window? — captured towers in the distance and a bit of smoke.

I turned off the captioning, switching to sound. The picture changed. A camera crew had gotten close enough to zoom in on a blackened scar venting tendrils of gray smoke. It angled through upper floors and stretched more than halfway across one side of the North Tower.

"David, look at that."

We both watched, trying to make sense of what was unfolding. We commented on the crater's shape, how you could tell where the plane's wings had slammed into the building. I don't think either of us grasped just how big the tower was, just how long that tear had to be. A private plane, I thought. Or perhaps a commuter jet.

That it might have been a Boeing 767 with dozens of passengers and crew members aboard was unthinkable.

The smoke turned thick and oily, licked here and there by hot little tongues of orange. More smoke began to seep from other sides of the tower.

I spotted Managing Editor Thom Fladung by the doors to the Beacon Journal's main staircase. I called to him and he hurried over to join the growing knot of people around my desk, all of us unable to look away from the disaster playing live on television. Editor Jan Leach, who had been about to attend a meeting of the paper's senior managers, joined us as well.

We speculated. What kind of aircraft? How could such an accident happen? Had a pilot become confused, gone off course?

Then another plane, clearly a full-size jetliner, appeared. A moment later, an enormous fireball blossomed from the adjacent South Tower.

The time was 9:03 a.m., 17 minutes after the first plane had hit. I stopped watching. I could no longer spare the seconds.

"It was just this cascade of knowing it was a very big deal.... It was going to be the biggest news event," Leach recalls.

We identified places where the public could watch the televised coverage and reporters shot off to get reaction, to capture the fear and horror that likely mirrored our own. Other reporters phoned government offices, police departments and schools to ask about security measures being put into place. Photographers and reporters headed for Cleveland Hopkins and Akron-Canton airports.

Reporter Thrity Umrigar, who would leave the paper a few years later to write best-selling novels and memoirs, reminded me that former metro desk colleague Andrea Louie had moved to New York City. Someone should call her, Umrigar said. Do it, I responded.

Everyone in the newsroom scrambled in similar fashion, but we didn't realize how quickly a deadline would be upon us.

Publisher Jim Crutchfield had arrived around 9 a.m. after attending a meeting at the East Akron Community House. He was working at his desk when his secretary told him to turn on the TV.

Footage of the fireball erupting as a jetliner hit the World Trade Center played on the screen. He thought he was looking at a horrendous accident until the news anchor identified it as the second strike by a Boeing 767.

He watched as people trapped on the uppermost floors of the towers began jumping to certain death.

He watched as the FAA grounded all domestic flights, diverting planes aloft to the nearest airport for landing.

He watched as a report came in about American Airlines Flight 77, the third of four jetliners seized by terrorists, slamming into the Pentagon at 9:37 a.m.

And he decided. The Beacon Journal would publish an extra, a special run of the presses.

"We were not scheduled to be out telling people what was going on until the following morning," he says. "That just seemed too far away, too late."

The extra would be the paper's first since Nov. 22, 1963, when President John F. Kennedy was assassinated. Before that, on Aug. 14, 1945, an extra trumpeted Japan's World War II surrender.

"There was always a question," Crutchfield says, "about the value of an extra... but I also knew that newspapers can get below the surface. I knew that there was a role for us as a newspaper and that people would be hungry for information."

And he thought people needed reassurance. "Your local newspaper, when it publishes, tells you that something is right with the world."

Crutchfield huddled with Leach and Fladung.

"We started talking about (the extra) at 10 a.m.... and in the classic Knight Ridder fashion, we just started organizing," Fladung recalls. "We determined the deadline right away. We got circulation and the press room, started just walking through the logistics."

The front and four other pages from that day's A-section would be cleared of ads and redone, then the entire paper would go to press again with the new edition distributed to newspaper boxes and businesses that sold Beacon Journals.

The goal was to get the extra on the street around 1 p.m. For that to happen, stories needed to be written, edited and laid out by noon.

Fladung assigned Bob Dyer to write the lead story, using material from wire services as well as local information and reaction gathered by other reporters. That decision drew criticism from some of Fladung's colleagues at other newspapers.

"It wasn't immediate. It was down the road," he says. "There were journalism types who particularly pointed to the Beacon Journal as 'you can't localize everything.'"

But Fladung wanted the main story to have an Akron feel. "I thought we had great writers and I wanted our great writers involved."

Other local stories began coming together.

Business writer Mary Ethridge rounded up the chaos ensuing in Akron and across the state — the emergency landing of a Boeing 767 in Cleveland because of fears a bomb was aboard, school closings, event cancellations, heightened security just about everywhere.

Jim Mackinnon, also from business, covered the economic impact.

R.D. Heldenfels and Terry Pluto provided columns — TV critic Heldenfels on the networks' coverage of the attack, and Pluto, who wrote weekly about religion in addition to his sports commentary, on the need for prayer.

Umrigar had an interview with Louie, who could see the towers from her Brooklyn apartment. "I just want to be able to turn it off," Umrigar quoted Louie as saying.

Fifteen other Beacon Journal reporters provided inserts for the bylined stories.

The redone pages in the extra also included an editorial and four wire stories.

Design of the front page commanded immediate attention.

Susan Kirkman, assistant managing editor for photo, graphics and presentation, had Kathy Hagedorn, the only newsroom artist on a morning shift, start designing A-1. A photo would cover more than half of the page, topped by a 2-inch tall, all-caps headline.

"The hard part is, we were waiting for some photograph because we knew we were on such a tight deadline and that we might not get real pictures," Kirkman says. "We didn't know if there were any real pictures."

Though New York photographers had rushed to the scene when the first plane hit, Kirkman had no idea how long it would take them to return to their studios to transmit their pictures. Falling debris could be making it dangerous to leave a vantage point of relative safety. Roads might be closed or blocked by emergency vehicles.

Then the Associated Press moved a "screen grab," a shot off a TV, from NBC's New York affiliate. It showed the smoking North Tower and the fireball eruption as the South Tower was hit.

The image was grainy, but it was what Kirkman was looking for — "the seminal moment, what's the most important picture that we can put there."

That big headline also would be very important.

Headlines are crafted by the copy desk, and Fladung started talking early with Jim Kavanaugh, the desk's chief, about both the extra and the next day's paper.

Every Beacon Journal reader wasn't going to see both, but Fladung and Kavanaugh felt there needed to be a difference, a progression, from one edition to the next.

"The extra was really going to be the shock and awe — what was happening," Fladung says. "We wanted the next day's paper to try to do more analysis."

For the extra's headline, they came up with "OH, MY GOD!" The quote was from Dyer's story, a reaction gathered from TV viewers at the University of Akron, but being heard over and over in the newsroom as well.

"WHO DID THIS?" would scream from Sept. 12's A-1. "That had to be the outstanding question of the day," Fladung says.

While enough reporters and photographers were available to write stories and take pictures, copy editors and page designers to put out the extra were in short supply.

Those editors and designers didn't come to work until mid- or late afternoon. Only a handful of those staff members were in the office on the morning of 9/11, mostly working on the features and weekend sections.

Calls went out to get editors in as quickly as possible. That almost wasn't necessary, though. A number of staffers came to work on their own once they learned of the attack.

Bruce Winges, then the night managing editor, had just started his vacation along with his wife, Bonnie Bolden, the newsroom's administrative editor. They canceled their plans and made it to the office around 10:30 a.m. Winges went right to work laying out pages.

"The urgency was," Winges recalls, "we've got to get the extra out.... The whole focus on these five pages was, let's get those done."

In all likelihood, the 9/11 edition will remain the last Beacon Journal extra ever printed. Newspaper websites are now the home for "read all about it" breaking stories once trumpeted by newsboys from street corners.

But in 2001, having a Beacon Journal reporter file a breaking story directly to the internet was at best a glimmer in a few far-seeing eyes.

Ohio.com was a separate entity of Knight Ridder Newspapers then, part of its Real Cities network. Stories by Beacon Journal writers appeared on Ohio.com's home page, but only after publication in the paper. However, if major national or international news broke during the day, the home page could be updated with a wire service story.

Michael Needs, who held dual positions as public editor and liaison with Ohio.com, posted breaking wire stories on the page more than 25 times on 9/11.

"For a lot of people who did not have access to a television," he says, "but who did have access to a computer, like in offices all around, there was a sense that this was a way that many people were getting the latest information…. It was possibly one of the first times that the internet was looked at as a source of instantaneous reporting."

Once the extra was sent to the pressroom, the newsroom's focus shifted to Wednesday's paper.

Sixteen full pages in the A-section, including the front and two editorial/commentary pages, were earmarked for 9/11 coverage, the majority of it focused on the Akron area.

Forty Beacon Journal reporters and seven photographers contributed material for those pages. The art department produced a center-spread illustration highlighting locations of the day's significant events.

As he had for the extra, Dyer wrote the main story from wire reports and local news-gathering efforts. Heldenfels and Pluto reworked their earlier columns. Mackinnon broadened his coverage on the economic impact. Ethridge's roundup fractured into at least five different stories on what was happening at airports, police stations, churches, schools, offices and shopping centers. New topics, such as reprisal concerns by the Arab community, were covered as well.

Paula Schleis filed a report from Somerset County, Pa. The fourth hijacked plane had crashed there at 10:03 a.m., turning picturesque countryside into scorched trees and a debris-strewn field. Accompanying her story was a photo by Phil Masturzo showing investigators combing through the wreckage of United Flight 93.

Local news columnist David Giffels had been working at home that morning on a long-range project. He got to the newsroom about 11 a.m. and was asked to write for A-1.

"I remember honestly feeling overwhelmed," he says, "like not knowing, like trying to say something and not knowing yet what to say."

He managed to write anyway, on the danger of not knowing who our enemy was and letting fear dictate our response.

Also working at home that morning was food writer Jane Snow. She had turned on the TV just in time to watch the second plane hit the World Trade Center.

"I watched in horror for about a half hour before I remembered I was a reporter and might be needed at the office," she recalls.

She came in and asked how she could help. I found her a desk and a phone in metro and asked her to gather accounts from area residents who were in New York or Washington and had witnessed or were otherwise affected by the attacks.

"How will I find them?" she remembers asking.

They'll contact us, I replied.

And they did.

Snow's most important caller that day turned out to be a Silver Lake man whose son, George Hessler, had escaped from the North Tower's 83rd floor, a few floors beneath where the first plane hit. She got Hessler's phone number and wrote a harrowing story of his descent down the stairs, of encountering firefighters on their way up, of making it to the second floor when the lights went out and the stairwell shook as the adjacent South Tower collapsed.

Wednesday's front-page photo showed the same moment as the lead picture in the extra. But this image of the second plane's strike was no screen grab. It was sharp enough to capture the rain of glowing orange debris beneath the fireball.

By early afternoon, pictures from New York and Washington were coming in. Kirkman estimates she looked at thousands of photos that day, selecting the best for possible use. One was an image that became known as Falling Man.

It shows a man wearing a white top and black pants plummeting head first toward the ground against the vertical backdrop of the towers. His arms are at his sides, his body also nearly vertical except for one bent knee. He was one of the estimated 200 people who jumped from the World Trade Center rather than die by fire.

Many newspapers ran the photo. Many others did not.

Kirkman wanted to use the picture, as did Fladung and Winges. Leach overruled them.

"It wasn't violent," Leach says. "It wasn't gory or sensational. But it was so human and I think everybody could look at that and say, 'What brings a person to that act of desperation?' And it felt to me like we were invading that person's privacy."

Kirkman offers a different perspective.

"For me, that picture represented the victims," she explains. "That was the only way the victims were represented because everyone else was a survivor — people walking away…. We had all these people represented, but not one picture of the people who died in the building."

Not all the 9/11 coverage ran on those 16 pages in Wednesday's A-section.

Much of the Sports front was devoted to the suspension of Major League baseball, the postponement of Saturday's Ohio State football game and the uncertainty as to whether Sunday's pro football games would be played. In the Business section, nearly all of the stories dealt with 9/11's impact on the local, national or world economy.

The Local front, however, had other news — stories that on any other day almost certainly would have run on A-1. A robbery suspect was killed and two Akron SWAT team officers were injured in a gunfight at Copley's Red Roof Inn. Two Akron councilmen lost their ward seats in the primary. Another Akron councilman was arrested on a felony drug charge of lying to a doctor to get painkillers.

Over the following days and weeks, the newsroom continued its expanded terrorism-related coverage. Columnist Jewell Cardwell wrote almost daily of area residents helping 9/11 victims. And through the newspaper, Akron formed a lasting bond with a New York City fire station.

On the day after the attacks, Crutchfield held a meeting in his office with his divisional and departmental managers. He doesn't remember why they had gathered, but it wasn't to discuss 9/11.

"The meeting was about to get underway," he recalls, "when Jan (Leach) comes in… and she said, 'You know, people want to know what they can do. They're just calling. The phones are going crazy out there.'"

John Murphy, director of marketing communications, suggested helping New York's first responders. Someone threw out, "Why don't we buy them a fire truck?"

The idea stuck.

After the meeting ended, Crutchfield contacted businesses and institutions about partnering with the Beacon Journal to raise money for a truck. He wanted the mayor's office involved as well. He also called Giffels into his office.

"I knew we needed somebody to be the reporter on it and David was just a reasonable, automatic candidate," he says.

Giffels jumped at the opportunity to provide what he had searched for in his Wednesday column. An answer.

"Personally, as a journalist, it was a relief because I had something to write about. And what I had to write about was real and providing some kind of an answer at that time when, like I said, I felt like I didn't have any answers."

On Sept. 16, Crutchfield kicked off the campaign with a page one Sunday column on the just-established Fire Truck Fund. The goal was to raise $350,000 for New York City, with $325,000 used to buy a fire engine and $25,000 for a police cruiser. Initial campaign partners were the city and FirstMerit Bank, which collected the donations. A coupon to mail in with a contribution ran at the bottom of A-1.

By Tuesday morning, when Giffels' first fire truck story was published, $22,325.77 had been collected already in addition to $25,000 that the Beacon Journal had pledged. By bank closing time Wednesday, the total had hit $218,952.75.

Other major partners — Akron Community Foundation, the F.W. Albrecht Co., Ohio.com and the University of Akron — signed onto the campaign. Continental General Tire offered to provide the fire truck's tires.

Children emptied their piggybanks. Organizations held vigils and passed the collection can. The Akron Fire Department sold patriotic T-shirts with proceeds going to the fund.

"I remember being taken, really taken, by how strong this response was," says Giffels, who saw homemade cards and drawings of fire trucks pile up on his desk.

The campaign ended on Sept. 30, with late donations accepted until Oct. 11. Nearly $1.4 million was raised, enough to buy two EMS vehicles, three police cars and a ladder truck with an $850,000 price tag. (Ten years later, Tom McDonald, a former assistant New York Fire Department commissioner, would tell Dyer that though donations poured into New York from all over the country, no other city contributed more than Akron.)

On Nov. 27, the brand-new truck stopped in Akron en route to New York from the Seagrave Fire Apparatus factory in Clintonville, Wisc. During an evening ceremony downtown, hundreds watched as the truck's 95-foot-long, flag-topped ladder rose over Dart Street.

Two days later, the Beacon Journal ran a 30-page special section listing every person, organization and business that had donated to the fund. Nearly 50,000 names were on the list.

The truck went into service on Dec. 13 at the New York City fire station in Queens that housed Ladder Company 163. A delegation from Akron, including Crutchfield, Mayor Don Plusquellic and FirstMerit Bank vice president Barbara Matthews, attended the dedication. Giffels wrote about Ladder 163's first run.

Giffels and Crutchfield each visited the station again over the years before the truck was retired on May 30, 2013. Many other Akron area residents dropped in as well whenever they were in New York.

They were always welcome to see, to touch and to sometimes climb on board Ladder 163, which bore a bronze plaque next to the driver's door: "A gift from the people of Greater Akron, Ohio, in honor of the victims of September 11, 2001."

Every U.S. daily newspaper, of course, has its own 9/11 story to tell — where reporters were sent, what headlines were written, which pictures were published. I can hardly imagine being in a New York or Washington newsroom on that day, worrying not only about getting a paper out but about whose name I might recognize once the dead and injured were identified.

There's one aspect to the Beacon Journal's story, however, that is unique.

For our newsroom, 9/11 also was about healing.

Healing. The word sounds almost offensive when linked with so monstrous a day, with so many lives taken, with the wars that would follow.

But it's the correct word to use.

On Sept. 10, 2001, ours was a newsroom still in mourning.

That spring, the chief librarian and eight members of the Newspaper Guild lost their jobs, victims of the first newsroom layoffs in the Beacon Journal's history. That summer, 18 more newsroom employees took company buyouts.

Twenty-seven of our colleagues — managers, reporters, copy editors, artists, librarians — were no longer with us.

In the years to come, there would be other layoffs and buyouts as the Beacon Journal downsized and downsized and downsized some more. But those losses of 2001 were the first and, as such, they cut the deepest.

They hurt the most.

The spring and summer of 2001 was a time of dress-in-black days, of frantic searches for job openings to share with co-workers who needed them, of group sessions to talk out our uncertainty and sorrow.

We never stopped doing good work, of putting out a newspaper we could be proud of, but our hearts and enthusiasm just weren't in it.

Then on a beautiful September morning, terror came down from the sky and we were jolted into remembering who we were. Giffels, perhaps, describes this best. "Probably almost every American felt this helplessness (on 9/11). In a newsroom, we didn't feel that. We had a job... a duty that it gave us."

Our numbers might have been fewer on Sept. 11, 2001, but our mission had never been greater.

We all pulled together and, in doing so, forgot to dwell on what had been.

# Chapter 9
## '20/20' Hindsight: When Geraldo Rivera Came to Akron

Tim Smith

Sometime in late 1979, (memory dims after a couple weeks, let alone after 40 years), two Akron police detectives — Helmut Klemm and Sgt. Ed Duvall — were investigating the reappearance of handguns that were supposed to have been tossed into a blast furnace. The story started developing after the Beacon Journal had run a series of stories about corruption in the sheriff's office. The series was written by Dick McBane, the Beacon's courthouse reporter, and Morse Diggs, the police reporter, joined by investigative reporter Keith McKnight, a curmudgeonly old bulldog I had hired from the Dayton Journal Herald (full disclosure: also my oldest friend).

McBane and Diggs had been hearing rumors about an investigation into guns missing from evidence lockers or showing up in pawn shops. Klemm and Duvall started leaking stuff to Diggs about the guns and how deep into the courthouse their probe went. They also wanted us to run some blind-source stories about their suspicions, of course without offering any hard evidence and nothing they would stand behind.

Imagine our reluctance to participate.

But Klemm and Duvall were serious cops, even if a little naïve about the news business and standards of proof before publication. And, of course, they were cops. They had the same trust level that lambs have with lions. (I doubt they would appreciate the imagery.) Still, they were able to convince me that the probe could reach deeper into the courthouse than we had been led to believe, including to judges and major local political figures.

After clearing their request with Editor Paul Poorman, I allowed the two cops to come to the newsroom on a Sunday afternoon when the place was vacant to examine our files on, among other topics, Probate Judge James V.

Barbuto and Akron lawyer Robert Blakemore, the former Summit County Democratic party chairman and a significant figure in state and national Democratic politics. The officers were there for several hours and I made copies of numerous newspaper stories — called "clips" — that later would come back to haunt me.

Though we were digging into the story, we weren't moving fast enough for the cops. In early 1980, they invited the ABC-TV investigative show "20/20" — and its star Geraldo Rivera — to Akron to dig into the story.

After we heard rumors that Geraldo had been spotted, I got a request to meet with his producer, Charlie Thompson. (I remember talking to him in my Beacon office, but I cannot remember how he got invited.) I was a newly minted night school lawyer (having passed the bar in 1977) and one of my law-school favorite clichés came to mind: "You knew it was a snake when you picked it up."

Charlie talked a good game about sharing and helping each other, but mostly he just kept trying to milk me for as much information as he could get about the main players we had been looking at for weeks. What I didn't know at the time was that the cops had already provided Thompson and his crew with copies of the clips I had given them. I guess with the hindsight of 40 years, I can't blame the cops. They didn't trust anybody: the prosecutor, the judges, certainly not the Beacon Journal and probably not some of their fellow cops (some of whom got caught up in the gun probe). And, hanging out with Geraldo was a lot cooler than with some local newspaper reporters.

It turned out that the gun probe was small potatoes compared to what the cops turned up on the local judge, Barbuto. They had women who were willing to testify about being pressured for sex, but they wanted a special prosecutor to handle the case because they didn't trust Prosecutor Stephan Gabalac, who had been Barbuto's chief assistant before taking over when Barbuto was elected to the bench. It didn't help that Gabalac didn't trust the cops, apparently fearing their agenda included bringing down as many Democratic officeholders as they could.

In the midst of all this, "20/20" producer Thompson was going around town, bad-mouthing the Beacon Journal at every opportunity, including doing the occasional radio interview. Taking shots at the local newspaper was always a popular game for other local media and some local politicians (except when they wanted an endorsement). You could hardly blame them.

By this time in the paper's storied history, it was probably at the peak of its influence and near the top of its local reach, circulating in five counties, with bureaus in Stark, Medina and Portage counties besides the headquarters in Akron.

The paper had long worked behind the scenes to influence issues in the city under the guidance of Executive Editor and Publisher Ben Maidenburg. Following his retirement, there was something of a revolving door in the editor's office until Poorman was hired in 1976. Shortly after the gun probe got underway, Poorman hired a tall, curly-haired, kick-ass type from the Philadelphia Inquirer named Dale Allen to be the new executive editor. Allen was soon caught up in the local intrigue surrounding the gun probe and the Barbuto investigation.

Not long after Dale's arrival, "20/20" aired its story about crime and corruption in Summit County. The gun probe barely figured in the story because the cops had shared their findings about Barbuto's sexual escapades while a sitting judge. And former Democratic Party chairman Blakemore provided the angle to justify doing a story about hanky-panky in the court-house: The Beacon clips showed a connection between Blakemore and the Kennedy family from the 1960s. Never mind that the connection was tenuous, and old, and unrelated to Barbuto, guns or anything else in the "20/20" story. The Kennedys were the hook. This was a story with national implications.

Well, not actually.

It was classic Geraldo. Barbuto was up to his neck in trouble, as subsequent events would prove. But the rest, as time would show, was made-for-TV razzle-dazzle. The program's most dramatic scene was Rivera chasing an alleged "hitman," Bobie Brooks, supposedly hired by Barbuto to intimidate witnesses, through a downtown hotel and through city streets. The show presented the event as a bold confrontation between the intrepid Rivera and the shadowy hitman. The hitman turned out to be a small-time crook with a conviction for manslaughter in his past. Even better, a picture later surfaced of Rivera sitting with his arm around Brooks at the Tangier restaurant, taken before the "chase" took place.

Another feature of the program was an interview with one of the witnesses against a young woman who had met with the judge. Rivera and his cameraman, lugging a hidden camera and mic in a suitcase, talked their way into the woman's house with a promise that she would not be identified or quoted by name. The whole segment was done with Rivera's voiceover while showing the young woman sitting in her house facing Rivera. The woman sued Rivera and "20/20" sometime later and the need for the voiceover became apparent. The cameraman had taped Rivera repeatedly reassuring the woman he wouldn't take her picture, use her name or reveal anything she said. Of course, he did all three. Hence, the need to pass on the tape recording and just stick with the video. (The woman won at trial, but lost on an appeal.)

Still, with all its faults, the show left the Beacon looking as if it had ducked a major story. Fact was, we had missed a major story about Barbuto's conduct. We immediately started playing catch-up, including an extraordinary meeting at Allen's house called by Poorman and attended by me, editorial page editor Dave Cooper and a local lawyer, Orville Hoover, who would soon be appointed special prosecutor. Hoover was a compromise appointment agreed upon after Gabalac and the common pleas judges ended a stand-off on how to handle the Barbuto allegations.

Years later, Dale admitted to some reservations about getting involved with community issues from the outside, instead of being the usual neutral observer. I can't say I was wild about it, either, but I had a much longer history with such conduct at the Beacon under Maidenburg, who had often acted as an arbiter when local rubber worker unions struck the local rubber companies, which they did like clockwork every three years. There was also a local chamber of commerce committee of bankers and other heavyweights who met in secret any time a city, county or school tax levy was being considered. Maidenburg attended and the rule was no endorsement of a levy that the committee dinged. All done in secret.

I know because when I was a county government reporter in the early '70s, Ben invited me to attend a committee meeting, off the record of course, to discuss county government finances, which were a shambles. On the walk back to the paper, Ben commented archly on county operations. Feeling a bit stung by the implication that my coverage was lacking, I allowed as how the presentation made by a chamber economist missed the problems of county government by a country mile.

Put up or shut up, Ben replied, leading to the publication of my series on county government that prompted the first formation of a county charter commission and a county charter (that got clobbered on the 1972 ballot

— another decade would pass before one was adopted). Ben's famous line about all that: "There's probably a special place in hell for those who manage the news."

So the meeting with Hoover, no matter how uncomfortable, was nothing new for me.

Meanwhile, Barbuto went on trial, got convicted, and was sentenced to prison. He got out a few months later on "shock probation." I often wondered whether he knew too much to be left in prison too long.

The gun probe that started it all ended more with a whimper than a bang. A few law-enforcement types got rounded up and procedures were changed to eliminate light-fingered treatment of guns confiscated in crimes.

Now, looking back 40 years at the story, I'm trying to focus on the lessons of my encounter with journalism from the receiving end. The Geraldo story itself was a whole separate trip, but, at bottom, it was just another story. Complicated, to be sure, and more than a little frustrating when you're caught between feuding public officials like the cops and the county prosecutor, with neither side trusting you and both sides trying to get you to spin the story their way.

But the enduring part — still crystal clear despite the passage of four decades — was my interview with Wall Street Journal media reporter Dan Machalba. He had heard about Geraldo stirring things up in Akron, resulting in some Beacon coverage about the tensions between the TV star and the local paper. He had already interviewed Poorman and Allen, but he wanted the perspective of the line editor, the one in charge of the staff having to deal with Geraldo.

"Why not," I remember thinking. "Just another reporter. How tough can it be."

So much for my predictive ability. What I remember most of the lengthy interview was what he didn't write down. When I made what I thought were substantive points about our coverage and the "20/20" team's less-than-professional approach to news gathering, Machalba listened politely, but he didn't take any notes. However, when I lapsed into one of my occasional smartass remarks (really out of character for me), he wrote it down.

I should have known. When his story appeared a short time later, in the middle column of page one in the Wall Street Journal, my worst suspicions were confirmed. The story accurately recounted my quotes, just not in the order that I made them, or in reference to the topics they involved. But they were good quotes.

For example, Machalba asked me about the reporting work the "20/20" crew was doing. I called it "sleazy," being charitable. Machalba placed it next to a reference to the show "20/20" aired, which didn't appear until long after my interview. It was, it turned out, a sleazy show, but that's not what I was talking about. Other quotes were also out of context. Made for a good story, but my sense was that it played more like how the little hick paper got rattled by the big time, if disreputable, reporter.

It was a lesson about how journalists can spin stories to fit a preconceived notion that stayed with me and influenced how I taught journalism for 30 years.

# Chapter 10
## How a Crooked River Shaped Environmental Coverage

Bob Downing

The Beacon Journal has been praised for some of the best environmental coverage in Ohio but in the early 1970s, the newspaper did not have an environment beat or reporter. Air and water pollution, along with toxic waste dumps, garbage-filled landfills and a burning river, were routinely covered as special projects by general assignment reporters or by reporters with geographical beats, if they got covered at all.

State desk reporter Bruce Larrick wanted to change that.

In August 1973, he wrote a thoughtful four-page memo to Editor Mark Ethridge Sr., calling for establishing such a beat with a full-time reporter like himself. Issues that need coverage, he said, included preserving the Cuyahoga Valley, air and water quality, solid waste, parks and open space, strip mining for coal, land-use planning, nuclear power, sewage, Lake Erie and endangered species.

At that time, the Cuyahoga River was a foul-smelling open sewer, and the air reeked from rubber companies in Akron and steel mills in Cleveland.

Larrick's memo came only four years after the Cuyahoga River had caught fire in Cleveland. It broke out on June 22, 1969, when hot steel slag that dropped from a railroad car ignited a slick of oil and floating debris. The flames lasted for 24 minutes and damaged two railroad trestles.

The fire got national attention and embarrassed Northeast Ohio. The Cuyahoga became a poster child for the environment. It led Congress to pass major environmental laws and for the government to create environmental agencies.

Larrick argued that the Beacon Journal was neglecting environmental issues and that the paper owed it "to our readers to have a reporter whose full effort is devoted to examining and explaining the environmental issues so the readers will have the information and insight needed to make the difficult decisions the quality of the environment has thrust upon us."

In his memo, Larrick said his proposal had been rejected by editors Terry Murphy and Al Fitzpatrick.

Publisher/Executive Editor Ben Maidenburg regularly told those in the newsroom that the Beacon Journal would get an environment reporter only over his dead body. And he was still very alive at that time.

The smells from Akron's rubber companies were the sweet smells of jobs and success, he had written.

Larrick got a polite response three weeks later from Ethridge. The proposal had been studied and Larrick's arguments were sound, but the paper was doing a good job covering environmental issues, Ethridge said.

"The specific questions you raise as subject matter remain, with or without an environmental reporter. And they're good. But I would prefer not to lump them under one beat. They either fall naturally into beat coverage already being done or to special assignment," he said in a memo.

Larrick's 1973 efforts failed, but two years later he was named the Beacon Journal's first full-time environmental reporter. It came, interestingly, after Maidenburg retired.

Bob Von Sternberg, Jim Carney and Susan Smith Gippin followed him as the paper's environmental reporters. I was named to the position in 1990.

The beat has changed over the years. In the 1980s and early 1990s, readers were most concerned about toxic-waste dumps. Later the concern switched to water pollution with dozens of grassroots groups springing up along small streams. Air pollution in Northeast Ohio is more complicated and still gets little public attention.

The coverage expanded, at times, to include parks, transportation, science, Utica Shale drilling and wildlife including bald eagles, peregrine falcons and white-tailed deer.

But no topic has gotten or deserved more attention than that burning river that had gotten so much attention in the years before Larrick's memo.

It is a small river with a big story.

During my 26 years on the beat, from 1990 to 2016, I filed 1,453 bylined stories on the Cuyahoga River. That far surpasses my stories on Lake Erie (942), ozone or smog pollution (400), Uniontown's Industrial Excess Landfill

(365), Akron's combined sewers (285), Stark County's Countywide Landfill and its fires (253), the Ohio & Erie Canalway National Heritage Area (204) and Ohio shale drilling (100).

The 100-mile-long Cuyahoga River and its tributaries flow through the heart of the Beacon Journal area and remain an international icon. It is a working river. It provides drinking water to Akron and its suburbs. It takes away treated sewage. It flows through the Cuyahoga Valley National Park and local parks.

It is an urban river surrounded by 1.7 million people. A major portion of its flow has gone through a sewage-treatment plant and industries still discharge into the river. After rains, billions of gallons a year of sewage-laced runoff flowed into the stream, although that is changing.

By some estimates, in excess of $7 billion has been spent along the Cuyahoga River to reduce sewage and industrial pollution since the 1969 fire.

The Cuyahoga River was, in the eyes of the Environmental Protection Agency, a problem because it was not fishable or swimmable, two key criteria for water quality.

Reporters had to pay close attention to fish and aquatic insects in the Cuyahoga River. That's because the Ohio EPA relies on fish and aquatic insects to gauge stream water quality. In general, the more species, the cleaner the water. Certain fish and insect species can survive only in clean water; these fish and insects are more desirable species than species that live in polluted water. Insect populations generally recover more quickly than fish populations.

The agency has electroshocked nearly a half million fish on the Cuyahoga and its tributaries. The fish are shocked with an electric current, examined and then released as the shock wears off.

At its worst, in 1968, no fish were found at 22 sites between Akron and Cleveland. Three species of fish (bluegill, blunt-nosed minnow and goldfish) were found by Kent State University researchers at an additional site just upstream of Akron's sewage plant.

The river was in major degradation between Akron and Cleveland, severely impacted by the Little Cuyahoga River, rubber-company wastes and Akron's troubled sewage plant.

In 1984, Ohio EPA sampling north of Peninsula found only 14 fish. There were 12 gizzard shad, one white sucker and one fathead minnow. Most were deformed. South of Peninsula, only eight fish were found, all deformed.

Similarly poor results were found at six other spots between Akron and Cleveland. In all, the EPA found about 2,400 fish and 18 species between Akron and Cleveland.

The results were shocking and the low point to the Ohio EPA that had just started fish testing along the river, says Steve Tuckerman, a retired river specialist with the Ohio EPA. The Cuyahoga River was "still in bad shape" in 1990, he says.

Then quietly and magically, in the late 1990s and the early 2000s, the fish started to return to the river as it slowly started to get cleaned up from earlier projects.

It was 2010 when the 47 miles of the river from Lake Rockwell through Akron to Harvard Avenue in Cleveland met the warmwater habitat designation for the first time. That designation meant the Cuyahoga met federal standards for fish and insects under the federal Clean Water Act.

In 2015, 61 species of fish were found between Akron and Cleveland from the nearly 18,000 fish collected by the Ohio EPA, said agency staffer Bill Zawiski. The most numerous were gizzard shad and emerald shiners. It also included clean-water species like steelhead trout, northern pike, walleyes and rainbow trout.

The recovery was almost miraculous.

"That's why we're giddy," Tuckerman said in 2008. "If you had asked me 20 years ago, I would have said there's no way that we'd ever see what we're seeing.... In the 1970s and 1980s, I didn't think it would happen in my career. The habitat was there, but the pollution was so severe and so pervasive. The change is that dramatic."

Water quality on the Cuyahoga between Akron and Cleveland in the 1970s was "pretty horrific," retired EPA staffer Bob Wysenski said in an interview. "It was almost an alien environment... with unbelievably bad things happening."

The Beacon Journal's Cuyahoga River coverage dealt largely with improving and expanding sewage treatment and solutions with big price tags for communities along the river. It also dealt with sewer overflows, industrial wastes and urban runoff.

That coverage was significant in the eyes of the Ohio EPA.

It was accurate, fair, balanced, thorough and reporters were willing to doublecheck facts to make sure there no errors in dealing with often-complicated federal and state mandates and procedures, Wysenski said.

That coverage helped build support for the river and the cleanup activities along the stream, he said.

Environmental groups "were extremely lucky to have you as our reporter at that time and we knew it," said Elaine Marsh of Bath Township, the long-time head of the Friends of the Crooked River, a grassroots group. "You made a huge difference."

The EPA has also helped create a new Cuyahoga River by removing four dams. A fifth was removed in 2020, and plans are taking shape to remove a sixth and the biggest dam: the 57-foot-high, 450-foot-wide Gorge Dam between Akron and Cuyahoga Falls. Removing that dam and the sediments trapped behind it could cost $70 million.

Dams create stagnant pools with low dissolved oxygen. Removing the dams creates healthier streams.

Taking down the Gorge Dam would create 60 miles of a free-flowing Cuyahoga River from Lake Erie to Lake Rockwell near Kent.

A dam in Kent was altered in 2004 and one in Munroe Falls was lowered in 2005-2006. In 2013, two smaller dams in Cuyahoga Falls came down. An 8-foot-high dam between Summit-Cuyahoga counties in the Cuyahoga Valley park was removed starting last May.9.

Such projects were recommended by the Ohio EPA with removals undertaken by various stakeholders and partners.

Those projects immediately improved water quality with fish and insects rebounding. Great blue herons, beavers, bald eagles and river otters quietly returned to the Cuyahoga Valley.

In 1992, I researched and wrote my first big story on Akron's overflowing sewers that impacted the Cuyahoga River. It was described as "a growing environmental nightmare" for David Crandell, manager of Akron's Public Utilities Bureau.

Those 38 overflow sites were found in older neighborhoods of Akron because there is only a single sewer to carry residential, business and industrial waste along with storm water to the city's sewage treatment plant. About one-third of the city or 160 miles had such sewers and at its peak the problem annually produced 1.2 billion gallons of polluted runoff, of which 10 percent was raw sewage.

The impacts of the sewer overflows on the Cuyahoga River were "real and serious," Wysenski said in that article.

The problem resulted in high levels of disease-carrying bacteria and viruses in the river for up to 72 hours after overflows. It added low levels of toxic chemicals, suspended solids and debris and depleted oxygen in the water.

The issue became an extended and expensive environmental and legal problem for Akron. The latest price tag is $1.2 billion. Sewer bills sharply increased. Unlike many cities, Akron must eliminate all overflows by 2027.

Work is 70 percent complete and is continuing with 20 projects complete, six ongoing (including a giant tunnel under downtown Akron) and three still to go by the deadline.

Stories on the Akron sewer issue focused largely on the fights between Akron and the state and federal EPAs and U.S. District Judge John Adams.

The City Hall reporter provided a share of the sewer coverage.

In 2006, Akron completed its first project to fight overflowing sewers: an oversized concrete tank along the Little Cuyahoga River in North Akron. The nearly $18 million Rack 40 Storage Basin handled 30 percent of the city's overflow. It was the start.

In 1990, I interviewed John Debo, superintendent of the Cuyahoga Valley park.

He lamented the fact that there was no one speaking for the Cuyahoga River that flows through his park. It had no constituency, no voice, no political clout. It was just part of the landscape and was largely ignored.

I prominently featured Debo's provocative comments in a story and a few weeks later the Friends of the Crooked River was created by paddlers including Elaine and Harold Marsh of Bath Township and Jerry Welch of South Akron. That group gave new voice and support to the Cuyahoga River.

The group has been "an absolute benefit to the river," Tuckerman said. "It educated people about issues and pushed them for their support. It cajoled and sometimes bludgeoned people. But it is a tremendous advocacy group and has done a lot."

Not everything I wrote was as well received as stories on the Cuyahoga River.

In 1997, I wrote an in-depth story on septage, the waste that is pumped out of local septic tanks. Much of it is spread on Ohio farmland and it can create health and environmental problems.

The story won a state award for best environmental coverage but no politician or environmentalist got involved in looking into septage. The story, surprisingly, went nowhere.

Covering the Industrial Excess Landfill in Uniontown required dealing with Chris Borello, the spokeswoman for the Concerned Citizens of Lake Township, a small grassroots group.

Dealing with Borello resulted in long telephone calls where you say very little and do a lot of listening. Later came superlong emails filled with great detail from Borello. She drove some Beacon Journal reporters and editors nuts.

Borello is bright, articulate, persistent, strong, demanding, stubborn, intense, obsessive and has a photographic memory. She was a straight shooter. She was also politically savvy. She didn't overstate, but she knew what she wanted.

She did not always like my stories. We fought over the years but later made up and resumed coverage of the 30-acre dump, a very political Superfund site.

My first Uniontown story was done in 1987 with co-worker Dave Adams.

Thirteen landfill neighbors had blood samples tested for toxic chemicals and they released the results on a Friday afternoon. The testing found six toxic chemicals. The samples were comparable to blood levels of petrochemical workers in Texas and Louisiana.

At Uniontown, the two sides remained at odds for years on what needed to be done and on radiation testing at IEL. What developed over many years were irreconcilable differences. It was a frustrating stalemate.

The dump, a one-time sand-and-gravel pit, got 1 million gallons of toxic waste from Akron-area rubber companies and an estimated 750,000 tons of trash from 1966 until it closed in 1980.

Twelve neighbors were moved out. Alternate water was provided because of a contaminated aquifer. Methane was collected and burned for a time. The toxic wastes were never removed. The aquifer was allowed to naturally cleanse itself.

Other topics covered over the years included Ohio's coal-burning power plants, unhealthy ozone pollution, Akron's old trash-burning power plant, toxic algae and invasive species in Lake Erie, and E-Check vehicle tests.

On the environment beat, you are mixing science, health, economics, business, law, education, weather, medicine, race, religion, nature and lots of politics. The beat is not black and white like many others. It is gray and the key is to accurately figure out which shade of gray best describes what's happening. Not always easy.

A good environment reporter is part educator, part watchdog and part public service provider. You must straddle a fence with trees on one side and factories on the other. You shine a light on problems, hoping that that those responsible will be held accountable.

In 2010, I added shale drilling to the beat.

I developed stories explaining what was happening and looking at the risks involved with Utica Shale drilling including air emissions, water availability, wastewater issues and the threat of earthquakes from injection wells.

Billions of dollars were being spent in Ohio on leases, drilling for oil and natural gas, building processing plants and pipelines. Ohio was benefitting in a big way from the shale boom, although a small group remained nervous about the risks from drilling.

It was a tough nut to crack because energy companies in general do not talk to the media or answer questions.

I also added a blog in January 2012 to provide readers with more information about Utica drilling. It was filled with the latest reports on what drilling companies were planning and doing in Ohio. I posted 1,500 short stories in 2012 and 2,500 stories in 2013.

It quickly became the No. 2 best-read blog at the Beacon Journal behind Nate Ulrich's Cleveland Browns blog. The shale blog, to which business writer Jim Mackinnon contributed, received 664,486 pageviews in 2013, its highest total. It died in May 2016.

In 2014, I came under attack from a social media activist for my coverage of the Summit Equipment & Supplies Superfund site in southwest Akron years earlier. Federal, state and local agencies were also attacked.

I was accused of whitewashing an environmental issue that was killing people in Akron — even though that never happened and there was no evidence to back up such claims.

About 70 people signed an online petition at Change.org that was filed by Toxic Avenger against me and two others. Facebook and YouTube attacks followed.

The chief organizer, an Akron native then living in Los Angeles, made a film about the site in 2013 and the petition came in 2016. I had spoken to him about the site once years before.

Agencies including the U.S. EPA reported no major problems at the site near Nesmith Lake where the initial cleanup took place from 1987-1991 with the final cleanup from 1998-2000.

There were soils contaminated with polychlorinated biphenyls (PCBs) from old electrical equipment and contaminated groundwater. There had also been unexploded ammunition on the site.

The Beacon Journal's top editors, Bruce Winges and Doug Oplinger, knew of my unhappiness about the online petition, but said it would be impossible to win such a social media fight. They ordered me to ignore the campaign.

One of my favorite environmental stories won no awards and got little response from readers.

It was a 2009 account of the strange late-summer gathering of purple martins that roosted nightly at the south end of Nimisila Reservoir in the city of Green.

The birds, as many as 15,000, flew away every morning, only to return again that night. The gatherings continued in August and September until the birds flew off to South America for the winter.

The Summit County roost was discovered by Larry Hunter of New Franklin. He took me and photographer Karen Schiely out in a boat to experience the martins.

Here's what I wrote: "It is a surreal, enchanting, almost indescribable experience with the sky overflowing with birds. To be near the roost at sunset is to be surrounded by a fluttering, chirping mass of feathers. They fly en masse in swirling, circling clouds at eye level. The sky is filled with black flecks. There are too many to count.

"The martins — known to be social and communal — are like wind-driven leaves on a late November day. Or a swarm of bees. It is a real-life, nonthreatening scene straight from director Alfred Hitchcock's 1963 film, "The Birds." The birds chirp and squawk madly. It is a raucous get-together... ."

Said Hunter: It is "an awesome natural sight." He added, "It's just unbelievable... . Words and pictures don't do it justice. It's something you have to experience."

Stories like that made it fun to be the environmental reporter.

# Chapter 11
## The Walk of a Lifetime Behind a King from Akron

Marla Ridenour

I will never forget the fear in Savannah James' eyes.

It was one of the most satisfying days of husband LeBron James' career, perhaps surpassed only by the Cleveland Cavaliers' historic upset of the Golden State Warriors in Game 7 of the NBA Finals on June 19, 2016.

Three days later, a million or so of James' adoring admirers packed the streets of Cleveland. They lined the cutouts of parking garages, climbed light posts and onto porticos of downtown businesses. There were no barricades, no portable toilets, no schedule — at least not one that anyone cared to follow.

This was the championship parade Northeast Ohio had been longing for since the Browns captured the NFL title in 1964, yet Cleveland seemed totally unprepared. The celebration of all celebrations could have gone horribly wrong, as Savannah James' glance revealed.

James and his wife rode in a Rolls Royce convertible with sons LeBron Jr. and Bryce, the boys at times wearing headphones (Beats by Dre, of course, since James made a reported $30 million when Apple bought the company in 2014) to block out the noise. Daughter Zhuri, four months shy of her second birthday, started out in the Rolls, but was soon carried to a Ford Super Duty truck behind them.

To try to keep the crowd at bay, a few police officers walked bicycles alongside James' car, but that idea was soon abandoned. James was trailed by photographers, a few members of the media and employees of the LeBron James Family Foundation. Even early on, the path through the street was barely wide enough to get the car through, so it crawled along.

The atmosphere could have been claustrophobic as fans reached out to James, some with phones in their hands to take pictures or video. This was the closest they would get to their King, and before the day was done there was a feeling that they felt they deserved it.

James seemed oblivious, drinking in the euphoria. Fans chanted "MVP!" and "Stand up!" and he frequently obliged. He extended his arms, emulating his pose in the Sherwin-Williams poster of himself at the corner of Ontario and Huron streets. He pointed when he spotted a sign on a building on East Ninth Street that read "Superman May Have Been Born On The Planet Krypton, But He Was Created In Cleveland." Clearly James wasn't thinking of the comic book version.

But Savannah James didn't share her husband's festive mood. She was focused on protecting their children. Occasionally she turned around to check on Zhuri, who slept much of the way. The car was in front of the Cathedral of St. John the Evangelist on East Ninth Street when she looked back, saw the crowd pressing even closer, and her eyes revealed a flash of panic. She was hit in the face by a beach ball.

The rest of the way, the media and members of James' foundation walked shoulder to shoulder with the people, who waved at those on the sidewalk to

Lebron James is the King of Cleveland as the city celebrates the Cavaliers' 2016 NBA championship. (Photo by Marla Ridenour)

join them. Outside a CVS drugstore, James was close enough to fist-bump a boy in a neon green T-shirt and high-five another.

Before the car turned onto Lakeside Avenue toward the rally at Mall B, the crowd became more aggressive and started to question my presence, so I bailed. I walked toward Lake Erie and looped around the masses as my cell phone died, protecting pictures I still cherish.

The parade did end in chaos as a 13-year-old girl was shot twice in the leg near Public Square and a 15-year-old boy with a gun tucked into his waistband was taken into custody. But it was an isolated incident most learned of on the news when they returned home. An afternoon that could have taken a disastrous turn instead became a momentous party.

### Dispatching the reporting team

I was there because of what co-worker and close friend Jason Lloyd of the Beacon Journal agreed was the worst choice of his sports writing life. Arguably, mine had come three days before.

Lloyd also worked for WKYC-Channel 3, providing post-game analysis. Because he would be going on the air after the ceremony, he chose to wait out the parade in a media pit near the stage on Mall B, and I got the spot in the parade allotted for a Beacon Journal sports reporter.

It quickly became an issue when James told Joe Vardon of Cleveland. com before the parade that he would return to defend the title the following season. A deadline was approaching for James to decline his player option for 2016-17, which he did, signing a three-year, $100 million contract that August that included another player option in the final year.

"I love it here. I love being here. I love my teammates," James told Cleveland.com. "Obviously my agent will take care of all the logistical things, but I'm happy. I've got no plans to go nowhere at this point. This is the happiest time in my life right now."

Lloyd texted me to get the same comment from James. I made my way to him, but he wouldn't repeat those words to me. So as the marching band from James' alma mater St. Vincent-St. Mary High School in Akron began to play, I took my place behind the Rolls for the walk of a lifetime.

The streets dirtied by police horses (a member of James' foundation threw out her designer flip-flops afterward), the crowd closing in on James, the hint of fear, the long walk back to the press box at Progressive Field to write, the dehydration on an 84-degree day, none felt like negatives. Instead, as James celebrated the culmination of his career, it seemed like mine as well.

Thanks to Lloyd's choice, I was able to make up for my monstrous gaffe on June 19.

I could blame it on deadline pressure, since I had to file a column on Game 7 about five minutes after it was over, which was about 10:30 p.m. EDT. While I had written a few thoughts ahead of time in case the Cavs won, I had nothing prepared if they lost. I frantically started the second piece at halftime and bounced back and forth between the two the rest of the night. It wasn't until a few seconds remained that Terry Pluto of The Plain Dealer said, "They're going to win." I can still hear the amazement, almost incredulity, in his voice.

I could also blame it on professionalism. I had covered Cleveland teams since 1981 and spent my life racing to locker rooms after games to get the instant reaction. So I did what I was trained to do.

After I transmitted my column on the 93-89 victory, capping an unprecedented rally from a 3-1 Finals deficit, I was in a fog. Flying back and forth to the West Coast had taken a toll. Coherent members of the Cavs media contingent drifted toward the court at Oracle Arena for the emotional celebration. Lloyd, a native Clevelander, was so moved that he had to find a quiet spot to compose himself afterward.

I walked to the bowels of the arena, dropped off my laptop and missed the celebration of a lifetime, catching only snippets on television monitors.

I made sure the hot pink swim goggles I had purchased that morning at CVS were around my neck in case I needed to shield my eyes from champagne. The rain hood in the collar of my jacket was easily accessible via zipper. While James was clutching the Larry O'Brien Trophy and Coach Tyronn Lue was crying on the bench, I waited in line outside the Cavs' locker room.

It was my 40th year as a sportswriter and I made the ultimate rookie mistake. I robbed myself of a chance to witness the unbridled joy I had waited to see for over three decades covering professional sports.

When the locker room opened, champagne covered the floor, a few empty bottles stuck back in ice buckets. Timofey Mozgov was enjoying a cigar. As we waited for player interviews, members of the media took photos of one another. But the better scenes were the ones on the hardwood I had missed.

*Pushing regrets aside*

I should have known better.

On the plane to Atlanta for the Eastern Conference semifinals, I dreamed that Browns' Hall of Famer Jim Brown presented the championship trophy to James, which happened on Mall B a month later.

I rarely sleep on flights, and if so, not well. Except for what I call "newspaper dreams," which involve some sort of deadline panic or missed test or assignment, they are rarely about sports. But this vision — so clear it seemed real — stuck with me long after we landed.

While it may have instilled a sense of hope, it didn't instill faith.

I had read about James' incredible skills at St. Vincent-St. Mary High School, where the son of a struggling single mother led the Irish to three state championships. I still have the Feb. 18, 2002, Sports Illustrated magazine emblazoned with "The Chosen One," when he burst onto the national and international scene. I had watched a St. V-M game against Oak Hill Academy on ESPN. I had covered James since the McDonald's All-American Game his senior year of high school.

I had seen him extend the Warriors to six games in the 2015 Finals when Kyrie Irving and Kevin Love were injured. Yet I don't think I fully comprehended what James was capable of, and to a lesser extent the fearlessness of Irving.

After the Cavs fell behind 3-1 in the series, the headline on my column read, "Cavs Not Built to Beat the Warriors." Somewhere among my 2016 championship souvenirs, I may have a couple clippings of that article I received in the mail, one with an envelope scrawled with I told you so's.

I'd had my doubts since a 34-point home loss to the Warriors on Monday, Jan. 18, of that season. The day before, Warriors star Steph Curry wondered if the visitors' locker room still smelled like champagne; Irving said the Cavs needed to make it a statement game. Then Cavs fans showed up at Quicken Loans Arena with more passion than their team.

Irving and Love were no factor. The Cavs trailed by 37 points after three quarters as fans headed to the exits on a snowy night. In my column, I asked some of the same questions I did when they stumbled through the first four Finals games. Did they have the right pieces around James? Did they have the right coach in David Blatt? Can they find a way to get Love more involved?

The following Friday, Blatt was fired and replaced by top assistant Tyronn Lue. While Blatt's success in Europe didn't translate to the NBA, he remained confident in himself until the end. Headlining his legacy was his quote in the wake of criticism following Game 4 of the 2015 Eastern Conference semifinals against the Bulls when he tried to call a timeout he didn't have and was physically restrained by Lue. "A basketball coach makes 150 to 200 critical decisions during the course of a game, something that I think is paralleled only by a fighter pilot," Blatt said the next day.

With the fighter pilot gone, the atmosphere in the locker room changed. But there were still questions about chemistry, about the supporting cast, about Lue.

That's why when the Cavs trailed the Warriors 3-1, I still had doubts. I saw how the Cavs appeared to seize momentum, stunning the Warriors 112-97 in Game 5 at Oracle, with James and Irving scoring 41 points apiece. Irving hit 17 of 24 field goals, five of seven 3-pointers and James added 16 rebounds and seven assists. They evened the series with a 115-101 victory in Game 6 at Quicken Loans Arena, with James totaling 41 points, eight rebounds and 11 assists, Irving 23 points and Tristan Thompson 15 points and 16 rebounds.

But it wasn't until the afternoon of Game 7, when I spoke on the phone to Stephanie Ocker, the wife of longtime Indians beat writer Sheldon Ocker and one of my best friends, just before I left my hotel room that I believed the championship drought was about to end.

### Getting access to LeBron

Through all the drama, Cavs beat writers Lloyd, Vardon and Dave McMenamin of ESPN had James' ear. While James was extremely cooperative with the media during his second stint in Cleveland — his biggest offense was the long time it takes him to get dressed after games — he was closer to those three, whom he jokingly called his wives. They could chat privately after the cameras had been turned off. If something was needed for a major feature, he would give them time. He has similar relationships with a few in the national media.

But James, who reads everything written about him, respects those who work hard, take pride in their job and understand the game, and I include myself in that group. James knew who represented his hometown paper. At the end of media availability at All-Star Games, which I usually covered while Lloyd and his wife took a short vacation, James would always ask if I needed anything else. And no subject was off limits. He would talk about the special shoes he wore (one in 2017-18 was modeled after Nike's first track shoe), his favorite players on the Browns (in 2017 he named only Joe Thomas and Duke Johnson), or how he would redesign the Browns' uniforms (black would be involved).

But covering James, with the crowd he draws, is a challenge.

I used rubber bands to secure my voice recorder to a selfie stick (copying off former Lexington Herald-Leader co-worker Steve Aschburner of NBA.com) to get it through the throng around James' locker. During the playoffs, I often packed two selfie sticks in case one broke.

Covering James is also costly. With newspaper advertising declining and the budget shrinking, the Beacon Journal still spent excessively to fly first Lloyd, then the two of us, then myself around the country to cover the James-led Cavs. A two-month playoff run to The Finals was very expensive since plane tickets were being bought at the last minute and hotel rooms in Boston, San Francisco and Toronto had the highest rates in the league. Even the year I took the NBA media charter to Golden State road games in The Finals, the cost was $500 each way (and my plane had ashtrays in the armrest).

Being around James brought attention, even for the media. One of my questions to James after a loss to the Celtics in Game 1 of the 2018 Eastern Conference finals landed me in a video clip shown during the monologue on "Late Night with Jimmy Fallon" on May 14 (check out the 1:46 mark on YouTube). I asked James about a crucial fourth-quarter surge by Boston, and he responded with a detailed play-by-play of the entire run. Not only did Fallon use it, but SportsCenter ran a fact-check of James' answer the next morning. It was the perfect example of how seemingly insignificant comments by James could go viral.

That included remarks at shootaround. James talked after nearly all of those sessions, at least during LeBron 2.0. Although Cleveland Clinic Courts is a mere nine miles from my house, I would leave an hour before the sched-uled interview to make sure I got a parking place. I always wore contact lenses and makeup because James often had an opinion on a hot topic that would be broadcast nationally in a matter of minutes. (During the 2018-19 season, with James gone to the Los Angeles Lakers, I wore glasses to shootaround.)

But that is part of the lure of covering James. It's not just his otherworldly basketball skills, it's his worldwide following, his fearlessness to take on topics that most athletes avoid. Renjun Bao of Tencent America once told me everyone in China knew who I was. (Obviously the Ohio.com paywall was no deterrent when it comes to reading about LeBron.)

With James, every minute seems relevant. Every night you might see him do something he'd never done or hear him say something that would be remembered for decades.

That's probably why James' second departure, his July 1, 2018, announcement he was leaving for the Lakers, hit me so hard. After finishing the news story, I sat in front of the television and watched James' highlights, despite the on-air comment from ESPN's Brian Windhorst, the former Cavs beat writer for the Beacon Journal and a good friend, who said, "I know no one in Cleveland is watching this."

I watched every gut-wrenching clip. The next morning, I wrote a column.

"I thought my heart was protected. I thought I was prepared for LeBron James to leave Cleveland again. But as I watched ESPN's highlight package of some of the best moments of James' career, I teared up…" I wrote. I revealed that when he walked out of Quicken Loans Arena after a Game 4 Finals loss to the Warriors on June 8, I thanked him for his amazing season and told him I got into this business to cover greatness; he bent over and gave me a peck on the cheek.

I cried all day after finishing that column. It might have been a catharsis of emotions pent up since the 2016 championship. I still don't know. That's happened to me only twice, the other while I wrote about the death of former Browns owner Art Modell; I was wiping tears from my glasses during that one. But on July 2, 2018, I felt like my days chasing greatness were behind me.

Now the Browns have given me hope. A Super Bowl before my career ends does seem possible. Perhaps another Jim Brown trophy presentation will push aside the "newspaper dreams."

# Chapter 12
## Coming Together for A Question of Color

Deb Van Tassel Warner

On the southeast side of the corridor leading to the editorial board offices at 44 E. Exchange St. sat a windowless room decorated top to bottom, walls, floor and upholstery, in deep shades of red.

Akron Beacon Journal employees referred to the room, obviously though not creatively, as the Red Room. Reporters took advantage of its seclusion to conduct interviews, hold confidential conversations and have spirited discussions over brown-bag lunches about the craft of writing. Editors used it for planning and training sessions, to deliver performance reviews, and occasionally to melt down privately from stress. No one remembers who deemed red suitable for the room's purpose. But as our cafeteria had been decorated in blue tones (yes, we called it the Blue Room!) in the same renovation, some decision-maker must have thought red was just the ticket.

On an auspicious day in mid-1992, seven staffers occupied the Red Room for an entire shift, not to be interrupted, to brainstorm ideas for a project on race relations, an initiative that two years later would win the newspaper the prestigious Pulitzer Prize Gold Medal.

The idea hatched after the April 29, 1992, trial verdict clearing four white Los Angeles police officers in the brutal, videotaped beating of Rodney King. Gathering community reaction, the Beacon had run a story of a white woman in Canton holding up a sign along a road that simply said: "I'm sorry."

In the newsroom, the verdict provoked a series of arguments between reporter Yalinda Rhoden and Assistant City Editor David Hertz, including a debate over which was more horrific, American slavery or the Holocaust. "It underscored, at least for Black Americans, the years of unfair treatment by police and the criminal justice system," Rhoden recalled.

Hertz saw parallels between anti-Semitism and racism, and "became convinced that the ABJ should examine race relations in our community and help the residents come to grips with racism."

He took the idea to senior editors, who called a meeting for input and buy-in from the entire newsroom. The staff packed into the hallowed John S. Knight conference room, and Hertz led the discussion.

"I was petrified," he said. A relative newcomer to the Beacon, 30-year-old Hertz was then one of the youngest editors on staff.

Everyone supported the concept, but agreeing on the project's scope proved contentious. A few staffers argued that any examination of race relations must include Akron's suburbs and other minority groups. Most favored limiting the project to Blacks and whites in Akron only. The rationale was twofold: The predominantly white suburbs would not illustrate the issues underpinning racial tension; and Blacks formed Akron's largest minority group. After all, the impetus was a Black man's beating at the hands of white cops.

At the time, the decision seemed to make sense. We knew it would be an enormous undertaking requiring deft management and skillful diplomacy to keep newsroom egos on task. Today, some of us would certainly support a broader approach. Ignoring Akron's other minority groups ran counter to the project's goal, which was to foster inclusivity.

After a second staff discussion, Editor Dale Allen and Hertz picked a smaller but diverse cross-section of newsroom talent to sharpen the focus. Black staffers were reporter Rhoden, local columnist Carl Chancellor and editorial writer Laura Ofobike. White staffers were Hertz, projects editor Bob Paynter, copy editor Sarah Vradenburg and myself, then the Sunday news editor.

That's how we landed in the Red Room for eight intense, emotional hours, launching the discussion with the experiences that had shaped our own attitudes about race. We challenged and teased each other. We were variously loud, angry, contemplative, sorrowful, joyful, tearful, confrontational. We stayed in the room for lunch, leaving only for bathroom breaks. At the end of the day, no one was dry-eyed.

I told of growing up in a lily-white, working-class suburb in New Jersey, where my interactions with Blacks were mostly positive. The worst racially motivated incident in my lifetime happened after I moved to Akron in 1982. I was driving through a seedy area of North Hill when a young Black man threw a lit cigarette through my car window and called me a white bitch. I learned to drive through the 'hoods with doors locked and windows closed.

Akron also gave me my most illuminating epiphany about race, at a baby shower for Yuvonne Bruce, a Black reporter who would become the copy editor on the project, at the Highland Square home of Cristal Williams, a Black assistant editor. There were as many whites as Blacks at the party when it began in the afternoon. By nightfall, the group had shrunk to about six or eight dedicated card players. I was the only white person.

I never felt unsafe. These were my friends, my colleagues. But I did wonder how I would feel if I were the only white in a group of Blacks I did not know. Then I realized this uncertainty about safety, about how one will be treated, is what my Black friends must experience most days of their lives as minorities in this country.

Rhoden, a versatile and gutsy reporter as well as a good friend, chuckled, and said something to this effect: You're right about that. When I started here I was covering northern Summit County. No one looks like me there.

A graduate of Akron's Central-Hower High School and Ohio Wesleyan University, Rhoden was the youngest in the room. Family members had strong ties to the rubber companies and ran a funeral business. She provided invaluable context, having witnessed firsthand the demographic shifts along Copley Road and Hawkins Avenue, the near west side, North Hill and other neighborhoods as tire jobs, Akron's economic spine, vanished.

She broke into tears recalling how one of her best friends in childhood, a white girl, told her they couldn't play together any longer.

Hertz, a native of Shaker Heights, recalled how older Black students would try to shake down the younger white kids every day at lunch time at Woodbury Junior High School. "I had to figure out a way to fool these kids, as they were much bigger than I. So I bluffed and told them I had no money, even though I did. I saw this as a racial thing, as everyone I sat with was white.... For years after I told this story, Carl Chancellor and I would joke about it. Every so often, he would come up to me and ask me for my lunch money."

So many years later, it is impossible to capture all we discussed that day. I am not the best person to be writing this chapter. I had been the business editor for about five years when Stuart Warner, my husband, got promoted to deputy managing editor, overseeing business and local news. As I could not report to him, I was named Sunday news editor, a new position without portfolio. Heck, for months I didn't even have my own desk.

I no longer created content or directed reporters, which is what I do best. I worked Tuesday through Saturday to plan and design the big Sunday paper, as well as elections and special sections. Mine were the last eyes on major projects, checking mainbars, sidebars, headlines, captions, page toppers, pull quotes, photos and graphics, before they went into the paper. For the first three installments of A Question of Color, a five-part series, that was my contribution. But I was never comfortable in the role and left for The Seattle Times in September, before the series concluded at the end of 1993.

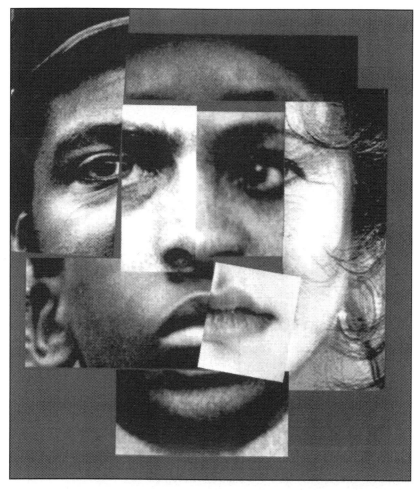

Art Director Art Krummel, working with Assistant Managing Editor/Design Susan "Mango" Curtis and Sunday News Editor Deb Van Tassel, created this award-winning design for the A Question of Color kickoff. (Beacon Journal graphic by Art Krummel)

Stuart stayed in Akron to see the project through. Key people involved in the project were not available to author this chapter.

Here is what I have reconstructed from my memories, Beacon Journal archives and interviews: We agreed to do something ambitious and important and with impact. It would be expensive. We would examine Black/white relations in Akron, a city where African Americans made up 25 percent of the population. We would inform our reporting using Census data and professionally managed focus groups of Blacks and whites. We would ask for polling money for the University of Akron to survey city residents about race, pivoting off the 30th anniversary of Martin Luther King Jr.'s "I Have a Dream" speech. We would use the polling, focus groups and Census data to drill down into what were likely to emerge as "hot-button issues": education, economic opportunity, crime and punishment, and housing. Hertz suggested a community component.

I proposed that the focus groups be racially mixed but got roundly shouted down; my colleagues said that Blacks and whites would hold back if we put them in the same room at the same time. To accomplish anything at all, they said, we needed to create a safe environment for people to discuss their feelings candidly. Ultimately, we decided on three focus groups for each installment — one white, one Black, and one mixed to be drawn from members of the first two groups.

Paynter, the venerable and highly decorated projects editor who introduced computer-assisted reporting to the Beacon newsroom, drew up a comprehensive proposal for Allen's review. Always supportive of big-picture projects with a strong sense of place, Allen signed off quickly.

Allen anointed Paynter to lead the project. He began working on the survey and drafting reporters, one Black, one white, for each topic. Officially, Paynter had carte blanche to ask for anyone he wanted and reached into the features, sports, business and local news departments. In reality, Stuart conducted delicate negotiations with more than one territorial editor. Fine writers who should have been chosen were not. Some could not be spared; others were casualties of hoary grudges.

The final team, however, a diverse collection of 29 writers, editors, photographers and artists, did superb work. Assistant Managing Editor Susan "Mango" Curtis oversaw the design and graphics. Chancellor and feature writer/columnist Bob Dyer sat in on the focus groups with Assistant Managing Editor Doug Oplinger and wrote for all but one installment, kicking off with "30 Years After the Dream." Paynter often shared a byline. Other writers were Leona Allen, Carole Cannon, Sheryl Harris, Michael Holley, Colette Jenkins, Kevin Johnson, Ron Kirksey, David Knox, Steve Love, Maura McEnaney, Bill O'Connor and Will Outlaw. Also rotating onto the team were news editor Gloria Irwin; photographers Mike Cardew, Lew Stamp, Paul Tople and Jocelyn Williams; and artists Chuck Ayers, John Backderf, Deborah Kauffman, Art Krummel and Terence Oliver.

I started styling prototypes with my dear friend Mango, who has one of the best eyes for design in the business. After hours of mocking up, which involves placing dummy type, photos and graphics on a full-page grid, I would unveil my work for her. In the blink of an eye, she would have suggestions for improvement: Change that font. Make that bold. Use two-line subheads. Lose this. Add that.

Another huge talent in the art department was its director, Krummel, who created the project's signature composite of a black-and-white face forming a ragged, ill-fitting puzzle, plus templates for all the infographics.

The project gestated during an interregnum of managing editors. Jim Crutchfield had left to be editor in Long Beach, Calif. Allen was searching for his replacement. The steadying presence of a managing editor might have prevented the blow-up that occurred during a status meeting before the first part was published in February of 1993, but probably not.

Mango and I simultaneously mentioned that we had to go beyond traditional reporting and somehow make a lasting, meaningful statement. We didn't want to do another big-ass spectacular package that landed with acclaim, won awards for reporting and design, then went nowhere. The novel concept of public journalism was invading newsrooms nationwide, for better and worse. Journalists either hated it or loved it.

Paynter hated it. He is a brilliant, ballsy, compassionate, dedicated journalist with a large personality and a mind for detail. He began to bristle as I was speaking.

"No fucking way are we doing anything that makes us part of the story. That's not our job," he said, or something like.

Mango and I pushed back hard, begging Paynter to let us talk our ideas through, maybe with a larger group. We screamed at each other. Finally, Mango and I shrugged and left. There was no point in staying if we wouldn't be heard.

Stuart watched it all quietly from a seat in the corner. He thought the idea had merit. He also understood Paynter's resistance. He described the

shouting match to Allen, who enjoyed an occasional donnybrook and probably regretted missing this one. Most important, he appreciated what Mango
and I wanted and figured out how to do it.

The solution, Allen told Stuart the next day, came to him in the middle
of the night. The Beacon would bring in a number of prominent people
from the community and put the question to them: "How could we take A
Question of Color beyond the reporting?" He invited 10 or so business and
political leaders and Stuart, a former religion writer, reached out to the same
number of religious folks and social activists.

"I can't remember who all was there," Stuart said. "Deputy Mayor Dorothy Jackson and the Rev. Knute Larson (pastor of The Chapel) for sure...
but a robust discussion took place. I remember the saintly Dorothy saying,
'The Beacon should be the facilitator, should bring people to the table, but
then get out of the way and let them decide a course of action.' That's what
happened and that's how the Coming Together part of the project was born."

Allen also built a firewall: None of the reporters or editors working on A
Question of Color, except Stuart, the project's supervisor, would be involved
in Coming Together.

"Solomon had indeed split the baby in two," Stuart said.

A Question of Color was published in five, multi-day installments from
February 1993 to December 1993. Day One opened with this introduction:
*"Many whites are tired of hearing about it. Most Blacks wish it would go away.
All seem powerless to move it.... Thirty years after the Rev. Martin Luther
King Jr. described his dream of a colorblind America, race seems as huge and
divisive a force as ever."*

The project concluded in January of 1994 with a 12-page supplement
bearing the names of more than 20,000 readers who accepted the newspaper's pledge to fight racism.

That was also the beginning of Coming Together Akron, the non-profit
formed through private and corporate memberships. While it operated, CTA
sponsored overseas missions to Africa and an annual race walk, as well as
workshops, forums, and theatrical and musical events to raise awareness of
Akron's diversity. It lasted almost 15 years, dissolving in January 2008 when
it ran out of money.

In 1997, though, CTA was still going strong. Citing its success, President
Bill Clinton launched his national conversation on race with a Town Hall

meeting at the University of Akron on Dec. 3, 1997. The choice was controversial — critics said the Midwest was too white and Akron was too small — but Clinton's visit did boost Coming Together's profile beyond Northeast Ohio. In a short time, numerous cities expressed an interest in developing local efforts, recalled longtime director Dr. Fannie Brown, and CTA became a model for a national project, Coming Together USA.

"I would estimate in excess of 3 million people were touched by the organizations," Brown said.

Sadly, hard feelings linger over the management of A Question of Color. Some resentment is justified, some not. A Black reporter said her editor blocked her from rotating into the project, yet forced her to turn over her contacts among business leaders to a white reporter. Badly done! Another reporter, a white man, sniped on social media, "While you guys were working on race, the rest of us were putting out the paper." Nonsense!

For the record, Paynter was the only one who worked exclusively on race — the project wouldn't have succeeded without someone's full-time attention. The rest of us, while hitting our marks on race, also were putting out the rest of the paper. I know. We still had a composing room with printers and engravers for cold-type production. And that's where I was every Saturday night as printer Mike Jewell placed type and photos on page one and the A-section. Deputy News Editor Tom Moore and I stayed well after midnight when the presses started rolling, to give the paper — every section — a final check, usually wrapping around 1 in the morning.

The Pulitzer Board awarded the 1994 Gold Medal for Meritorious Public Service not to named individuals but to the Akron Beacon Journal, for the newspaper's "broad examination of local racial attitudes and its subsequent effort to promote improved communication in the community." Everyone in the newsroom made it happen and shares the kudos, now as then. Stuart and I were both in Seattle by then, in another time zone. Paynter and I traded congratulatory voicemails. Stuart called Allen, who told us to have a celebratory dinner and send him the bill.

Examining race relations seems to be a prize-winning formula for newspapers. In an ironic twist, the New York Times wrote of the Black/white divide in the Beacon's own newsroom as part of a series on contemporary racial attitudes across America. That series won the 2001 Pulitzer Prize for national reporting.

Has any of it made a difference? Carl Chancellor wonders, "So here we are 56 years since Dr. King's iconic March on Washington; 25 years since the Beacon's last Pulitzer Prize; in the wake of Tamir Rice, Ferguson, Missouri, Mother Emanuel Charleston Church Shooting, Black Lives Matter, Orlando Castillo, Eric Garner, Charlottesville, [Colin] Kaepernick, Trump, and the question still remains to be answered: What becomes of a dream too long deferred?"

Fannie Brown thinks it would be worthwhile to revive Coming Together Akron.

"Many acknowledge the need for it and offer accolades for the work we were able to accomplish," she said. "I can easily say it was the most important work of my life. The students we worked with continually share with me that diversity-related concepts learned as a part of the project have and will continue to govern the way they live their lives.

"What can top that?"

*Carl Chancellor and David Hertz contributed to this chapter.*

# Trying to Get It Right
# (But Not Always Succeeding)

# Chapter 13
## We Were Family — and Families Make Mistakes

Thrity Umrigar

The Beacon Journal. I say those three words to myself and a rush of warm memories floods me — whipping around after feeling the sting of a rubber band shot across the newsroom, only to see a look of faux innocence on Dave Adams's face; engaging in philosophical conversations with Chuck Klosterman, the general weirdness of the topics exceeded only by their madcap humor; being tormented by my buddy David Giffels' impressions of Harvey Firestone, in between discussions about Nirvana and R.E.M. and Patti Smith; jumping on rolls of bubble wrap in the women's restroom with Regina Brett to hear their soul-satisfying *ratatat*; sitting in the lunch room with other colleagues like Paula Schleis, Kathy Spitz, Susan Smith, Marcia Myers, Mary Beth Breckenridge and so many others, and giggling helplessly when Craig Wilson inevitably sneezed that single, shotgun sneeze.

God, we were so young once.

And so very lucky to have been hired during the last golden age of print journalism.

Lucky for another reason, too: As embarrassingly clichéd as it sounds, we were more than just friends and colleagues. We were family. We hung out with one another, went drinking together, saw the Beacon children grow up before our eyes in that newsroom — Naprie and Denise and Gabe. I personally experienced the caring of that family within six months of starting at the Beacon when, while on an out-of-town assignment, my lower back dramatically gave way and I was unable to drive for several months. In her characteristically competent, no-drama way, Metro Editor Kathy Fraze arranged for a rotation of reporters to pick me up and drive me to my physical therapy appointments.

That caring never waned. When I became a U.S. citizen, artist Chuck Ayers drew me one of his iconic cards and almost every person in the newsroom signed it. That afternoon, they threw a party for me in the newsroom, with the mandatory white sheet cake.

A few years later, when I earned my Ph.D., a big group took me out to dinner to celebrate. And when I was awarded the Nieman Fellowship to Harvard University — after Editor Jan Leach stayed up late into the night to write me a letter of recommendation because, in true journalistic fashion, I'd waited until the last minute to apply — people came up for days to congratulate me.

Family.

There were divisions of race, of course, but even those conversations seemed friendly and, in retrospect, oddly tepid. We weren't using terms like *white privilege* and *systemic racism* back then. Or perhaps that was true for me, occupying a no-man's land, being neither Black nor white, the only two major fault lines that seemed to exist in 1990s Akron. And so, I found myself, a brown girl, safely ensconced in the sorority of my Black sisters: I could enjoy Lynn Rhoden's deadly, wicked humor and Cristal Williams' quiet, steady warmth; Marilyn Miller's big sister protectiveness and Leslie Ansley's wry, trenchant observations. I loved joking and chatting with the impossibly suave Carl Chancellor, Akron's own answer to Don Johnson.

And then, there was the corner of the newsroom where I truly felt at home — the photo department, that glorious collection of the zaniest, most colorful and eccentric people in that newsroom. (Of course, the art department had Derf, a one-man army of zany and eccentric.) There was photographer Ed Suba Jr., who drove in and out of the parking deck at such breathtaking speed that it's a wonder it wasn't a site for daily mass murders. There was Ott Gangl, the gruff German-American with the heart of gold, who had survived World War II as a child and rightly felt invincible for the rest of his life. ("I survived the Nazis," Ott used to say to editors. "What're you going to do? Fire me?") There was my dear friend Robin Witek, smart, funny, brilliant, no-nonsense. There were my friends Susan Kirkman and Don Roese and Lew Stamp and Mike Cardew and to walk into that room and hang out with them for a few moments was to feel your spirits lighten.

A few other random memories: The sound of the coins jiggling in Editor Dale Allen's pocket as he strode through the newsroom like Colossus, the jiggling his own special calling card. Getting chastised by reporter Terry

Oblander when he found out that I had not yet opened a 401(k) account. Catching the eye of Managing Editor Thom Fladung as we rushed past each other while putting out an extra edition on 9/11, both of us stopping just long enough for him to whisper, "God, I love this business." Nobody outside a newsroom could understand such a comment on such a sad day. But nobody working in a newsroom could fail to agree with it.

And then there was Fran Murphey, a battleship of a woman, a towering legend, a woman who most likely would have been a misfit in any profession other than journalism. It was as if the newsroom had birthed Fran whole, and she had emerged from the darkroom fully dressed in her signature denim overalls and firemen's boots, with her mop of white hair and that handsome face, the keen intellect and that great, big heart. She was our everything — our mascot and our resident specter, our inspiration and our cautionary tale. If Fran didn't exist, we would've had to invent her. When she retired, she took with her a chunk of the pre-standardized, pre-journalism school, pre-corporate, newsroom culture. After she left, we became what we'd always feared we'd be: Bland.

Yes, we were once young and we were family.

"Bless This Mess" was a motto that longtime Beacon Journal columnist Fran Murphey lived by. She was a pioneering figure for women in the newsroom. (Photo by Roger Mezger)

And like family, we made mistakes.

In 1993, the Beacon Journal devoted a year and considerable resources to its epic series, A Question of Color. Early on, an editorial decision was made to confine the discussion to the Black and white racial divide. Of course, thanks to the historic presence of the rubber industry in Akron, the city had its fair share of other minorities, including Asian Americans. Even a few stories about the unique challenges facing that population — immigration, say, with all its ensuing legal, economic and emotional complications, or questions of identity, or the burdens of being considered a model community — would have deepened the conversation. As one of the handful of Asian Americans on the staff — and as someone who had already demonstrated such a keen interest in issues of race that I would eventually earn a Ph.D. in African American literature — I could have helped. Indeed, it is hard to imagine such a narrowly conscribed undertaking today. I remember sitting in on the early planning meetings, bubbling with ideas and then, the slow dawning that there was no place for me at that particular table.

But if we were clueless about how to think about race, we were even more so when it came to the issue of sexual minorities. To put it bluntly, not only was there no real desire to cover the concerns of the local gay community, there was also no attention paid to the hiring of gay reporters. The argument that had been made for the recruiting of racial minorities — that one needed the newsroom to look like the larger community one covered — was non-existent when it came to hiring gay journalists.

And so, what happened was absolutely predictable. Except for a couple of shiny examples of courage in the face of what was indifference at best and hostility at worst, the rest of us hid in the closet. We devised our own Don't Ask; Don't Tell long before it became a national slogan.

Postcards of a Life from Inside the Closet: While straight reporters complained openly about their divorces and breakups, gay reporters in long-term, loving relationships referred to their partners as friends and used the all-purpose "they" when talking about their weekend plans. One colleague repeated her mantra: "They may suspect something but as long as they don't have the proof, it doesn't matter." Two other friends went to incredible lengths to keep their relationship a secret. It is all very sad and very normal.

I myself lived an increasingly double life, one split between my home in Kent and my work in Akron; between my gay friends and my straight colleagues; between the life of the mind as I began to work part time on my

Ph.D. and my full-time job in the "real world" of journalism. Sometimes, I would still lose myself in the camaraderie and playfulness of life in the newsroom; other times, I felt like I was walking a tightrope: One spill and it would all come undone. I told myself that I had a lot to lose: My special interest was writing about social issues — the raging AIDS epidemic, the crisis of homelessness, the stigma of welfare and poverty. I was aware that behind my back people referred to me as the bleeding heart of the newsroom. And that they didn't mean it as a compliment either. I lived in constant fear that any indication of my sexual orientation would mean that I would never have another opportunity to tell the stories I felt most compelled to tell.

I had heard vague scuttlebutt that Bill Bierman was openly gay. But Bill was on the copy desk and older than I, so our paths didn't cross much. Indeed, for me, there was only one shining exception to this culture of silence: Photographer Robin Sallie. African American. Female. Proudly, openly queer. Comfortable in her own skin. Which, of course, meant that it made the rest of them uncomfortable. There were scandalized whispers about how she was "rubbing her gayness in our faces." There was much rolling of the eyes when she matter-of-factly referred to her partner as, well, her partner. In fact, Robin's simple, quiet insistence on equal treatment was considered to be either a provocation or the source of much amusement. And for the rest of us, spies in hostile territory, their rebukes and outrage were a call to silence. I spent the rest of my days in that newsroom ricocheting between unspoken admiration for Robin and self-loathing at my own cowardice.

After all this time, I don't know who to blame for this unnecessary human misery. The unenlightened age we lived through? Our own lack of courage? The newsroom culture?

One incident stands out in memory. One morning, my editor assigned me a crime story about a suicide-homicide. But this story had a twist. The murdered woman was a trans drag queen. She was also, I found out in my reporting, a beloved figure in the gay community because she had raised thousands of dollars in the fight against AIDS. But the main reason we were covering this story was because of the crime angle and the sense of bereavement her murder had produced in the gay community.

Reader, I cannot tell a lie.

I wrote the living hell out of that story.

All the editors loved it. They went out of their way to tell me so. The managing editor decided to run it above the fold of page one on a Sunday.

And then, all hell broke loose: Canceled subscriptions by readers who were offended to read about such degenerates over breakfast. Condemnations from the pulpit by pastors against the newspaper for running such a story on the Sabbath. Phone calls to the top editor, filling up his voice mail.

Editor Allen, who had been out of town when the story ran, was blindsided by the outrage. The managing editor was red-faced. Suddenly, I was the pariah of the newsroom, even though my immediate editor tried telling me that I had written a wonderful story and had nothing to apologize for. But then things became even more surreal. Columnist Bob Dyer weighed in by chastising the editors for running such an inflammatory story. Nobody thought of giving me the heads-up before his column ran. And then Allen used his Sunday column to issue a mea culpa for the newspaper's lack of judgment.

For two, painful weeks I had the dubious honor of holding the newsroom record for the most canceled subscriptions. Two weeks. Then, a miracle happened. The Beacon decided to stop running a popular syndicated comic strip and even more subscriptions were canceled. Just like that, I was dethroned. Thank you, beloved fickle readers.

But the scars from this incident remained. I felt hung out to dry over a story that had been assigned to me. It was clear to me now that my whole rationale for being a journalist — to give voice to the voiceless — would constantly have to be defended.

The final straw came after I returned to Akron at the end of a blissful year at Harvard. I had resolved to no longer live a double life when I got offered the Nieman fellowship. And for a year, I experienced what it was to live in a culture that didn't see diversity and difference as something to tolerate, but to celebrate. When I returned to Akron, I invited my immediate editor to lunch and came out to her. I told her that I was no longer able to pretend to be someone I was not. Still woozy from the freedom of Harvard, I was not prepared for her answer. I could do whatever I wished, she said. But as my friend, she should warn me that I would no longer be able to write about the social justice issues I cared so passionately about.

I hid my tears as we drove back to the newsroom. A white male reporter could cover any topic without anyone questioning his professionalism or objectivity. But a brown-skinned, gay immigrant was immediately suspect. The irony was that in 17 years as a journalist, no source had ever accused me of twisting their words or misquoting him or her. This much was clear — in order to continue writing the stories I cared about, I had to re-enter the closet.

No way of knowing then about the enormous social changes that the next two decades would bring. No way of predicting that gay marriage would become the law of the land and that my former conservative colleagues would become increasingly staunch defenders of equal rights. It was a different era, a darker age, one that we have thankfully left in the dustbin of history.

But back then, we were all facing bigger and newer challenges — layoffs, buyouts, shrinking news space, budget cuts, contentious Guild negotiations. In the face of an existential crisis, we did what families do in times of crisis — we came together, supported one another, cried on each other's shoulders, told each other about job leads elsewhere. We ate copious quantities of that white sheet cake as friend after friend left the newsroom.

It was the end of an era and the divisions of race and gender and sexuality seemed to pale under the class divisions of which we were now aware — all of us, editors and reporters alike, battling increasingly distant corporate bosses who resided in their glass towers thousands of miles away.

And despite the coming apocalypse, and perhaps despite our many shortcomings and imperfections, we continued to work side by side to put out the best damn newspaper we could, day after glorious day. It is those memories that will make me forever proud to have worked at the Beacon Journal alongside some of the best colleagues one could hope for.

As for me, I lasted at the Beacon until 2002.

And then I left, slamming the closet door behind me forever.

# Chapter 14
## A Long Climb to the Mountaintop for Women

Charlene Nevada

I was just 23 and had been at the Beacon Journal only a couple of months when my rude awakening came from a colleague, who sat a few feet away from me in a very small Action Line office, a floor below the main newsroom.

Our job was to help readers and answer questions, but I wasn't prepared for the note I was passed one morning.

"Nevada," it said, "I started to call your number last night...."

It then gave me four little multiple-choice boxes.

"Would you have:

"Talked to me.

"Hung up on me.

"Told me you aren't into Black-white relationships.

"Told me to go fuck myself."

I felt the blood run to my face. The race of my colleague wasn't the issue. He was twice my age, an ex-con (armed bank robbery) and had a live-in girlfriend who was a bruiser. (She grazed him in the shoulder with a bullet a few weeks later during a fight.)

I left the office and went to the restroom to collect myself. I felt vulnerable. This senior co-worker had been invited to sit in on my official job interview. He was working at the Beacon Journal because the editor at the time believed in convict rehabilitation.

Though I was tempted to check Box No. 4, I instead passed his desk on the way back to my seat and simply said: "Don't call me."

He didn't, and any ongoing anxiety I might have had disappeared a couple of months later when FBI agents led him from our office in handcuffs. Seems he and the girlfriend had stolen paychecks from a defunct gas station and were cashing them to buy heroin.

That was in 1970, and except for being pinched on the ass by another colleague in a hallway a few years later — and somehow that was more ornery than threatening — the note from my co-worker was the worst example of sexual harassment I ever experienced during my 35 years at the Akron Beacon Journal. Some women fared worse.

A few "me-too" examples:

One new copy desk hire was invited to lunch by a (married) senior co-worker, who drove to a restaurant-hotel complex in downtown Akron. "Should we have lunch or just go to bed?" he asked. Thinking quickly, she replied she was hungry, and then made up an excuse to walk back to the office after lunch.

An editor asked a young female reporter to lunch on another occasion. He gave her an address and said he would meet her there. She realized when she pulled into the drive it was his home and he had more to offer than lunch.

Another (married) editor gave a (married) female staffer a ride home from a luncheon one day and said: "We should go to the zoo sometime."

In short, the Beacon Journal did indeed have its own Bill O'Reillys and Matt Lauers. And while sexual harassment is not confined to any particular decade, there were lots of opportunities in the 1970s and 1980s as women pushed into a news business traditionally staffed by men.

Those of us around (meaning alive) today will never know what our earlier sisters went through to raise women to positions of respect. But we can see how they paved the way for us.

The first female reporter of note at the Beacon Journal was Helen Waterhouse, who was hired in 1928. She had been selling stories "freelance" to the Beacon. When John S. Knight realized she was making more money than some staff reporters, he hired her.

She was a "sob sister" and a star, scooping and drawing the attention and dislike of people including nationally recognized radio commentator Walter Winchell. (He called her the "Akron disaster.")

Her background was in aviation. With Knight's blessing and his checkbook, and her ambition and friendship with Charles Lindbergh, she traveled to New Jersey to cover the 1935 trial of the man accused of kidnapping Lindbergh's son.

She scored the only interview with the convicted kidnapper, Bruno Hauptmann. Back home, she was a confidant and supporter of Sam Sheppard, the Bay Village doctor accused of killing his wife in 1954. She had a special way of putting things, once describing the unwed pregnant women at the old Florence Crittenton Home near East Market Street as having loved "well but not too wisely."

The Waterhouse era ended in 1965, when she died from a cerebral hemorrhage driving to work one day.

By then, there were a few more women in the newsroom. The biggest change had happened during World War II, when women were offered "temporary" jobs to fill in for the men in uniform — with the understanding that the job would end when the GIs came home.

However, by the war's end, the single women, who had no man to support them, were generally allowed to stay. Polly Paffilas and Fran Murphey were among those. While Murphey gravitated to covering suburban news, Paffilas wound up as the food writer in what was often referred to as the "women's pages."

In those days, no one thought about the lack of women in top management or the idea of a glass ceiling.

But there was a glass partition — a wall separating the newsroom from the reporters who worked for the women's pages. For much of that time, only Waterhouse and Murphey were on the news side.

"I tried so hard to get through that glass partition," says Nancy Yockey Bonar, who covered fashion, the teen beat and beauty from 1960 to 1966 in the women's news department. There was only one opportunity to cross the partition. The ladies room was on the other side of the newsroom. Then again, it had only two stalls. More were not needed.

Presiding over the women's news side of the newsroom was Betty Jaycox, who came from a prominent family and was hired by Knight to write about his carriage-class friends. She did run the department, but her chief job was to be a columnist, know and connect with the VIPs in the community, and make sure all the important charity events were covered.

As the women's movement took hold in the late '60s, some of the department's younger reporters — Janis Froelich, Pat Ravenscraft and Joan Rice — considered the liberation fight "their beat." Froelich recalls Editor Ben Maidenburg being opposed to the women's page reporters covering the women's movement.

Instead, she and the other reporters were being sent to cover events like a "wives-of-lawyers" luncheon.

"We said, 'This is what women are like in the '70s. You can't keep just covering Day at the Races,'" says Froelich, who did subsequently get to cover a major march on Washington and other women's events. When Wendy Sclight was named executive editor of the section in 1975, the focus began to shift to consumerism and health.

On the other side of the wall, change was slow as well. To be sure, there were anomalies. Editor Maidenburg hired Mickey Porter from Evansville, Ind., to be a columnist in 1966. Porter's wife, Suzanne, was the city hall reporter for the Evansville paper. Once she and Maidenburg talked — and he learned how much she knew about the workings of a city government — he hired her, too, and assigned her to Akron City Hall. She stayed until she became pregnant and the city hired her away.

One big obstacle to the hiring of women on the news side was De Nobili-smoking, high-energy Pat Englehart, the editor in charge of suburban coverage. He once said he needed "a tough man" to cover sewer problems in Canton. "Goddamn woman" was part of his lexicon. There is a note in Newspaper Guild files in which Englehart threatened to bite a reporter's "tit off" if she didn't get a story.

Englehart, however, didn't always get his way. In 1969, Maidenburg hired Kathy Lally and then-husband Russ Lilly. Lilly was sent to the city desk and Lally to the state/suburban desk. She recalls Englehart grumbling: "Why didn't they give me the man?"

Lally, who would later spend years co-anchoring the Moscow bureau for the Baltimore Sun, was on rewrite on May 4, 1970, when National Guardsmen opened fire on students at Kent State University. She talked to reporters at the scene and helped shape the Beacon's same-day stories. Later, when the newspaper won a Pulitzer Prize for its coverage of the event, 16 reporters were singled out. Only two were women: Lally and Helen Carringer, the education writer who would become the first woman editorial writer in 1976.

Things hadn't changed much in the suburban news department when Ann Sheldon Mezger was hired in 1972. Early on, Mezger was sent to interview a suburban police chief. She remembers Englehart chomping on his cigar before she left the office: "When you go to interview a police chief," he advised, "always wear a short skirt."

Kathy Fraze was hired in 1973 and a year or so later was assigned to the Ravenna bureau. Her late husband, Bruce Larrick, was also a Beacon reporter. One particularly busy day, there was a huge gas leak in Portage County. Fraze was digging in when Larrick came skulking into the Ravenna office to announce: "Englehart sent me out here to do the gas leak." So much, she recalls, "for marital harmony."

Still, Lally, Mezger and Fraze all say today that once they established themselves as solid reporters, Englehart treated them fairly. The issue was getting in the door.

A major change happened in 1974, when the city and suburban desks were merged under Metro Editor Scott Bosley. He put a woman, Cathy Strong, on the police beat. He assigned me to cover county government, a first for a woman. Englehart became editor of an investigative team that did have a woman reporter, Melissa Berg.

While women were making inroads in the 1970s, there was still gender discrimination.

In June of 1977, a sewer exploded in the middle of the night and tore up a cemetery and streets in near West Akron. It also tore up the Beacon Journal newsroom.

The early a.m. calls went out to reporters. Medical writer Peggy Rader answered the phone and the editor asked to speak to her boyfriend, Bob Von Sternberg. Soon, she recalls, he was getting into his work clothes and mumbling about manhole covers flying in the air. Von Sternberg was called out to cover the story but Rader was not, even though she was clearly available. Eleven reporters — all men — were credited in the next day's paper. The only woman involved in the coverage was photographer Marcy Nighswander. The female reporters were furious and demanded an explanation.

In retrospect, Tim Smith, the assigning editor who made the calls that night, says he would have handled things differently. Given the darkness and the area of the city (high crime), he worried about the safety of female reporters. Now, he says, he would have given female reporters the choice of whether or not to head out in the night.

Smith did allow me to cover a murder a year later, when I was about seven months pregnant. The police radio alerted us that a woman had been shot inside a church in West Akron. The shooter was believed to still be inside. It was lunch time, and there were only two reporters in the office

— me and ace rewrite guy Don Bandy. Better for him to stay behind and write the story on deadline. I volunteered to cover the scene, Smith nodded and out the door I went.

Maybe the cops didn't think I was really a reporter. They did tell me the shooter was no longer in the building, then shooed me to the sidelines, where I found lots of church members who provided me with the name of the dead church secretary and information about her and her family. We got it all in that day's paper.

That isn't to say I didn't experience my share of gender discrimination.

The Cleveland school system was set to begin busing and desegregation in the fall of 1979. I was the education writer, anticipating I would cover the event, when I learned an assistant editor had assigned another reporter to cover the first day of cross-town busing. I demanded an explanation. It seems the male assistant metro editor felt it would be a long day and "Char would want to be home with her kids." The answer didn't go over well with higher-up editors. I was in Cleveland on Day 1.

Another major change came in early 1980, when Bosley moved to the Detroit Free Press as Sunday and features editor. Dale Allen, an associate managing editor of the Philadelphia Inquirer, was brought to Akron as the executive editor. By the fall of 1980, Allen was ready to do some reorganizing.

Ann Mezger, who had been the lifestyle editor since 1978, was promoted to oversee both lifestyle and features/entertainment. The male assistant metro editor, who a year earlier had decided I shouldn't cover Cleveland desegregation, was assigned to be Mezger's assistant, overseeing lifestyle coverage, which included food, fashion and home furnishings. As I remember hearing, he declared he could do better than "editing Tupperware stories."

He left the paper shortly thereafter, but before his departure, Mezger saw an opportunity. She suspected that her salary was not up to par with some of the men managers in the newsroom. She told Allen she didn't know how much money her assistant-to-be made but she would find out and hoped her salary would not be lower than his. "I got the biggest raise I ever got," she recalls.

That reorganization put Colleen Murphy Tigelman, a features copy editor with a master's degree in modern diplomatic history, as the first woman in the national editor's slot. Not long after that, the Beacon had its first woman copy desk chief, Joanne McLaughlin. Up to that point, Mezger and head librarian Cathy Tierney had been the only woman in management meetings.

And while the women had been welcomed into management meetings, they weren't invited to the table. John S. Knight died in 1981. A year later, a room at the Beacon Journal was dedicated in his honor. All the executives from Knight Ridder in Miami flew in for a banquet. The Beacon bought a table — but invited only its male editors.

While women were breaking into management, testosterone prevailed.

Every female had to deal with Editor Paul Poorman, who was hired in 1976. He was notoriously sexist and always made comments about women wearing pants. The best way to describe Poorman is to explain his situation: He had eight kids — six boys — before he got a vasectomy, and then entertained female staff members at a party one night by describing it. ("I went home, sat on the end of the bed and said to my wife, 'Sylvia, it's the end of a dynasty.'") He most always had something inappropriate to say at news meetings. On more than one occasion, he referred to Tierney, the head librarian, as "Tootles."

Still, Poorman listened in the early '80s when Assistant Metro Editor Marilynn Marchione approached him about females being made to feel uncomfortable in the newsroom by a certain male editor. He wanted details; she refused to give them, except to say: "You have a problem, and it has to stop." Indeed, Poorman called all his top male editors into a meeting and the overtures did stop.

But the old-boy humor remained for years. There was the time that some of the guys challenged some of the younger women to a volleyball game. The guys even had special shirts made for the females — white with a blue Superman shield across the chest. Instead of an S, there was a big BJ inside the shield. The ladies canceled the game when they realized the BJ stood for Big Jugs, not Beacon Journal.

Then there were the birthday strippers: A Mae West imitator for Tim Smith, a male stripper for Colleen Tigelman and a scantily clad 300-pounder sent to the office by radio personality Stan Piatt for columnist Stuart Warner.

Those appearances were short-lived. The anatomically correct and nude blow-up doll that appeared in the office of Assistant Managing Editor Bill Winter was another matter. It/she stayed there awhile until someone pointed out that Winter's office — with the door open — was in the direct path from the parking deck to the photo department, and lots of senior citizens passed that way when they came into the paper for their complimentary golden anniversary photos. Deflation came at last.

About that same time, some women faced another stumbling block: their marital status.

Based on a problem Allen had with a newsroom couple in Philadelphia, he decreed: no new spouse hires. But when the Philadelphia Bulletin folded in 1982, the Beacon offered jobs to a number of staffers there. It was no secret two of the reporters ultimately hired had been dating and moved in together once both were in Akron.

"Is that the message you want to send?" an assistant managing editor asked.

Allen relented.

Lifting that ban led to the hiring of two talented editors. Bonnie Bolden (the late wife of now retired Beacon Editor Bruce Winges) would fill roles including features, suburban and hiring editor. Years later, Margaret Corvini (wife of then Sports Editor Bill Eichenberger) would be the features editor.

Women (some men, too) also spent years fighting the title war: They simply wanted to call women by their last names, as men were referred to in stories. Having to ask a woman her marital status — so a Miss, Mrs. or Ms. could be attached — was awkward and not often relevant.

Kathy Fraze, who through the years held a number of editing positions, including copy desk chief, remembers a big fight on the copy desk with one older man insisting that married women wanted to be called Mrs. and deserved the title. "They worked for that," he argued. The honorariums finally disappeared, but not until about 1990.

Titles aside, women made strides in the 1980s — even earlier for Carolyn White, who became the first woman sports writer for the paper in 1979. She later was hired by USA Today. In 1983, Mary Grace Poidomani was assigned to the Beacon's Columbus bureau. Katie Byard, a student correspondent from Ohio State University, was filing stories from Columbus as well. The Beacon had a women in the city hall beat (Kathy Byland), and I was covering the labor beat, probably the first female to cover the United Rubber Workers negotiations. Marilyn Geewax, later a business news editor for NPR, was covering the steel industry for the business news department. A few years later, Susan Smith became the first female political writer, and in 1987, Deb Van Tassel was named the first woman business editor. Susan Mango Curtis was in charge of design and graphics and later, Susan Kirkman Zake directed the photo department.

There remained, however, another big issue: Salary disparity.

Manager salaries were not available information. However, payroll records for union-covered employees had to be shared with the officers of the Akron Newspaper Guild.

Over the years, guild officers had seen a pattern. Upper managers — traditionally male — valued sports writers and columnists almost like franchise players and paid them much above the top union scale.

It became an issue during salary negotiations in the '90s, when the paper's management wanted to take some of the money it would have put toward across-the-board and experience increases and instead use it for merit raises.

Then-guild president Paula Schleis says guild negotiators did not trust the company to parcel out the money fairly, given what she knew.

So the guild prepared a list of the 10 highest-paid union-covered workers and their salaries. The list included sex but no names. All 10 were male.

The list went up on the Akron Newspaper Guild bulletin board in the newsroom. At the next negotiating session, Schleis says, the proposal was off the table.

It was about that time that food writer Jane Snow, a franchise player in her own league with multiple (and prestigious) national awards, got a job offer from another Ohio paper. She had had offers before, but none so close to home or as tempting. Snow remembers Ann Mezger, who after stints as the suburban and magazine editor had returned to the features editor position, advocating for her — going to top managers and reminding them not only of Snow's reader following but that Snow (a former guild president) had access to salary records and knew exactly how much those sports reporters were making. Snow recalls getting a raise of more than $200 a week!

The final step to the top for womankind began in 1997, when Editor Dale Allen took an early retirement. Publisher John Dotson was upfront in saying that choosing Allen's successor would be the most important decision he would ever make at the Beacon Journal. He sought lots of staff input.

Many of us hoped for a woman at the top. Some suggested the voice of a working mother.

In the end, Jan Leach, the managing editor of the Cincinnati Enquirer (and a mother of three), was named the first female editor of the Akron Beacon Journal in 1998. The glass ceiling had been broken.

And it stayed shattered. When Leach left five years later, her successor was another woman, Debra Adams Simmons.

As for me, my career was full and fulfilling, if not occasionally bizarre. I once saw a man cut in half at the Cathedral of Tomorrow, the result of a stage accident. I watched doctors transplant human skin at Akron Children's Hospital. When Ohio's POWs from Vietnam were released, I was at the airfield when they landed on American soil. I once spent 30 hours (straight) covering very difficult labor negotiations when a strike at the Twinsburg Stamping Plant shut down Chrysler nationwide.

I got to meet two presidents (George H. W. Bush and Bill Clinton) and travel to Washington, D.C., when city officials convinced the National Inventors Hall of Fame trustees to move the shrine from Washington to Akron. No matter what happened later, that was a career highlight. I worked out with Jane Fonda and drank with mayors, county and party officials. And when they screwed up, I helped skewer them. I met my husband, artist Art Krummel, at the Beacon.

My hit-home memory came on a snowy December night in the early '70s. I was working the late Saturday shift and my boss sent me to a Mensa meeting at a local restaurant — open to the public — where the minister of a fairly large church in West Akron was talking about how he had been communicating with a Martian named Astume Gastula, who had been patrolling Earth in his flying saucer, checking for fault lines. (This was in the days before we knew the red planet was a dead planet).

The Martian whisperer turned out to be the preacher who had officiated at my marriage a year earlier!

Life at the Beacon Journal was never dull.

# Chapter 15
## The Guild-ed Age of Journalism in Akron

Roger Mezger

In the fall of 1985, contract negotiations between the Beacon Journal and the union that represented most newsroom employees had reached a stalemate. The company was determined that a key union perk, double-time pay for Sunday work, part of the contract since the 1950s, had to go. The union, Local 7 of The Newspaper Guild, was just as determined to keep it.

Gerald "Jerry" Chattman, a labor lawyer who had been guiding Local 7 through contract bargaining since the early 1970s, was unimpressed when company negotiators declared that they intended to kill Sunday double time no matter how long it took.

"My union has an iron ass," Chattman glowered across the bargaining table, "and we'll sit here for months if you like!"

Local 7 voted to authorize a strike and broke off talks. In a matter of days, many of Local 7's members — at the time, about 125 reporters, editors, photographers, editorial artists, clerks and librarians as well as a small number of maintenance workers — were sporting "My Union Has An Iron Ass" T-shirts featuring a knight in shining armor. Not wanting a strike, the company dropped the demand. Talks resumed, and Sunday double time remained part of the new contract agreed to three weeks later.

It was one of the last significant wins for the union at the bargaining table. Changing dynamics at the Beacon Journal and its corporate parent, Knight Ridder Inc., and in the newspaper industry at large, soon would force Local 7 to play defense more than offense. Negotiations were about to become far more adversarial. Before the end of the decade, Sunday double time and other union-friendly contract language would be gone.

"That was the last respectful negotiations we had," recalled Jane Snow, a former food writer who was a union negotiator in 1985 and Local 7 president when the contract next came up for renewal in 1987. The pivotal 1987 negotiations would drag on for more than two years, destroy morale in the newsroom and set the pattern for more drawn-out bargaining in the future. "Our negotiations were brutal. We never got a contract on time," remembers Paula Schleis, a reporter who was elected president in 1994.

But in 1985, Local 7 — commonly called simply the guild — was still riding high. At the unsatisfying conclusion of the contentious 1987 to 1989 negotiations, Chattman would wistfully look back on the 1985 contract as the best he had seen to that point in his collective bargaining career. Under the 1985 contract, reporters with the most experience received pay raises to $694 a week, equal to more than $1,600 in 2019 dollars. Reporter pay at the Beacon Journal, already the highest in Ohio, had now surpassed that at many big-city newspapers, including the Washington Post and papers in Detroit and Seattle.

"The company made so damn much money back then that it wasn't hard-nosed about sharing that with the workers," said Tim Smith, a former managing editor who bargained for the company from 1977 until leaving the paper in 1986.

Still, Beacon Journal and Knight Ridder money managers could not have been thrilled with the 1985 settlement. It was just the latest in a string of contracts favorable to Local 7 starting in the early 1970s. But the nonunion newsroom managers certainly were pleased. Among them was Executive Editor Dale Allen, who joined the Beacon Journal in 1980 from Knight Ridder's Philadelphia Inquirer with a goal of turning a very good regional newspaper into an excellent one. In an unpublished memoir, Allen wrote that he had been ecstatic about the 1980 contract, which provided $40-a-week raises in each of its three years. He knew that would help him compete with bigger papers in recruiting the best journalists.

"We often heard from other journalists about how good our pay was," recalled Doug Oplinger, who held both union and management jobs over more than 45 years at the paper. "We were very attractive. There were good people who wanted to work here. That really did give us the opportunity to hire the best."

The plush 1985 contract had padded the hiring advantage. But half a century earlier, there was no satisfaction with wages, benefits or working conditions in the Beacon Journal newsroom — or just about any other newsroom in the country.

*John S. Knight once offered to join*

As the Great Depression deepened in 1933, waves of job and pay cuts became the norm in the newspaper industry. News workers slowly began to realize that banding together in order to further their own interests was just as suitable for reporters as for printers and pressmen. Reporters at the Cleveland Press and the Cleveland News were the first in the nation to organize, forming what would become Local 1 of the American Newspaper Guild. Akron journalists at Scripps-Howard's Times-Press and the Beacon Journal soon followed Cleveland's lead. Meeting at the Mayflower Hotel on South Main Street and at the Hub Café on South Howard Street, they established what would become Local 7 of the new union. At the time, even the best-paid among them were earning less than $40 for workweeks that often stretched to 60 or 70 hours, with no overtime.

At first, it was unclear to some whether the guild was a labor union or a professional organization. Managers, including Beacon Journal President and Editor John S. Knight, applied for membership, only to be advised by guild headquarters in New York that they were not eligible. "Not wishing to cause you any embarrassment whatsoever," Knight responded in April 1934, "I am very glad to comply with your suggestion that I withdraw from the Akron Newspaper Guild."

The Akron guild soon found that negotiating contracts would not be easy. Knight "is very stiff-necked about any concessions and indicates very definitely he does not intend to come even close to an agreement until absolutely forced to do so," Local 7 Secretary Ray Sutliff, a Times-Press reporter, advised New York in April 1935. Not until 1937 did the guild sign its first contracts with the Akron papers. A year after that, Knight bought and closed the Times-Press, which had a larger guild unit than did the Beacon Journal.

*Years of steady gains*

By 1972 the American Newspaper Guild had shortened its name to The Newspaper Guild. That year also marked the beginning of a 15-year run of steady contract gains for Local 7. Feeling that the union needed more firepower on its negotiating committee, Local 7 President Harry Liggett, an assistant state editor, had hired Chattman, a 29-year-old suburban Cleveland labor lawyer, as point person.

Chattman's hiring paid immediate dividends. The contract bargained in 1972 was groundbreaking. The Newspaper Guild's national publication for members, The Guild Reporter, trumpeted its achievements in a front-page story: paid maternity leave, believed to be the first such provision in a guild contract anywhere; unlimited sick leave; protections for workers displaced by automation; a program for hiring and training minorities; guaranteed protections for reporters against forced disclosure of sources; seniority rights in the event of layoffs; and many other gains in benefits and working conditions.

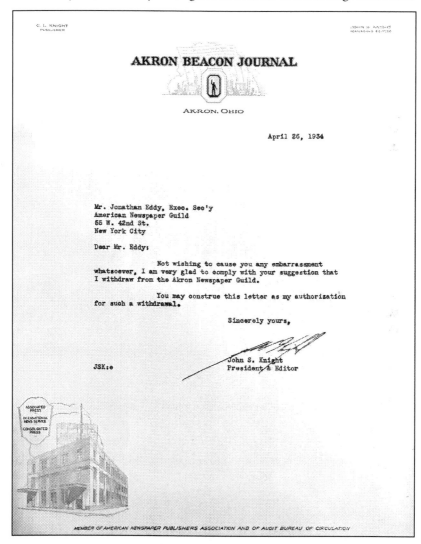

Memo from John S. Kight to the American Newspaper Guild. (Courtesy of Newspaper Guild Records, Walter P. Reuther Library, Archives of Labor and Urban Affairs, Wayne State University)

Circumstances were just right in the early 1970s for the growth of Local 7. The Beacon Journal was on the journalism map after winning a Pulitzer Prize in 1971 for its coverage of the 1970 Kent State shootings. The newsroom was filling up with young reporters hired straight out of college. The Beacon Journal even ran a promotional ad touting its "Under 30 Generation" news staff in 1971. That generation had challenged authority; union activism seemed a natural fit.

Despite occasional labor turmoil in other local industries, the Beacon Journal had never experienced a strike by any of its unions. Then on May 1, 1974, the union representing truck drivers and circulation district managers, Teamsters Local 471, walked out. The guild voted to honor the picket lines. When the Teamsters threw bricks at trucks trying to leave the plant with papers and scattered nails in their path, the Beacon Journal fitted one truck with unbreakable glass and puncture-proof tires. That truck managed to haul papers to the post office for mail delivery to subscribers, effectively ending the strike after six days.

### New publisher changes the battlefield

For several years after Knight died in 1981, relations remained business-like between the guild and the Beacon Journal. But sudden change rocked the Beacon Journal in March 1986. Tony Ridder, head of Knight Ridder's newspaper division, introduced John McMillion as the paper's new publisher. It didn't take long for word to spread that McMillion had earned a reputation as an aggressive cost-cutter and tamer of unions in Duluth, Minn., where he was publisher of Knight Ridder's News Tribune & Herald.

Even so, McMillion soon earned praise in the Beacon Journal newsroom for standing up to auto dealers who temporarily pulled their ads from the paper after a story told readers how they could save money shopping for a car. He also supported the paper's Pulitzer Prize-winning reporting on the attempted foreign takeover of Goodyear Tire and Rubber Co. in 1986. He was approachable and unpretentious, even taking part in an on-site exercise class with his employees.

But the gravy train that Local 7 had been riding for 15 years was about to be flagged to a screeching halt. The guild and McMillion would spend more than two years staring each other down in the highest-stakes contract bargaining since the union's earliest years.

McMillion officially threw down the gauntlet to the guild in September 1987. The union's contract with the company was due to expire on Nov. 1, and negotiating teams from both sides met to present their proposals. The guild went first, asking for, among other things, a pay increase, more time off, a bigger company contribution to the retirement fund, and a reduction in the number of newsroom employees exempt from union membership.

Then it was the company's turn. McMillion wanted to eliminate the experience-based pay scale and replace it with merit raises only. He wanted to cut sick leave to a maximum six weeks per illness from 104 weeks. Vacation time and the retirement fund contribution would be slashed. The clause governing guild jurisdiction would be rewritten in a way that eliminated nearly half the bargaining unit. And guild members would pay a significant portion of their health-insurance premiums for the first time. In all, the concessions the company wanted from the guild covered 13 single-spaced typed pages.

"I had never seen a contract proposal as radical as the one McMillion submitted to the Akron Guild," Allen, who died in 2019, wrote in his unpublished memoir, noting that it had been put together "with virtually no input from newsroom managers." To help members understand the scope of what the company was demanding, reporter Terry Oblander, a guild vice president, copied the contract onto poster boards he displayed at a membership meeting, then dramatically crossed out all the provisions McMillion wanted to eliminate. "It was almost the whole thing," Snow says.

Over the next two years, the relationship between Local 7 and the Beacon Journal — and, by extension, Knight Ridder — steadily spiraled down. The company's new hard line "was indicative of an end of an era for Beacon Journal employees," Allen wrote, and the beginning of an erosion of loyalty and trust in the newsroom. When Allen had arrived in Akron seven years earlier, he noted, "you could still feel a sense of belonging that permeated the newspaper, its genesis traceable to the days when John S. Knight walked its halls, building trust and pride among managers and employees." Now things were going to get ugly.

As negotiations dragged on, the months turning into years, the guild continued working under the expired contract, looking for ways to involve the community in its cause. Informational picketing in front of the building attracted attention, as did a byline strike and a full-page ad the guild bought in the Beacon Journal after the first year of unproductive contract talks.

Guild members also targeted major Beacon Journal advertisers — O'Neil's department stores and car dealerships — as informational picketing sites in an attempt to get advertisers to pressure the paper to settle.

Before one picketing event at an O'Neil's store, Snow explained to the volunteers that the store might call the police and, if that happened, they could get arrested. One enthusiastic picket, though, misunderstood Snow's use of the word "could." The member returned disappointed, feeling that she had failed. "When the police came, I told them that you said we could get arrested, but they wouldn't arrest me," she lamented.

All this activity drew the attention of other media outlets, both local and national. Columbia Journalism Review published a story titled, "Trouble in Rubber City." None of this, though, appeared to faze McMillion, who "seemed mostly amused by the antics of the guild," Allen wrote. But if nothing else the guild had done managed to get McMillion's attention, its ambitious subscription cancellation drive surely did.

The guild connected with dozens of labor unions and community groups and encouraged their members to sign cards directing the Beacon Journal to cancel their subscriptions. The guild also held free car washes and used the time it took to suds, rinse and dry to persuade drivers to sign cancellation cards. The guild planned to hold on to the cards it collected and present them to the company if all else failed. The threat of massive subscription cancellations was really the only leverage the guild could muster. The problem was, signed cards were coming in very slowly. About 30,000 cards had been distributed, but after many months only a few hundred signed ones were in hand.

The solution: Make a mountain out of a molehill. At Oblander's suggestion, guild officers identified mid- and low-level managers in the Beacon Journal's non-news departments and went door to door on the streets where they lived, asking neighbors to sign subscription cancellation cards. Guild officers knew that these lower-level managers would report the activity to their bosses, and that McMillion would soon hear about it. Though it appeared to management that the guild was canvassing all over the region, in reality it was targeting just a block or two at a time.

Ted Schneider, an assistant news editor and a guild vice president, pulled off an equally brilliant ploy. Schneider, who worked nights, was in charge of keeping track of how many cancellation cards had been distributed and how many signed ones had been returned. With so few signed cards in hand, he decided that some creative accounting was in order. One night, Schneider doctored his totals to show that the guild had collected 20,000 signed cards. Before heading home, he left his fake tally on a copy machine, knowing that it would find its way into management hands in the morning.

During this time, Knight Ridder was promoting a company-wide effort to improve customer service. That initiative, and also perhaps some concern about the increasingly toxic labor situation, brought Tony Ridder to the Beacon Journal newsroom for a pep talk. The guild hastily ordered a huge banner reading, "BJ CANCELLATION HQ," that it draped from the International Typographical Union hall across the street, clearly visible to Ridder from newsroom windows. When Ridder encouraged the newsroom crowd to "be flexible" and to "bend over backwards to please the customer," Snow couldn't keep quiet. We'll help you with customer service when you help us reach a fair contract, she told him. "I felt like Norma Rae," Snow remembers, referring to the union organizer played by Sally Field in the 1979 movie of the same name. "But I was scared shitless." Within days, Local 7 members were sporting big red buttons announcing, "Flexible NOT Breakable."

Just months before he arrived at the Beacon Journal, McMillion had married for the second time, having been divorced a few years earlier in Duluth. With an assist from the Duluth Guild, Local 7 learned from McMillion's 1983 divorce filing that he intended to retire in January 1990, just after turning 60. So even as talks dragged on forever, the guild knew that an agreement was likely before the end of 1989. As it turned out, a new contract was signed on Nov. 1, 1989.

But there was no celebration. The guild had spent more than two years and $30,000 fighting McMillion — more than $60,000 in 2019 dollars — for an agreement that pleased no one.

Harry Liggett, who with Chattman had negotiated the trailblazing 1972 contract, thanked the negotiators for doing all they could. But he aptly summed up the situation when he grumbled, "This is the lousiest son-of-a-bitchin' contract we've had."

"I put two years of my life into that contract," Snow replied, "and nobody feels worse about it than me."

McMillion did retire in January 1990, just as planned. In 2019 he was 89 and living on the Lake Superior shore outside Duluth. He was not available for an interview, but his wife, Melanie Higdon McMillion, said there was never anything personal about his battles with unions. He enjoyed the challenge of negotiating contracts and viewed the task almost like a game of chess. "He was trying to do what was best for the paper, which was also… in the long run good for the employees as well," she said.

### 'Blue-collar mentality'

From the 1970s into the 2000s, when contentious issues arose, the guild rallied the troops by slapping slogans on buttons and T-shirts that members wore in the newsroom. When a newsroom manager accused the guild of having "a blue-collar mentality" by insisting on sticking to contract language on overtime pay, members sported blue T-shirts proclaiming "Blue-Collar Mentality — And Proud of It." "We weren't old union bosses with stogies," Snow says. "The only power we had, came from the members."

The union's annual summer picnic was another morale booster, one year even featuring a roast pig. "We ate that roast pig down to its squeal," copy editor and columnist Mickey Porter reported afterward. Then, during the dark days of the 1987 to 1989 contract negotiations, when spirits hit rock bottom, the guild started a new tradition: a Christmas party featuring skits that became more elaborate over the years. One staple was the annual dramatic reading of what was known as the Ann Hill Letter.

Ann Hill was a bright young woman with two years of newspaper report-ing experience and a master's degree from Ohio State University. She arrived at the Beacon Journal in the early 1970s for a reporting tryout that editors grossly mismanaged. After an arduous day and evening of work lasting more than 12 hours, she sat at a typewriter and left a letter blasting her overlords. "I did not come to Akron or the Beacon Journal to do shit work or to run an obstacle course," she seethed. Mixed in with the legitimate outrage was a bit of youthful hubris: "Experienced newspaper people who now teach at OSU consider me the most talented student they've ever taught." After several beers at the Christmas party, a dramatic reading of Ann Hill's no good, very bad day at the Beacon Journal qualified as entertainment.

Thirty years after Ann Hill pounded out her frustrations, another letter of protest became part of the Christmas party festivities. In February 2001, for the first time in its history, the Beacon Journal laid off newsroom employees, the result of corporate-mandated budget cuts. The seniority clause that became part of the guild contract in 1972 kicked in, which meant that the most recent hires — eight of them — had to go. One was Mark Schlueb, a reporter who had moved his young family to Akron just 10 months earlier, eager to work at a paper with a reputation for excellence inspired by John S. Knight.

On his last day, Schlueb fired off a parting shot to Tony Ridder, who had taken over as chairman and chief executive officer of Knight Ridder. Schlueb railed about "faceless corporate hacks" ordering "arbitrary budget cuts" that hurt the Beacon Journal. "My only regret is that you haven't come to visit the Beacon Journal," during Schlueb's brief time there, the letter concluded. "I would have loved to piss on your shoes."

But there was an even more remarkable response to the 2001 layoffs. To mark the sad occasion, guild members planned a protest in which they dressed in black, decorated the newsroom with black balloons and stood silently at their desks for several minutes. This time, even nonunion newsroom managers, equally upset about the layoffs, also wore black and posed for a photo with guild members.

### Numbers dwindle

That sour start to the new millennium foreshadowed a long, slow decline for the Beacon Journal's proud newsroom union, already coping with radical change. Running the union had steadily become much more time-consuming, as union-management relations had remained rocky since the late 1980s. In addition, substantial legal bills racked up in the early 1990s had further drained the union treasury. Facing those challenges, Local 7 voted in 1995 to merge into Cleveland-based Local 1, which had a paid, full-time executive secretary to run day-to-day operations.

Meantime, as newspaper employment continued its relentless decline, the international union, The Newspaper Guild, was dealing with its own viability issues. In 1995 it merged into the Communication Workers of America, becoming The Newspaper Guild-CWA, later known as NewsGuild-CWA.

A year before the 2001 layoffs, the guild bargaining unit at the Beacon Journal had reached an all-time high of 170 full-time members, plus 27 part-timers on the sports staff. After several rounds of layoffs and buyouts under subsequent Beacon Journal owners Black Press Media and GateHouse Media, guild membership stood at just 30 full-timers and three sports part-timers at the end of May 2019. More layoffs were feared after GateHouse merged with Gannett later in the year.

In 1934, following a troublesome period during Local 7's precarious early days, President Don Strouse reassured New York in a letter that, "The immediate crisis has passed and the Akron Guild is still in existence." Eighty-five years later, staring at the harsh realities of an industry in decline, the guild must deal with the crisis of vanishing membership. And once again, existence is at stake.

# The Departments

# Chapter 16
## An Intern's Journey: The Soap Box Derby and Beyond

Bob Fernandez

I arrived in Akron in the Tire Bust of 1987, an intern right out of Ohio Wesleyan University and boarding with a super-nice West Akron widow with a beloved black cat that peed all over the house. She let me use her son's bedroom. It was only my second time to Akron. The first was for a Beacon Journal tryout in the spring when I banged out a short daily about University of Akron AIDS activists who were handing out safe-sex leaflets with condoms stapled to them — which meant they were perforated condoms and not safe at all.

The Beacon Journal had just won a Pulitzer Prize for its coverage of Sir James Goldsmith's takeover run at Goodyear Tire and Rubber Co., which punched Akron in the civic gut. Editor Dale Allen and Managing Editor Larry Williams, both former Philadelphia Inquirer newsroom leaders, were remaking the Beacon into a mini-Inquirer, replicating its flashy projects, features and hard news.

I fell flat on my face. Two stories I recall doing in those early weeks were the Beacon Journal's switch from afternoon to morning publication, which I put zero effort into, and an obit on a teenage boy wearing Army boots who drowned in the Cuyahoga River. His parents mailed a kind note to me, thanking me for the story.

Editors told me about mid-summer that the 50th running of the All-American Soap Box Derby would be my last assignment at the Beacon. There were some encouraging words like come see us in a few years, yada, yada, yada.

As derby time came around, I had one foot in Akron and the other in Columbus, where I'd found a reporting slot on a business weekly. On the Sunday of derby week, the Beacon published my kick-off story with this headline: "At 50, the Derby Is Gathering Speed Again." Chief Librarian Cathy Tierney helped immeasurably with the research. And her guidance shone through as my lead introduced the topic with sweep: "The story of the 50th All-American Soap Box Derby is ... a 20th Century American folk tale. It's about rapid and spectacular success; a big corporation withdrawing its big money; a scandal; and a period of self-evaluation and consolidation."

It wasn't Tom Wolfe. But the story crackled with analysis and quotes. Editors buzzed. Williams talked with Deb Van Tassel, my editor, about it.

Then I let loose a flurry of derby dailies. A West German kid who hadn't made the trip to Akron the previous year because he couldn't pay for it. Akron's all-girl racer contingent. The fabulous Franers from Texas, who had ordered $300 of exotic Appalachian sitka wood, cut it into strips and glued them together for the shell of the derby car. Whew, a beauty. But derby rules called for cheap plywood. On Aug. 13, the paper published "Texas Car Goes by the Boards, Wrong Wood, Fast Overhaul" — not groundbreaking journalism, but a lively read.

On Thursday, John Greenman, the assistant managing editor for metro news, called me into his office. He offered me a staff writer job on the business desk. I stammered that I'd have to think about it. That night, my dad in South Jersey counseled me over the phone against it. But I liked Akron.

I rented a one-bedroom on West Market Street in Highland Square for $275 a month and U-hauled my things out. Over the years, Beacon reporter and editor Charlene Nevada always laughed that, "Bob got hired for his derby coverage."

### Starting a career, losing my keys

The business news desk was in the back of the newsroom, next to the sports department. Regina Brett sat next to me. We were both rookies. She would blaze a storied career as a columnist in Northeast Ohio. Doug Oplinger was business editor. Barb Currence was secretary and assistant. The only person I knew in Akron was Yalinda Rhoden, a metro reporter. We were both graduates of Ohio Wesleyan.

I had an Oldsmobile Omega with 110,000 miles that I drove all over Akron and Canton and Cleveland. My life could be scattered as a young man and I'd regularly lose my keys — oddly, in the middle of the day. Reporters would drive me home. My elderly neighbor, Helen, kept spares. And that became a big joke in the newsroom. Where are Bob's keys? One day I asked a bank teller on South Main where I deposited my paycheck if they had a lost and found. She reached under the counter and pulled out a shoe box loaded with keys. "Somebody keeps leaving them."

Across from the Beacon Journal, the Printer's Club became my go-to joint for beer, gossip and fried-walleye sandwiches. Food writer and guild president Jane Snow, Don Fermoyle, Bill O'Connor, Gloria Irwin, Bill Bierman, Mickey Porter and other newsroom staffers would be hanging out. Longtime and respected editor Pat Englehart had a skin condition. He'd be telling a story and yelling and laughing and itching and trying not to scratch.

In the newsroom, tire treads ran through the veins of Larry Pantages. His father, Billy, had owned the General Cafe and then Leo's Café in East Akron, near General Tire and Goodyear. So Billy and the Pantages family had a front-row seat to the economic vagaries devastating Akron's tire industry. CEOs shifted production to Southern states, away from the heavily unionized Akron plants. The popularity of Michelin's radial tires and high gas prices in Europe and Asia meant growth for Japanese car company Honda, which built a manufacturing plant in Ohio in 1982, beginning an assault of foreign automotive businesses on U.S. soil. Foreign-owned car companies often used tires from foreign manufacturers.

Pantages was the tire-industry reporter and had watched the dismantling and distress of the hometown tire firms so dear to his family: Goldsmith's raid on Goodyear; Carl Icahn's predatory investment in B.F. Goodrich; Bridgestone's takeover of Firestone; Michelin's purchase of Uniroyal Goodrich; Continental AG buying General Tire.

"Akron was the loser every time in those deals," Pantages said. "Goodyear stayed independent but it had to sell off its parts. But, "it was a heyday for us chasing news."

On the business desk, we were a tight group with reporters Stuart Drown, Lornet Turnbull, Mary Vanac, Katie Byard and me competing for stories and scoops with The Plain Dealer, The New York Times, The Wall Street Journal and The Washington Post. Shortly after I joined the team Oplinger was promoted to assistant managing editor for features and Van Tassel replaced him as business editor.

I was at my best when I had to find stories and write them quickly. I wrote a story a day for years in Akron, covering the closing of the downtown

O'Neil's department store, the bankruptcy of LTV Steel, the boondoggle of a state-funded rehab facility in Cleveland and the decommissioning of the nation's first nuclear reactor in Shippingport, Pa.

In early 1988, the European press broke the story that Italian tire company Pirelli was negotiating to buy Firestone Tire and Rubber Co. Pantages covered the story. I helped. Someone faxed me an image of a European newspaper's front page with a Pirelli executive in shirtsleeves hoisting heavy dumbbells emblazoned with Firestone over his head. The implication: Firestone was too big for Pirelli. The headline said "Pista Pirelli." Pantages and I joked about that for years, not knowing to this day what it meant.

Japan's Bridgestone Co. waltzed into the fray, winning Firestone for $2.6 billion, and launching the company globally.

I continued to cover Pirelli even though it had lost Firestone to Bridgestone. I wrote a feature about its celebrated Cal, a limited-edition glam calendar featuring scantily clad models. Pirelli distributed it as gifts to customers and celebrities. Goodyear had gray blimps. Pirelli had racy calendars. The Italian company generously sent us one for my story.

Page designer Ted Schneider pored over the photos for our big Monday section. He chose a model in a long dress that plunged in the back, exposing the top of her butt. "I think we can get away with this," he said. I liked it and nodded. The last I saw of Schneider that day was as he headed back to the glass wall for a talk with top editors about whether the photo should appear in a family newspaper.

For fun, I replaced the dignified Beacon Journal calendar hanging on the center pillar in our department with the Pirelli Cal. This was well before we'd been counseled about sexual harassment and the PC movement, but women were finding their voice and several complained to Allen and Williams, who chose to stay out of the dispute. The women flamed Van Tassel with objecting emails. She thought the Cal was classy and artistic — the models formed signs of the Zodiac — and left it up. One morning, she found it crumpled up in the windowless back room that served as her office.

A newcomer to the department confessed he'd removed it because he was tired of all the complaining. Van Tassel took it home and hung it in her kitchen.

Later that year, Pantages was promoted to assistant business editor and I inherited the coveted tire-business beat, with its cavalcade of major stories and travel. So when Hurricane Gilbert tore through Jamaica and badly damaged a Goodyear factory, I flew there with Beacon Journal photographer Ed Suba Jr.

Shattered glass covered the hotel patio and grounds. The Goodyear hourly workers practically rioted in the first factory meeting with the plant manager. Many of them had no homes. Gilbert's winds had torn them off like metal lids on tin cans.

Goodyear soon presented another opportunity for travel, this time to South Africa. While other Fortune 500 companies sold off their South African subsidiaries under shareholder pressure because of the country's apartheid policies, Goodyear maintained ownership of its South African tire business as it was locked in a global battle for market share. Every tire sale was a big deal.

The Beacon editors approved a reporting trip. I told Goodyear and applied for the visas. Because of the required vaccinations, I sweated through a night of mild symptoms of yellow fever. But the day before I was to depart, Goodyear called me with news. The tire giant was selling the South African business. Editors immediately canceled the trip.

More than 30 years later, I spoke with long-time Goodyear spokesman John Perduyn, now in his 80s, and asked him if he remembered South Africa. "Yes," he chuckled.

"Why didn't you tell me you were selling it?"

"It was part of the agreement. We couldn't let you know until it was signed."

"But I had to take those f------- shots."

We both laughed.

I moved on. Bridgestone was relocating its U.S. headquarters to the Firestone campus in Akron. What exactly was Bridgestone? What was the company like? What could Akron expect?

Managing Editor Jim Crutchfield approved a two-week reporting trip to Tokyo for me, metro reporter Carl Chancellor and photographer Robin Witek. Bridgestone public relations officials arranged the schedules. The newspaper paid the airfare and hotels. We flew to Tokyo and rode the bullet train to Bridgestone's home city. Every meal was an adventure. One night, Chancellor and I sang "Girl From Ipanema" in a Tokyo karaoke bar with boozed-up Bridgestone executives.

### Behind the Iron Curtain

On Nov. 9, 1989, NBC's Tom Brokaw broadcast "Freedom Night" from West Germany. East Germans streamed across border checkpoints for the first time in 28 years. West Germans danced congas on Berlin streets. I watched on a rented TV in Highland Square.

The fall of the Berlin Wall fired Van Tassel's imagination. She developed ideas for a project looking at Eastern European consumer demand and potential growth for U.S. companies as well as state-owned rubber companies now facing western competition.

John S. Knight's paper had attitude and ambition. Akron itself had the characteristics and history of a big city with corporate headquarters, an art museum, a big university, a (rundown) downtown, neighborhoods, a booming retail/commercial western flank in Montrose, and hospitals.

The Beacon sent the music critic to Japan, China and Europe. Reporter Will Outlaw lived for a month on general assistance and slept wherever he could. Allen's strategy was to "outfox The Plain Dealer and set us apart from all the other little papers around here," he told me decades later. "We were trying to make a name for ourselves and have fun doing it."

I faxed the Iron Curtain rubber companies memos introducing myself. I reached out to their U.S. agents if they had them.

Early on, I told the editors I had to go with longtime Beacon photographer Ott Gangl, who was raised in Germany, spoke the language, shot excellent photos and laughed a lot. Because, let's be honest, an American reporter and photographer from Akron, Ohio, driving around Eastern Europe in the early 1990s looking at tire factories and asking questions would look suspicious.

Van Tassel and I emphasized an approach to the stories that editors could see us easily pulling off: the takeover battle between Continental AG of Germany and Italian tiremaker Pirelli. (There was Pirelli again!) The local connection was General Tire, which Continental owned. We would come back with *something*.

"They told me look at the rubber companies and look for pollution and take some pictures," Gangl, now 87, recalled recently in a phone interview. "They said here is $5,000 for you and $5,000 for Bob."

### We asked; Michelin said no.

We flew into Frankfurt and did a quick story on a Rubbermaid factory hiring East Germans as laborers. We attended an hours-long Continental

AG shareholder meeting in Hanover. One day I interviewed a Continental executive on the problems at General Tire. Gangl struggled to find the proper words for translation. What came out was — "When we shit, we stand beside it." We roared with laughter. So did the German guy, though he didn't know why.

I had told editors we'd take a run at reporting on Michelin's big tire-manufacturing complex in France. Gangl and I drove to Paris. Over dinner at the top of the Eiffel Tower, a Michelin spokesman told us we couldn't tour the company's factory complex. Gangl snapped photos of each new course of French cuisine. Gangl recalls the Michelin spokesman telling us: "DeGaulle wanted to go there. Hitler wanted to go there. We wouldn't let them. Why do you think we would let you?"

Disappointed but not surprised, we headed back to Germany in our rented Euro compact. Gangl and I had burned through most of our $10,000. We wired the Beacon for more cash and then thrillingly crossed into East Germany and the town of Massow, which wasn't even on maps because of the Stasi secret service compound there. Goodyear had leased part of the Stasi compound for a tire warehouse. Why? "It's the old Stasi antenna to Berlin on the roof," German Goodyear employee Manfred Garbrecht told us. The antenna was one of the few ways in East Germany at the time to connect to the West.

Next, we drove to East Germany's state-owned Reifenwerke Furstenwaldehas, which manufactured Pneumant brand tires in a factory 40 miles east of Berlin and located near a Russian military base that freaked us out when we made a wrong turn. The tire company had slashed 65 percent of its 11,000 employees over the prior 18 months.

An East German worker compared Pneumant managers to hated Stasi agents. "Under the old regime you could not say what you wanted because the Stasi would come and handcuff you and take you away," he said. Now Pneumant managers sit "in their soft chairs, and they're waiting for people to make mistakes so they can let them go."

In Krakow, Poland, we hired an English-speaking school teacher and drove three miles toward the Russian border. Farmers were still plowing fields with horses. Police stopped us on the road and asked us what we were doing and checked our papers. They thought we might be spies and considered contacting the secret police. But they realized the secret police had been disbanded. We raced on.

At the 6,000-worker Stomil factory in Dębica, tire workers used Akron machinery from the 1930s. Stomil managers had cut jobs and working hours. They closed factory-owned schools, stores, tennis courts, sports stadiums, housing and daycare. To raise $100 million to modernize, Stomil asked its 35,000 workers to contribute nearly two years of wages.

Taurus Hungarian Rubber Works, in smoggy, dazzling Budapest, was nationalized in the late 1940s. But in the 1970s, managers anticipated socialism's end. Taurus grew a brisk export business and modernized its factories with $30 million and employee cutbacks — or 45 percent of its workforce — through early retirements and layoffs.

The final destination: Munich. Gangl had relatives there. We visited them, drank beer and shopped. We caught a flight home. The stories were published in two parts. Many images of the trip stayed with me for years. One was of 20-year-old Elzbieta Stepian, who wore pink canvas shoes as she cut strips of rubber for a radial tire in an all-woman section of the Stomil factory. She spoke for many when she told me: "I'm afraid."

### Goodyear staggers; Beacon doesn't blink

Back in Akron, Goodyear's woes wouldn't relent. One day in early June 1991, Allen walked over to the business desk. The distance between his office and the business department was a city block. So when Allen made that trek, it was something big.

Goodyear had called. The board ousted CEO Tom Barrett. Stan Gault, a former top General Electric executive and Rubbermaid CEO, was replacing him. Goodyear planned a press conference. "We better get over there," Allen said.

Goodyear faced tough times by the late 1980s and early 1990s. Yeah, it had staved off Goldsmith. But doing so ruined its balance sheet. The company staggered under $4 billion in debt. Goodyear had been the world's No. 1 tire company. Now Michelin and Bridgestone owned big chunks of the global tire market through acquisitions and selling high-quality tires. The trends didn't look good.

I covered Goodyear relentlessly and fairly. It peeved me that Barrett wouldn't schedule an interview with me. I had a good relationship with the company generally, though.

At the press conference, an Akron TV news reporter asked Gault if he was a "Miracle Boy" who could save Goodyear. Gault, 65, deadpanned that he didn't know about "miracles" but he certainly was no "boy."

Gault told the journalists there to give him 90 days to develop a plan. Former Goodyear spokesman Perduyn recalled walking out of the press conference with Gault. They both looked up in the sky. A Goodyear blimp flew over the corporate headquarters. Perduyn had asked for years for the company to brighten the blimp with blue and yellow so that it would pop in the sky for consumers. But Goodyear officials insisted on the gray because the company still sought to sell the blimp to the military. A marketing wizard who sold everything from home appliances to plastic storage bins, Gault thought the brighter colors were a good idea.

In my remaining time at the Beacon, I reported on Gault's restructuring plan — selling off non-tire assets, opening its sales channels to big-box stores to sell more tires, developing the Aquatred rain-gripping tire and, yes, repainting the Goodyear blimp blue and McDonald's yellow.

### Goodbye, Akron, they were great times

In early 1993, I accepted a job with the Philadelphia Inquirer with Allen's blessing. I left Akron with regret. So much news. So much excitement. So many colleagues. The only comparable time in my career — yes, I am still a business reporter, still at the Inquirer — was covering Comcast Corp.'s deal for NBCUniversal with its public hearings in Washington, and Comcast's proposed deal for Time Warner Cable that exploded on social media. Federal regulators blocked it. Those were crazy days, too. Just like Akron.

To this day, I troll parking lots fascinated with tire brands — Hankook, Kumho, Kelly, Pirelli, Goodyear, Bridgestone, Firestone, Uniroyal, Cooper. I know the stories behind them all.

Writing this, I was saddened to hear that the Beacon Journal had to leave 44 E. Exchange St. under its current owner, the new Gannett. A developer tore down my former apartment building in Highland Square on West Market Street for a Mr. Zub's restaurant and bar. Does Highland Square really need another bar?

Goodyear opened a new world headquarters in 2013 in Akron — hooray. And Bridgestone has said it will open a new plant in Akron to manufacture racing tires for IndyCar. The first ones will roll off the line in 2020. And you can bet, the Beacon Journal will be there to report it. Photos! Story!

# Chapter 17
## Cooking Up Delicious Journalism in the Food Section

Jane Snow

I remember cooking a 2 1/2-pound beef roast on a car engine.

I remember naming the sauerkraut ball Akron's iconic food and Gino's its best pizza.

I remember making a Jell-O mold of my face for an April Fools' column and leading an Olympic-style Spam "torch" run through the streets of Akron to celebrate the canned meat.

In 24 years as the food editor of the Akron Beacon Journal, I amassed a lifetime of memories. I held the position from September 1982 through November 2006, the latest in a line of writers that stretched back to the 1930s.

In the Food section's heyday, from the early 1980s to 2014 when the last full-time food writer left, we wrote about local food entrepreneurs, kept track of grocery prices, taught readers how to cook, reviewed cookbooks, sorted out nutrition claims, offered original recipes and profiled chefs.

Our food coverage spilled into other newspaper sections, including the front page. We covered sports nutrition, contaminated food imports, dangerous diets, supermarket price wars and mad cow disease. We also critiqued restaurants in six Northeast Ohio counties.

The newspaper's food coverage wasn't always so lush. From the paper's founding in 1897 until Polly Paffilas became the food reporter in 1961, food coverage was almost entirely limited to recipes from readers and advertisers.

Beloved food editor Glenna Snow (no relation) is remembered for her two cookbooks of readers' recipes published in 1938 and 1942. The *Glenna Snow Cookbook* is still available in Akron area used-book stores, and remains popular enough that the University of Akron Press reissued a version in 2010.

Paffilas is the reporter who took food coverage beyond the kitchen. She had almost two decades of reporting behind her when she began chronicling the area through food. On her first assignment, an out-of-town trip to a Chicago food writers' conference, she tracked down New York Yankees star slugger Roger Maris for an interview about his food preferences. Maris, the toast of the country at the time as he chased Babe Ruth's single-season home run record, was in Chicago for a doubleheader with the White Sox.

Paffilas wrote about women whose bake sales helped fund church repairs, time-saving recipes for increasingly busy cooks, and during the deep recession of the 1970s, how to stretch a food budget.

When women picketed supermarkets in 1966 because of rapidly rising food prices, Paffilas began the newspaper's first quarterly grocery price checks. She wrote plenty of recipe stories, too, and her prose sparkled: "Happiness is homemade grape jelly, shimmering like an amethyst," she wrote in one Sunday column.

Paffilas wrote about food until she couldn't anymore. In 1973 she was diagnosed with diabetes. After struggling for two years, she gave up the food beat. Her editor, Betty Jaycox, wrote at the time, "The success of our food columns has continually grown thanks to Polly Paffilas. And will continue to grow thanks to the foundation she has laid."

Her successors continued to dive deep into the issues and personalities of the local food scene, first in the witty columns of Connie Bloom and then in the rigorously reported — and sometimes hilarious — stories of Charlene Nevada.

American cooks were beginning to venture beyond meatloaf and green-bean casseroles when Bloom wrote the food stories from 1975 to 1980. Julia Child's TV program, "The French Chef," had whetted America's appetite for French food and for cooking in general. Bloom responded with upscale recipes for such dishes as coq au vin and ratatouille.

Seasoned government and education reporter Nevada took over in 1980, breaking free of the last remnants of the "home ec" era of food writing with reporting that went beyond recipes — in part because, initially, she wasn't a good cook.

When Nevada was asked by Editor Paul Poorman to take over the food beat, "I remember at the end of the interview I said, 'You never asked me if I could cook.' He said, 'I don't care. You're a journalist, you can learn.'"

Poorman wasn't as sanguine when Nevada trooped through the news-room one December day with a wreck of a gingerbread house she had made at home and brought to work to be photographed.

"I honestly didn't think it would be that bad," Nevada recalls. "The icing was so stiff it broke my hand mixer. Clumps of gingerbread kept falling off."

The story and photo ran anyway. "Everyone loved it," she says. "They called in and said, 'That's what it would look like if I tried it.'"

Nevada's biggest contributions were away from the stove. She wrote about the decimation of the country's meat inspection system, expanded the newspaper's quarterly food price checks from one to three stores, convened reader panels for blind taste tests and created Recipe Roundup, a reader-rec-ipe swap that was popular for decades.

Nevada was an inspiration when I took over the food beat in 1982. Following her example, I was determined to cover all the ways food touched our readers' lives. I was an avid cook and would write many recipe stories, too.

I stepped into the job at an auspicious time. The country's nascent food revolution was gathering steam, and before the decade was out would carpet America with goat cheese and arugula. People cooked for more than just sustenance; they began cooking for recreation. In some circles, knowing how to peel asparagus was a status symbol.

I attempted to appeal to both adventurous and traditional cooks with stories that ran the gamut from how to prepare meat loaf to how to make caviar roulade.

Akron-area cooks were more savvy than their peers in many other Midwest cities, thanks to a core of residents who broadened their palates by traveling internationally for the rubber companies and also to Russ Vernon's West Point Market, at the time the largest fancy-foods store in the country. Readers could get almost any ingredient there, which influenced the type of recipes we could publish in the newspaper. Pink peppercorns? No problem.

Readers also had access to many of the best chefs and cooking teachers here and abroad at the Zona Spray Cooking School in Hudson. In addition, a parade of the world's best chefs found their way to our area for interviews, or we found our way to them.

I interviewed Julia Child over lunch in Cleveland and in a phone call to her second home in France (I treasured that telephone number until I retired). I met Martha Stewart at a Kmart in Medina, where we sat on packing

Russ Vernon's gourmet store, West Point Market, was one of the treats of covering the food beat at the Beacon Journal. (Beacon Journal photo by Ott Gangl)

crates in a stock room. I had lunch with Cajun chef Paul Prudhomme in his restaurant in New Orleans, and with the legendary French chef Paul Bocuse at a restaurant in Cleveland.

Lacking competition from the internet and the Food Network — neither were in play when I began covering food — the newspaper became a valuable source of information about food trends. To keep up with readers' increasingly voracious appetites for recipes and food news, the Beacon Journal steadily expanded its coverage. In the late 1980s, for the first time since the paper's inception, food had its own stand-alone section.

While interest in gourmet cooking was rising, food in general was becoming more complicated. What we knew about nutrition changed almost weekly in the 1980s and 1990s as nutrition research accelerated. We tried to cover the most important revelations, often interviewing the researchers themselves.

Our digging did not make everyone happy. In a story about the fat content of deli meats, I took Oscar Meyer to task for its misleading label claims. The article ran in other newspapers through the Knight Ridder News Service. A week or so later, Editor Dale Allen dropped by my desk to tell me the CEO of Oscar Meyer had telephoned the CEO of our parent company, Knight Ridder (reaching him on the runway in his jet) to complain about my story. Allen asked if I stood by my story. I told him yes. That's the last I heard of it.

Nutrition charlatans proliferated, and we tried to protect readers from them in stories about diet books and products. A favorite memory is an interview of a married couple who had written a best-selling diet book. I was skeptical of their advice, such as to avoid eating fruits before noon, and consulted dietitians who debunked the book's tenets. I checked the authors' credentials and found their "nutrition" degrees were from a company that provided diplomas by mail. The authors were more surprised than upset when I confronted them. No one else had looked into their claims or background, they said. Why would I?

Also complicating readers' lives at the time were increasing threats to the nation's food supply, which came thick and fast beginning in the 1980s. After a network TV news magazine reported in 1987 that more than 30 percent of raw chicken in stores was contaminated with salmonella, we shipped local supermarket chickens to a lab for testing (almost 40 percent contained the bacteria). Concerned about an uptick in food poisoning traced to produce, I tracked contaminated raspberries to fields in Guatemala where sanitation practices were horrible and inspection was nonexistent. The story resulted in a nationwide embargo of Guatemalan raspberries by the U.S. Food and Drug Administration. Irradiated food, contaminated eggs, dirty supermarket produce misting gear — we covered it all. It was a sprint; usually I had five days to investigate and write a story, squeezed in around other duties.

The Beacon Journal newsroom was a large, open bullpen with separate offices for the editorial artists, editorial writers and the reference librarians, and a suite of rooms for the photographers. What we did not have was a test kitchen, despite repeated budget requests by Bill Hunter, chief photographer in the 1980s. Hunter's staff was doing award-winning work for the Food section, which transitioned from black-and-white to color photographs in 1987. Lighting food was tricky. Composition was important. Often a photographer would be allotted a full shift to take a photo that would run large and be wired with the story to other newspapers across North America.

Without a kitchen at work, I had to make the food for the photos at home and transport it to the newspaper, where I styled it for the photograph.

I ferried everything from Thanksgiving dinner to a six-layer wedding cake in a succession of Ford vans.

Ed Suba Jr. and Paul Tople were among the photographers assigned most often to take the tricky food photos. We worked together in the photo studio to make the food look good. I attended food-styling classes and learned to paint steaks with Kitchen Bouquet to enhance grill marks, and spray vegetables with glycerin to make them look dewy-fresh.

One trick brought the fire department. I partially roasted a turkey for a Thanksgiving photo one year (fully roasted birds look wrinkled in photos), and started to bronze it in the photo studio with a blowtorch. The smoke alarm wailed, maintenance workers arrived with a ladder, and we were told the fire department was on its way. From then on we disarmed the smoke detector before heating anything.

For a recipe story I would create three or four dishes in one day. My refrigerator at home was stuffed but limited in variety. One week it would be filled with four pasta salads. The next, with maple, pumpkin and cranberry cheesecakes. The newspaper paid for my time and ingredients. I often shared the leftovers with the photographers and my co-workers in the features department.

The job was hard on my waistline. I gained and eventually lost 100 pounds during the course of my career. In the line of duty I once sampled every food item sold at Sea World, Cedar Point and Geauga Lake Amusement Park in the span of five days. I judged hamburger contests, brownie contests and even the North Carolina State Barbecue Championship, where I ate an estimated six pounds of meat in one afternoon.

Temptation was everywhere. Other reporters got letters from politicians. My mail contained slices of fruitcake from Texas and cases of cookies from the Keebler Elves. Not a day went by that someone didn't try to feed me. Readers left cookies and homemade cakes in the lobby. The lobby guard, for crying out loud, brought me samples of his wife's lasagna.

I was always on a diet — hard when you must review restaurants. I tried the Wild Weekend Diet, Weight Watchers and the grapefruit diet. I tried pills and was hypnotized. I wrote about all of it.

I eventually gave up restrictive dieting and in 1996 invented the Akron Diet, a healthful eating plan that ran as a 26-part series in the Beacon Journal and in newspapers nationwide. I worked with three local dietitians — Donna Skoda, Tish Galbraith and Evelyn Taylor — and exercise physiologist

Carolyn LeVan to devise small weekly changes that would lead to long-term results. Editor Jan Leach reprised the Akron Diet in 1999, partnering with Akron General Medical Center to offer it twice as a 15-week course I led at the hospital's Wellness Center.

At its peak in the early 2000s, my beat included writing not only the lead Food section story, a weekly recipe swap column and the quarterly food price survey, but a food news column (Tidbits), a Quick & Easy recipe, Ask Jane (a reader question and answer), a Sunday recipe story and an internet food newsletter, Second Helpings, as well as a weekly restaurant review, answering readers' emails and phone calls and writing the occasional breaking food news story (I once covered an attempted strangling over a chili recipe).

Locally produced food coverage also included a weekly item about food on the internet by Connie Bloom and a brief wine column by staffer Tricia Schellenbach. In 2003, copy editor Debby Stock Kiefer took over the Recipe Roundup column to add yet another voice to the food pages.

"We did a lot of cool stuff," recalls Leach. "It was not a typical food section. You could find stuff about health, nutrition, farmer's markets...."

The food articles were packaged in a visually appealing section designed by assistant news editor Dennis Gordon and before him, Ted Schneider. Various features editors over the years had ultimate authority over the section. Best among them was Ann Sheldon Mezger, who had a killer instinct for news and a firm but non-abrasive management style that drew the best from her reporters.

The effort and money the newspaper invested in the Food section resulted in national recognition and many local fans. In 1999, 2005 and 2006 when I was food editor and in 2009 under Lisa Abraham, the Beacon Journal's Food section was named the best in North America in its circulation category by the Association of Food Journalists.

Readers gave it a thumbs-up, too. Market research in the early 2000s showed that after the Sunday paper, the Wednesday paper, when the Food section was published, led in single-copy sales, according to Leach.

The restaurant reviews were popular with readers, too. Connie Bloom created the Dining Out column in the 1970s. Bob Downing was the critic when I took over in 1981. Except for a 14-month breather in 1987-1988, when Katherine Spitz handled the job, I wrote the Dining Out column and local restaurant features for the length of my tenure.

The job was not glamorous. I wore a disguise and had a credit card in an assumed name (Betsy Rose) so I would not be recognized. I looked like a dowdy older woman in my red wig, glasses and dumpy polyester dress. I tried to slip in and out of restaurants without being noticed. The newspaper paid for my meals and I was forbidden from accepting anything for free, even when I was not reviewing.

Before I got the pseudonymous credit card I was always in danger of being outed when I paid the bill. Managers would be summoned. Chefs occasionally rushed from the kitchen. I would either be fawned over or kicked out.

Then there was the manager of an upscale restaurant in Stow who had a unique reaction. He returned my card to the table and asked how much it would cost for a good review.

"It doesn't work like that," I told him as my friend and I quickly shrugged into our coats.

"How about a free dinner?" he implored as we rose from our chairs. "A drink," he yelled at our retreating backs, "just a drink!"

I took restaurant reviewing very seriously, toiling over each one for up to eight hours to get the facts and tone right. I was aware I was critiquing someone's life's work. I also knew who I was writing for — the readers, not the restaurants. I had to be honest. Some restaurant owners and chefs took it very personally.

A group of restaurateurs started an advertising boycott that lasted several months in the mid-1980s. To their credit, the editors of the newspaper shielded me from the ire of the advertising department and never mentioned the boycott to me.

The editors also had my back after I reviewed Tangier restaurant in 1986. My meal was disappointing and expensive. I was blunt in the review: "Tangier is a lot of things — an entertainment center, an exotic piece of architecture, a tourist attraction — but it is not a first-class restaurant. Peel away its veneer of elegance and you are left with mediocre food."

The day the review appeared I got an anonymous phone call at work: "We know where you live and we're going to kill you." I was shaken. Dale Allen called the police. The mystery caller was never identified; no one tried to slit my throat.

As serious as we were about the restaurant reviews and many of the food stories, we also tried to have fun. One way was to involve readers.

When I asked for stories about the worst things in their freezers, Carrie Goddard of North Canton told me about her son's pet iguana, wrapped and frozen after its death so it could have a proper burial when the ground thawed in the spring. That summer, long after the burial, Goddard found the iguana in the freezer and realized the family had buried a roast.

When I asked bakers in 1990 to send me fruitcakes if they thought they could convert me from a hater to a lover, I expected to get a dozen or so. The cakes began arriving in waves. The day before the contest cutoff, we clocked the flow at 20 per hour. Stuart Warner (assistant managing editor of features at the time), radio host Stan Piatt and I, fruitcake haters all, ate fruitcake steadily for hours to choose the winner. Never again.

The Food section was popular with a variety of non-traditional readers. I once got a phone call from an irate man who had organized a boycott of the newspaper by taping the coin slots closed in single-copy boxes at the General Motors Lordstown Complex in Trumbull County, where he worked. The Food section had been missing from the Wednesday paper for several weeks.

"A lot of single men work here and we need those recipes," he said.

Readers remained loyal even when the food coverage began shrinking. First went the restaurant reviews in the early 2000s in a round of budget cuts. Then the quarterly food price surveys were dropped when I was no longer physically able to dash through three supermarkets in one morning.

The food-price survey was not resurrected when Lisa Abraham took over as food editor in 2006, and Recipe Roundup was allowed to die when Kiefer left the paper shortly after I did. Still, the Food section under Abraham flourished. Then she left the newspaper in 2014 and was not replaced.

By 2019, the Food section was mostly wire copy except for a lively local food news column by reporter Katie Byard and a craft beer column by reporter Rick Armon.

I'm glad I was there when the aroma of turkey wafted from the photo studio in November, and Christmas contest cookies clogged the conference room table every December. I'm glad I worked for editors who were comfortable with a food editor who wrote not just about pot roast but avian flu, upscale dog bakeries and feeding time at the zoo.

It was a delicious career.

# Chapter 18
## The Copy Desk: Adding Some Life to Deadlines

Kathy Fraze

Why would anyone *ever* eat a cicada?

To make deadline, of course.

Reporters and photographers are the public face of a newspaper, but working furiously behind them is an equally talented crew of editors, artists and designers. They often have the worst hours (nights, weekends and holidays) and they don't get much public recognition, so sometimes it takes a little insanity to goad them to deadline.

At least that's my excuse for the shenanigans at night during much of the '90s and 'oos, when I supervised the desk that edited stories and wrote the headlines and photo captions.

I was taught the need for a little lightheartedness by longtime Barberton reporter Tom Ryan. Tom spent his last years at the Beacon Journal as the night rewrite man, and to amuse himself during downtime, he nosed around in search of staff birthdays. (This was in the days before the internet, so it wasn't as easy as it might sound.) Every month, he would anonymously post a list of birthdays on the bulletin board in hopes that people would take the time to wish their colleagues a happy day.

I was Tom's night editor, and I visited him when he was hospitalized with cancer. Though he may not have known he was dying, he did know he wouldn't return to the Beacon Journal. So he made me promise that I would continue the birthday list for him. And I did — for *decades,* whether co-workers liked it or not.

The birthday list prompted people to bring in treats and cakes for their colleagues, and then, because that was so much fun, to organize full-blown parties. No one got engaged or married, had a baby, celebrated a promotion, won an award or left the department (or the paper) without a party, often including a potluck dinner.

The insanity that occasionally broke loose on the night desk first surfaced in a cutthroat Christmas decorating competition with the business news desk in 1994. It started out innocently enough with tinsel and a few strings of lights. But then one side or the other declared that "our decorations are better," and the other side immediately upped the ante with more lights and more sparkly baubles. Suddenly, everyone was bringing in all the ugly Christmas decorations they could find at home, in thrift stores or on curbsides, and the two departments turned into a mad Winter Wonderland. There were Santas and elves racing around every computer terminal, there was "snow" drifting across the aisles, there was a life-size reindeer sitting on the national desk, and there were so many strings of lights hanging down from the ceiling that you had to bat them out of your face just to get to your desk. Some of the lights never even made it out of their packaging. And they blinked. Incessantly.

The final tacky straw was probably the blowup doll (attired in a very *tasteful* red holiday outfit).

The next Christmas, we were strongly advised to leave our decorations at home. And it was *years* before we allowed some modest ornamentation to creep quietly back onto our desks.

Alcohol fueled some desk traditions, like Miller Time. Back when the Beacon was still an afternoon newspaper, the production desks were fully staffed at night only on Saturday, when the Sunday morning paper came together. It was thirsty work, so as soon as the last page left for the composing room, there was a stampede across Exchange Street to the Printers Club. (One or two designated adults stayed behind to keep an eye on the wires and an ear on the police radio in case World War III erupted.) There was only half an hour or so until people were needed back in the newsroom to update the final edition, but it's amazing how much beer can be downed in that amount of time. The sharp-eyed, sour journalists who dashed to the Printers Club were often giggling and full of good cheer by the time they wandered back to proof the first papers off the press.

As the switch to morning publication in 1987 made night shifts the norm and a different collection of people moved onto the production desks, Miller Time morphed into Thursday Nights at Larry's Main Entrance, a bar on West Market Street in Wallhaven. Executive News Editor Mike Needs and later Bruce Winges would secure the big table in back, where server Nancy would bring the night crew breakfast with beer until long after the front door was locked.

On Election Night, voters anxiously await the names of the winners and losers. At the Beacon Journal, we eagerly awaited the posting of the fake congratulatory memos from our "bosses."

"I think they started because reporters (happily cynical sorts) felt the congratulatory memos from editors were patronizing," said writer Bill O'Connor. The fake memos were written on letterhead notepads swiped from real editors, and were wickedly spot on when it came to the style and attitudes of the bosses they were mimicking. O'Connor and columnist/copy editor Mickey Porter wrote the memos for many years, editing each other so they didn't stray *too* far out of line. However, the identity of the person(s) who purloined the stationery remains a guarded secret.

Food was at the root of many desk traditions. "What I remember most about the copy desk in my early days (1996-2000) was the food," said copy editor Mary Kay Quinn. On Saturdays, a clerk would take orders from the entire newsroom and pick up the food for us so we could work through our dinner breaks. During the week, copy editor Tim Hayes would frequently make dinner runs to Spaghetti Warehouse.

"There were massive sandwiches with heaps of sides from Jack Horner's, or maybe massive salads from Rockne's," Quinn said. And bowls of Hershey's Kisses on the chief's desk, and home-baked goodies from Debby Stock Kiefer or Olga Reswow.

Which brings us to some of the ironclad food rules on the copy desk.

On her second day at the Beacon Journal, copy editor Beth Thomas Hertz mentioned to her new colleague Mary Beth Breckenridge that she liked to bake. As Hertz remembers it, Breckenridge "immediately perked up and said, 'Oh, didn't anyone tell you? We require all new people to bake cookies for us.' I knew, of course, that she was kidding, but when I woke up the next morning, it occurred to me how funny it would be if I acted like I believed her, so I went to the store and got the ingredients to make chocolate chip cookies."

"She saw my bluff and baked cookies for everyone," Breckenridge said. "Henceforth, newbies were informed of their cookie responsibilities on their first day, and most complied."

That was the start of the Rookie Cookie Rule, followed by Deserter's Dessert five years later, when Hertz baked another batch of cookies to say goodbye to her colleagues at the Beacon.

Holidays forced a lot of us to miss family celebrations, so we almost always had a potluck at work instead. And these weren't measly meals. There were picnics for Memorial Day, the Fourth of July and Labor Day and full-course dinners for Thanksgiving and Christmas. We'd commandeer the empty desks of folks lucky enough to spend the holiday at home and pile on platters of appetizers, dips, salads, sandwiches, chili, casseroles, rolls and desserts. Everyone contributed something, even if it was just a bag of chips or a package of paper plates. But the most amazing contribution came the Thanksgiving when copy editor Dan Thom, who wasn't even working that day, brought in a whole roasted turkey.

Halloween was my favorite holiday because people always dressed up and the costumes were awesome — and newsworthy, like the year copy desk chief Jim Kavanagh was the space station Mir because it was "deorbiting," or the year copy editor/columnist Mark J. Price dressed up as Col. Simon Perkins, entrepreneur and son of Akron's founder, because of a controversy over moving Perkins' statue from Grace Park to the University of Akron. One year, Quinn colored herself from head to toe as a piece of candy corn, while then-copy editor Joe Thomas was a blinding yellow Pikachu. Another year, copy editor Monica Thomas was Princess Leia and copy editor Susan Gapinski Price was a spelling bee. But the king of costumes was the late photographer/page designer Ted Schneider Jr. I never thought he could top his roadkill costume, which included a tire track running across his chest, but the next year he showed up as a flasher, wearing a trench coat and a strategically placed smiley face. I thought we'd both be fired.

We didn't need an official holiday for an excuse to eat. If it was really hot (or really cold) outside, someone would produce cartons of ice cream and bottles of chocolate syrup. If the desk was especially cranky, doughnuts or cookies would magically appear. If it was going to be a particularly frantic night (like the opening of high school football season or an election), there would be pizza or sub sandwiches for the entire newsroom. If it was going to be a *really* hard night (like the introduction of a phenomenally difficult computer system), there would be trays of lasagna. Sometimes the bosses arranged for it, sometimes a leprechaun or two did. No matter — we never went hungry. Usually, there would be one mass feeding, then the leftovers would be deposited in the "usual spot" in the newsroom, underneath a cartoon of a man saying, "Mmmm, bread crusts." We'd graze all night long.

And chatter to each other.

"Scott wrote a good head!" the slot editor would shout.

Everyone would respond with one loud clap.

"I guess the idea was that we were so busy that we only had time for one clap," Mark J. Price said. "If a car horn honked outside, someone inevitably said: 'Your ride is here.' Or if a siren wailed outside: 'News happening.'"

"You people laugh at the same jokes over and over!" one intern complained. (Her complaint, of course, turned into one of those jokes, copy editor Joe Kiefer remembered.)

There were sunset alerts, when we'd race to the windows to watch a particularly brilliant sunset. Occasionally we'd ignore deadline to ooh and ahh over the fireworks at Canal Park. And to relieve the tension on a tough night, there'd be some pretty intense rubber band fights.

Headlines don't come with bylines, so I would post the best (and their authors) on the bulletin board. Every month we'd vote on the best of the best — not just the cleverest headlines but also the ones that told the best story in a tight space — and the winners would get traveling trophies to keep on their desks until the next month. We'd also publicize great catches. (It would be hard to top the night Debby Stock Kiefer saved us from printing a photo that inadvertently focused on the back end of a well-endowed bull elephant.)

There were aggravations to working nights. We missed a lot of family events. It was hard to maintain friendships because we lived at the wrong end of the clock. Years of prime-time TV passed us by. We couldn't watch our favorite sitcoms and sports teams. But then Deputy News Editor Tom Moore introduced us to a newfangled thing called a VCR, and suddenly we could keep up with "Friends" and "Law & Order." Still, it wasn't easy. Former editor/reporter Dave Scott remembers avoiding televisions in the newsroom "at all costs and hoping no one mentions the results when one of my teams was playing a game that I was recording."

With aggravations like that, was it any surprise that we used any excuse to party?

"When the copy desk moved from one side of the room to the other, we had a bon voyage party," recalled copy editor Maria Averion, who dressed up for the occasion as Gilligan.

When the sports copy desk merged with the main copy desk, we choreographed a "jumping the broom" ceremony in the JSK Room.

"There was never a theme night or potluck I didn't enjoy, although I wasn't a huge fan of getting stuck working behind the slow cooker full of chili while I was pregnant with twins," copy editor Elissa Murray said. "One of my favorites was the Pajama Night we had during my first few years at the Beacon. There's nothing better than wearing a robe and slippers at work!"

For the 1992 Olympics, we staged our own Newsroom Olympics, including sprints to the Blue Room and back. Copy editor Todd Burkes remembers that event was especially challenging because the runners had to stop long enough to buy a drink, then get it back to the newsroom without spilling a drop, all while dealing with the bewildered reactions of the people they dodged in the halls.

If a holiday wasn't handy, we made up our own celebrations — like Orange Food Night, when every contribution to our potluck dinner had to be orange. Quinn made a variation of tuna salad with salmon and orange French dressing. Mark J. Price remembered "lots of Cheetos, orange pop, cheddar cheese and carrots."

We also tried a Green Food Night, but the results didn't look nearly as appetizing.

We once had Bad Poetry Night, when Joe Kiefer offered a burred twist on a Robert Burns poem titled "To a Mouse." Kiefer's version described how his wife, Debby, dealt with a bat problem in their house. "My sister-in-law and her family request performances of it regularly just to hear my burr," Kiefer said, "especially on 'Hand me down yon racquet de "tennie" / Strung with the guts of a kitty.'"

Then there was Talent Night. (Or was that Stupid Human Tricks Night? Whatever.) Copy editor Tania Fuentez stacked an amazing tower of cookies and former copy editor Cliff Pinckard astounded us with vanishing cigarette tricks. And Strange Footwear Night. (My favorite was Kerry Clawson's high-heeled sneakers.) And Prom Night. And Oscars Night.

Occasionally, we went on road trips. We hiked the Summit Metro Parks trail south of the Mustill Store before it was transformed into the Towpath Trail. We explored the National Inventors Hall of Fame before it became a school. We took in a baseball game at the new Canal Park.

We also had a strong competitive streak. (Don't forget that Christmas decorating fiasco.) Whenever the Associated Press produced an updated stylebook, I'd challenge the desk to find a typo or style error. It rarely took more than one shift for someone to win.

One year, we had a baby photo contest. People throughout the newsroom brought in their baby pictures and we competed to identify each chubby little face. Another year we tried the same thing with childhood Christmas photos. And high school yearbook images.

We tested ourselves repeatedly, taking turns to create quizzes about local geography, local history, weather, election laws and pop culture. There was always a tasty prize for the winner.

Sometimes our competitive spirit was channeled into a good cause. One year, we competed against departments throughout the building to see who could bring in the most canned goods for a local food drive, and the result was a wall of cans around the copy desk. And after a vicious elimination round in the old Red Room, we fielded the first Beacon Journal team for the Project Learn Corporate Spelling Bee (which we won, by the way).

Good deeds weren't confined to the night desk. For years, the Features Department organized an auction of "freebies," supervised by Features Editor Lynne Sherwin. "Every newsroom gets free stuff," Sherwin said. "Book publishers and record companies send review copies. Corporations send shirts, satchels and leather binders imprinted with their logos. Food writers get spice mixes and chocolates, gadgets and small appliances.... Journalists struggle with what to do with it all, since keeping it is both unethical and impractical.

"In 2001 the Features Department started stocking a cabinet with books, CDs, DVDs and other items for staffers to purchase, generating several hundred dollars a year for the Akron Press Club's scholarship fund. But what to do with oddball and bigger-ticket items?"

The answer was a holiday silent auction, with all proceeds going to charity. The Graft Auction generated an estimated $25,000 between 2003 and 2017.

Sometimes the newsroom channeled its generosity to one of its own. In 1984, we pitched in to send Tom Ryan, a veteran of the Normandy invasion, back to France for the 40th anniversary of D-Day.

The newsroom also pitched in to give the late copy editor Donn Gaynor an unusual retirement gift. "His idea of a fun afternoon was to drive to Sharon, Pa., to get Pennsylvania lottery tickets to add to his Ohio ones," Beth Thomas Hertz said. "So for his retirement...we asked the entire newsroom... to reach out to friends/family in other states and get them to buy a $1 instant ticket and mail it to us.... We got about 40 tickets from about 25 states and had so much fun presenting them to Donn! He scratched them off slowly over the course of his last night at work, and he had two winners! OK, they were for a combined total of $4, but he was tickled by the whole project."

The night desk's alleged willingness to eat anything once fed a news story. A report by the National Academy of Sciences' Institute of Medicine in 1995 concluded that soldiers weren't exactly cleaning their plates when it came to Meals Ready to Eat, their staple in the field. About a dozen night folks volunteered to eat some MREs to find out why, and as Steve Love reported in a Beacon Journal story: "The consensus? Yuck." Even the night crew draws the line somewhere.

But apparently not at cicadas.

In 1999, cicadas crawled out of the ground of Northeast Ohio after a 17-year nap. They were big, noisy and ugly, so of course, the night desk threw them a welcome back party. The evening's buffet included Nymph Pilaf (a Joe Thomas specialty that tasted a lot like green bean casserole), twice-baked cicadas, cicada shells (which could have been pork rinds) and extra crunchy cicada legs (which bore a striking resemblance to pretzels). But the *pièce de résistance* was the cake decorated with a close-up photo of a bug-eyed cicada, courtesy of photographer Michael Chritton.

We chirped all the way to dessert. Then we dug in for 17 more years of night shifts.

# Chapter 19
## From the Biz Beat to Beyoncé

Glenn Gamboa

Legendary music producer Quincy Jones once told me that his approach to the recording sessions with Michael Jackson that would become "Thriller" was to have everything in place to do good work. "Then, you have to leave space for God to walk into the room," he said.

It's an approach that doesn't happen much in music any more, an industry where declining sales have led to prioritizing efficiency over risk-taking. And it's an approach that is even rarer in journalism.

But it comes close to describing what happened with the Beacon Journal's business staff in the '90s. Even the job that I was hired to do in 1993 signifies that something special was happening in Akron in those days.

Basically, I was hired to cover how the health-care reform proposed by President Bill Clinton's administration would affect Northeast Ohio. My beat was defined as "the business of health care," which meant I covered the business decisions of area hospitals, insurers and pharmacies, including the then-Twinsburg-based Revco D.S. Inc. The main focus, though, was to cover President Clinton's Health Security Act, an ambitious plan to reimagine health care spearheaded by Hillary Rodham Clinton. I read all 1,342 pages of the plan, looking to explain how the changes would affect both the patients and the providers. It's the kind of coverage generally expected from the nation's biggest newspapers — not from a paper battling to be the fourth-largest in Ohio. Of course, The Beacon Journal, as the founding paper of the Knight Ridder Newspapers chain, had long been more ambitious and better-funded than much larger competitors. Its business staff had helped the paper win a Pulitzer Prize for its coverage of the hostile takeover of The Goodyear Tire and Rubber Co.

When I joined the business staff in 1993, I was in awe of my surroundings. I was 25 years old — with three years of business news experience as the business editor of the Morning Journal in Lorain, Ohio — and I became the seventh reporter in a department already filled with respected journalists. Stuart Drown, who went on to become California's deputy secretary for innovation and accountability after numerous leadership jobs in journalism and public policy, was covering the tire industry. Lornet Turnbull was winning awards with her coverage of the auto industry, as was Mary Vanac as she pioneered a new way of reporting on small business and Mary Ethridge on retail. And business editor Geoffrey Gevalt, who went on to become editor of the Burlington (Vermont) Free Press, was quickly adding reporters to build on the department's reputation — including Maura McEnaney on banking and Janet Moore, who had just graduated from the prestigious Knight-Bagehot Fellowship at Columbia University, on manufacturing. Shortly after I was hired, Gevalt also added another Knight-Bagehot fellow, Sandra Block, to cover personal finance, Melanie Payne to cover workplace issues, David Adams from metro to cover the business of sports, and columnist Diane Evans.

All that firepower helped great journalism happen. It was the Quincy Jones adage come to life. When all the bases are covered, you get the chance to focus on the work and approach it in the best way possible, getting the chance to be inspired.

Moore said her decision to come to Akron following her fellowship in 1993 was an easy one. "The paper was much more sophisticated in terms of business coverage than most," said Moore, now a transportation reporter at the Minneapolis Star-Tribune. "There were already 10 people in the department and you could see there was a commitment to business news."

That commitment led to numerous department-wide projects — including The Beacon Journal Top 100, which ranked the top-performing public companies in Ohio — that helped readers make sense of the growing flood of information that was now available to them through the Internet. It also gave reporters the opportunity to branch out, even allowing some in the department the chance to cover Cleveland Indians home games as the team made its playoff run in 1995 and its return to the World Series in 1997.

"I came in knowing the business news section was really respected and I came in with the goal to make it better," said Gevalt, who came to the Beacon in 1991 from The Patriot Ledger in Quincy, Mass. "It was really a good time for that. Business news was becoming the thing in newspapers. It was a trend. I came in with carte blanche, but I also learned from Stuart (Warner, the Beacon's deputy managing editor at the time) and Dale (Allen, the paper's editor) the art of making proposals to corporate. It was a way to expand stuff.... It was the spirit of that newsroom. It really was a place where you could propose something, no matter how outlandish it was, and if you could prove it was really needed, it would happen."

That spirit was infectious. I received plenty of opportunities to branch out myself. For years, I had followed the development of the internet as a hobby and when there was interest in a story about its growth, I volunteered since I was already on several internet bulletin boards and had already seen some of the earliest World Wide Web pages. In 1994, it was clear that the web was going to transform the way people communicated and I was eager to cover that change. In January 1995, I launched Net Rider, one of the first weekly columns about the internet and its culture. And it was that column, as well as support from the Beacon Journal and local governments, that encouraged Time Warner to invest $150 million in the area and launch its first high-speed internet service, Road Runner, in Akron in 1996, a move that made the area one of the most-wired communities in America.

The investments the Beacon Journal had made in its business department were paying off. When the Society of American Business Editors and Writers launched its "Best in Business" awards in 1995, the department was honored as one of the top sections in the country. In 1998, it was one of only four newspapers in the country to receive two awards, both for spot news stories — one on the surprise sale of Revco to a competitor and the other on an international spy ring stealing trade secrets from Avery Dennison Corp. "The judges had no hesitation in giving two awards to the Beacon Journal," the judges said in their comments. "Their work was way ahead of the rest of the contestants." (Maybe the more telling judges' comment was on the Avery Dennison story: "The judges never thought we would have been so interested in a story about adhesives.")

When Drown was promoted to deputy business editor, I was promoted to be his replacement on the rubber beat. To cover tires in Akron may not quite be the same as covering cars in Detroit or theme parks in Orlando, but it was certainly an honor. Though Akron had certainly diversified its economy by the mid-'90s, an overwhelming number of readers either worked for a tire company or a supplier or knew someone who did. The responsibility to keep them all informed about those companies weighed on me, especially when there was a strike, like the lengthy one at Bridgestone Firestone that I covered, or a product launch, like Goodyear's run-flat tire, which was also part of my beat.

However, the most memorable event of my tenure as the tires reporter was only tangentially related to the beat. In 1995, I was in Noblesville, Ind., a suburb of Indianapolis, covering a strike at the Bridgestone Firestone plant there. It was weeks after the Oklahoma City bombing and there was still a question about whether Timothy McVeigh and Terry Nichols were the only ones responsible for the 168 deaths. Authorities were still, theoretically, searching for "John Doe No. 2," a dark-haired man seen near the bomb site.

Motel employees in Noblesville thought that maybe I was "John Doe No. 2." They were suspicious because I was in my room three days in a row when they wanted to clean it and I turned them away each time. That happened because I would go to the plant in the morning and write my story for the next day's paper in the afternoon. I was on the phone with Gevalt answering questions about my story when the police knocked at my door. Apparently, the motel manager had called them so they could search my room, presumably for firearms and explosives. I was, after all, a dark-haired man, though the fact that I was not white in a very white part of Indiana may have also played a part.

Gevalt stayed on the phone the entire time, while the police interviewed me and searched my room, which didn't take long. When he was sure I was OK, he told me to pack because I was leaving that motel. I tried to explain that because of the Indianapolis 500, there probably wouldn't be any other rooms in the area. It's what the apologetic motel manager told Gevalt when he called to complain. However, Gevalt wouldn't take no for an answer and soon I was at another motel and he was writing letters to the CEO of the motel company. Truthfully, he was more upset about it than I was, perhaps because I was already used to that kind of treatment.

But it's an incident that still sticks with me decades later. I wasn't just an employee. I was part of something bigger, a makeshift family at the Beacon Journal that stuck together. As important as the monetary investment was to the business department's success, the feeling of belonging made already-strong journalists want to try even harder.

"It was an incredibly cohesive department," Gevalt said. "You all really liked each other and pushed each other in a good way.... There was something going on that was unusual. And we had readers who gave a shit. They called us if we got something wrong. We were part of the community. That was the specialness for me. There was this incredible connection between the history and the community. I really appreciated that circle."

Moore said that, decades later, she is still in contact with many from her time in Akron. "We were just so close, maybe because we were young-ish then and many of us were single," she said. "I didn't have the same relationship with co-workers in other places. There was such camaraderie there and the freedom and time to think big thoughts."

That feeling continued even after Gevalt was promoted to deputy managing editor and Drown took over the business department, with Roger Mezger as his deputy.

I had been working on longer-range projects with Mezger before his promotion, as well as joining Pulitzer Prize-winning projects editor Bob Paynter on an investigation of prominent Akron businessman David Brennan. I had my own projects as well, on how the area's middle class was suffering and what parents could do to keep their children safe online.

Moore said many of the issues that surprised pundits during the 2016 presidential election were already things we covered in Akron in the '90s. "The fights from the labor movement, the decline of the middle class, people feeling disconnected from the growth in the rest of the country — we were already covering those issues at that time, before people started writing about them in 2016," she said. "We lived there. We could see it for ourselves."

The effect of globalization on once-thriving manufacturing cities like Akron became part of one of the most ambitious projects I have ever seen a newspaper undertake, "Wheels of Fortune," a history of the rubber industry in Akron. The series, written by David Giffels and Steve Love and edited by Deb Van Tassel, who had been the business editor in Akron and at the Seattle Times, involved producing a special section every Sunday in 1997 about the rubber and tire industry's growth and decline in Akron and how it helped shaped the region. I was fortunate enough to be one of the reporters on that project, and it pulled together all sorts of storytelling and journalism opportunities that almost seem impossible now.

The combination of business reporting and projects work was a path I would have been happy to stay on, but the one opportunity that I wanted more unexpectedly arrived. Kevin C. Johnson, the Beacon's award-winning music critic, had taken a job at the St. Louis Post-Dispatch in 1998, and I applied to replace him. A lifelong music fan, I got my start in journalism writing album reviews and interviewing artists for Alternative Press, the Cleveland-based magazine dedicated to underground artists. I had continued writing about music in college and even as a freelancer for Cleveland Scene once I graduated and occasionally for the Beacon, when Johnson had too many events to cover at the same time.

I had always dreamed of being a full-time music critic, but I never really thought it would happen. When I interviewed for the job, several editors questioned whether I would feel fulfilled in features, considering how much I enjoyed business news. It was actually a genuinely kindhearted question, but covering the region's music scene I grew up in and the Rock and Roll Hall of Fame in Cleveland offered so many exciting possibilities, I just couldn't resist it.

As part of the search to replace Johnson, editors had found Chuck Klosterman, a promising young reporter from North Dakota, but decided that they would give me the music critic's job and that they would hire Klosterman as a general assignment reporter who would help out with music coverage.

That move also represented my time at the Beacon. Not only did the paper give me the chance to try something new, something I had long wanted to do, it also brought on new talent.

With the support of my editors, Joan Rice and Ann Sheldon Mezger, I was able to quickly make the music beat my own. I launched a weekly music column on local music, including hometown hero Chrissie Hynde of The Pretenders, and because of the coverage I was giving local acts, promoters were putting many of them in larger venues. Through our ongoing coverage of the Rock Hall, I was able to interview Paul McCartney and Public Enemy's Chuck D, as well as Justin Timberlake and Canton's Macy Gray.

Those high-profile stories got me noticed by several news organizations, including NPR, which had me talk about Akron's Joseph Arthur on "All Things Considered" and WAPS, which gave me a weekly radio show.

Less than two years after starting the music beat in Akron, Newsday hired me to cover music in New York, a job that was beyond my wildest dreams. (And Klosterman, who became a noted author and journalist with memoirs like "Fargo Rock City" and "Killing Yourself to Live," replaced me on the music beat for a time before leaving to be a staff writer for Spin.)

It wasn't long after my arrival at Newsday that my training in Akron paid off. When Newsday's editor Howard Schneider asked for a serious look at hip-hop, I proposed an ambitious, Beacon-style project that showed how hip-hop had become part of the fabric of nearly every facet of American life.

To my delight, the project was approved. My experience from working with Bob Paynter in Akron led me to receiving the infamous "hip-hop dossier," information about hip-hop stars gathered by the Miami Beach Police Department after I filed a Freedom of Information Act request. I traveled to Slope County, N.D., the county with the fewest minorities in America, to search for hip-hop's influence. In the end, Newsday ran a four-day series about hip-hop that involved contributions from throughout the newsroom. It won national awards, became the subject of stories by Fox and the BBC, and was named a Pulitzer finalist for explanatory reporting in 2005. It was praised by Pulitzer judges "for its serious, energetic and substantive series examining three decades of hip-hop music in American life."

The series was yet another example of what can happen when you cover all the reporting bases and then leave room for inspiration and ambition. It opened plenty of doors in the music industry for me, leading to invitations like covering the Live 8 Festival in London as one of only two credentialed American journalists and interviews with Beyoncé, Jay-Z, Billy Joel, Mariah Carey and nearly every other major musician in the last two decades. I became a regular music pundit on NPR and on local TV stations and I found myself in the middle of all sorts of stories.

I was there when Kanye West interrupted Taylor Swift's acceptance speech at the MTV Video Music Awards, even catching a glimpse of a stunned Swift huddling with her mom in a hallway afterwards. I was questioned by pre-President Donald Trump about why I had better seats at a Duran Duran concert on Broadway than he and his family did. I was hugged by President Bill Clinton on a red carpet for asking him about his commitment to music education. Yes, there is a clip of me getting yelled at by John Mayer as part of a story on "The Daily Show," and if you watch "The Real Housewives of New Jersey" very closely, you can see me chatting with Christie Brinkley and in the crowd at The Plaza watching Alexa Ray Joel perform.

It's not clear whether journalism will ever recover or if the current wave of cost-cutting will remain an unfortunate necessity. Hard work and covering all the basics in journalism are now more important than ever, as newspapers are forced to cut back on even the most crucial of coverage areas. There are papers in major metropolitan areas that have news staffs that are barely larger than the 10-reporter business staff that the Beacon Journal had in the '90s.

Maybe it was an anomaly, a confluence of resources and ideas that can't be duplicated. Or maybe it can serve as a reminder of what is possible when you manage to save some room for the occasional bit of inspiration to work its magic.

# Chapter 20
## Oh, to Be a Fly on the Ceiling of the Art Department

Art Krummel

Whenever I think of the Beacon Journal art department, I think of flypaper. Flypaper because years ago, when the building's air conditioning was either nonexistent or not working, artist Walt Neal insisted on opening the windows to cool off — inviting in the flies. To combat the flies, he hung flypaper. Lots of strips, suspended from the drop ceiling.

I first encountered the flypaper in 1967, just a few weeks after Chuck Ayers, who would later famously draw the cartoon Crankshaft, and I had been hired. We were on a crash course to learn how to retouch photos because the sad and sudden death of Chief Artist Byron Fairbanks left the department short-staffed. Chuck and I could not yet be left alone to handle the deadline photo retouching flow, so we worked with Joe Grace, the new chief artist. On Saturday mornings Chuck and I worked with Joe through the deadline for the Saturday afternoon paper.

This was our second Saturday working with Joe. As soon as Joe headed home after the deadline rush, Chuck and I decided to have fun with Walt's flypaper. We took a three-ply Strathmore drawing board — very expensive — and Chuck began to draw giant flies and I cut them out.

Then Chuck climbed up on a desk chair and hung the paper flies as I handed them to him.

Abruptly the door opened and in walked Joe. Chuck and I froze — caught red-handed. "Forgot my hat," Joe mumbled as he quickly snatched the hat and without a word was out the office door.

"'Aw, crap, we're screwed," we said to each other — in stronger language.

Not a word was ever said about the flypaper incident. That was our introduction to how wacky that department was and would continue to be for decades.

I first joined the Akron Beacon Journal in 1962, fresh from hitchhiking all over the country after high school. A friend who was leaving for college tipped me off about a job at the Beacon — a copy boy, a.k.a. a gofer, filler of glue pots. The sound of someone shouting "copy" would prompt an immediate response from me or another copy kid. Reporters and editors would ask for a cup of coffee (machine made), supplies or to carry a message to another department. It was a fun and exciting job watching how each day's newspaper was created and then feel the building vibrate as the presses began to run, the newspaper's heartbeat starting another day printing the city's source of news.

As I was shown around the newsroom, we came to the door to the art department. Throughout my adult life I longed to be an artist so excitement grew as I opened the door to the artists' section. WHAT'S THIS???? A DENTIST'S OFFICE? The artists' main job was to retouch photos with an airbrush (their choice a Paasche AB). Every photo had to be retouched. The process helped the photos reproduce better, but the airbrushes sounded like the high-pitched whine of a dentist's drill. It was a sound I came to appreciate and hear in my dreams.

Later I happily became aware that all four of the artists drew cartoons and illustrations, too (retouching photos did not fit my image of an artist). At that time Fairbanks was the head of the department. The other artists, Joe Grace, Bud Morris and Walt Neal had all been hired in the 1940s and 1950s and were World War II veterans.

My journey to join them first took a detour. One day on the elevator while still a copy boy, Landon Knight — the son of John S. — asked if I knew anyone who could type and wanted a job. Lanny, as he was known, ran a subsidiary business out of the Beacon that provided supplies to Knight newspapers. I went home that weekend, rented a typewriter and borrowed a Gregg typing book from the library and on Monday applied for and got the clerk job. I immediately enrolled and attended night classes at Cooper School of Art in Cleveland, including a class in airbrush. And when I didn't have class after work, I would hang out in the art department.

When Fairbanks died, I was offered a job there. Such fun colleagues I was joining. Bud was a true Texas gentleman. Walt was a wacky, offbeat character who was so finicky he would only eat chicken if it didn't look like it was once part of a chicken (i.e., no legs or wings or big bone-in breasts). Joe was the tolerant boss with a quick laugh. Also hired was Dennis Haas, who had been an artist at the Canton Repository and was serving his active duty (Army Reserves) during the flypaper incident.

Haas returned from his active duty stint and Chuck, after graduating from Kent State University in 1973, joined Dennis and me as "the kids." Joe took on the role of illustrator while drawing a weekly TV-based comic, Please Stand By. Bud drew the sports comic, Jest Sports, and Walt took over the comic that Fairbanks drew, calling it Saturday Showcase.

During the late 1970s and early 1980s, our focus changed from cartooning and retouching photos to helping to illuminate stories. A story about depression during the holidays needed an illustration. Draw us a picture, editors said. The high cost of buying a house. Do us an illustration. No cameras allowed in the courtroom? Send an artist to do sketches.

And still every photo had to be retouched.

One of the first news sketches I remember was for the tragic Who concert in Cincinnati, where 10 people died after a mob of fans rushed the locked gate at the sold-out concert. I received a phone call at 1 a.m. to come into the office to create an image of what that event might look like. All I had for reference was a couple after-the-fact photos of the gate showing empty beer bottles and some discarded programs. By daybreak, I had illustrated a crowd of people with arms raised, some holding beer bottles with one clearly trapped young woman with her head turned, panic on her face.

We now had a role in presenting the news.

Another new role for us was courtroom sketching. When six men were charged with the mob-related murder of Danny Greene in Cleveland, I was sent to do drawings in federal court. It was chilling when an entourage of large men in dark overcoats came into the courtroom and grimly stared at me, trying to see what I was drawing. I had to catch quick glimpses of defendant and mobster James Licavoli and then do a lot of drawing. Very unnerving.

The federal hearings in 1981 on the deportation of John Demjanjuk, the Ukrainian immigrant believed to be a Nazi war criminal, brought a new challenge. The judge was Frank Battista, and he demanded that every man working in the courtroom wear a tie. People who work with paint and ink all day don't dress up. Only the bosses wore ties in the art department, and I had no idea about the judge's rule until I showed up in downtown Cleveland a half hour before the beginning of court. The bailiff wouldn't let me in. Panicked, I ran down the street and found a Woolworth's. Please have a tie, I thought. I ran in and found a rack of cheap clip-on ties! PERFECT! I clipped it on and made it back to court in time to be seated before the doors were closed. Fascinating, captivating testimony describing the evil of the extermination camps and the brutality of the guards, including one called Ivan the Terrible, who some believed was Demjanjuk. When I showed up for work the next morning at the art department, all of the guys wore ties to work in my honor — having a good laugh with me.

In December 1984, there was a massive explosion at Akron's Recycle Energy Plant — the place where trash was turned into steam heat. Three workers died and six others were injured. Our mission was to diagram how the plant worked and where the explosion occurred, so that readers could understand what happened.

As our jobs changed, so did the department. In 1973, Chuck Ayers snared the editorial cartoonist job that remained open after longtime cartoonist Ned White left the Beacon Journal. Joe Grace retired in 1978 and Dennis Earlenbaugh, who had been in advertising art, was hired. Bud Morris, who took over as chief artist, retired in 1984 and Neal retired a few years later. Dennis Balogh was hired from the Columbus Dispatch to replace Morris and I became the chief artist. Chuck returned to the art department in 1987. Chip Bok, who had recently arrived in the art department, took over the editorial cartoonist job. We hired our first female artist, Deb Kauffman Barry, in 1988.

In early 1990, the Beacon hired the first assistant managing editor to oversee graphics and the first African American in the department, Susan "Mango" Curtis. She came from a suburban paper in Washington, D.C., and played a major role in overseeing the redesign of the paper and of our new weekend entertainment section, Enjoy! I was named art director about that time, and she also worked with me in overseeing operation of the art department.

As we moved more into computer illustration, it became necessary to have someone almost full time assigned to MacIntosh technology and upgrades, a role Dennis Haas embraced (along with the historic houses he sketched for the paper each week.) Haas did such a good job with the technology that the Knight Ridder Washington Bureau lured him to its headquarters. I chose to follow in the technology route. Terence Oliver, who was hired from the Plain Dealer, became the new art director.

Other faces joined us over the next decade. Kathy Hagedorn was hired in 1994, shortly before Ayers left to concentrate on co-creating and drawing the nationally syndicated cartoon strip Crankshaft. Rick Steinhauser was hired soon thereafter. Others came and left. Jamee Tanner and Jamal Ricky Brinson, who later became LeBron James' brother-in-law, were with us for a while. So was Phil White, who took over my MacIntosh job when I moved to the position of newsroom technology manager in the mid-1990s. Brian Shellito initially interned with us in 1993 and joined the staff years later. He was the sole art department survivor, working in sports design and drawing the Sunday editorial cartoon as well as handling other design requirements, until he was laid off by GateHouse Media (now Gannett) in September 2019, after winning Cleveland Press Club awards for his political cartoons.

One of our more interesting part-time hires during the 1990s was Derf, born John Backderf. He came to us from the Plain Dealer and became associated with one of the most sensational stories in Akron's history.

Former Bath resident Jeffrey Dahmer was arrested in 1991 in Milwaukee and charged with kidnapping, murdering and dismembering 17 young men and boys. He and Derf had been friends at Revere High School. At the time Derf refused all requests for interviews. And many years later he created the graphic novel, "My Friend Dahmer," about growing up with Dahmer. The novel catapulted Derf to international fame and resulted in a movie as well.

He discussed the experience before the movie came out in 2017 in an email interview with former Beacon colleague Stuart Warner. "I remember a week or so after his arrest, I was standing in the checkout line at a grocery store in Cleveland, where I live," Derf wrote. "I glanced over at the magazine display and every... single... cover had a photo of Dahmer staring out at me. This was a guy I sat next to in study hall and gave rides home from school! I just left my cart and bolted out of the store. It was too much for me."

I was assigned to do a graphic illustration of Dahmer's apartment, showing where he stored the dismembered body parts (i.e. his refrigerator) and his power tools. I produced it based on the coroner's report from Wisconsin, and the graphic won a prestigious national award. I was so proud I had the original artwork framed and hung in my family room — much to the horror (and interest) of my friends and relatives who came to visit that Christmas. Dennis Balogh also won several awards for his watercolors that illustrated the section.

Now here was the thing. Although the original wacky and fun guys I worked with left over the years, the new people were equally entertaining. You don't put six or eight artists in a room and not have fun figuring out how to make a goofy looking 6-foot Christmas tree out of old rolled-up newspapers.

Actually Walt Neal was the first to make such a tree, but it became a Christmas tradition in the center of our office. Newsroom folks as well as artists could hang nearly anything (nothing mean or obscene) on the tree: pennies, doctored photos of former editors, column sigs with a Grinch pasted in or blah blah blah printed on it.

And woe be the person who happened to walk into our space when we were throwing pieces of kneaded erasers at each other or darts at the dart board. Once an editor came in while we were trying our left-hand darting skills. His elbow caught a dart and he was NOT happy.

At one point, we even had a fish tank, with two sharks named for our two bosses, Mango and another assistant managing editor named Joette Riehle, who didn't always see eye to eye. Our two fish — Fango and Chew-ette, chased each other around the tank all day.

The laughing really never stopped, but we did know when to get down to business.

In 1986, British financier Sir James Goldsmith attempted to take over the Goodyear Tire and Rubber Co. It was huge news, and we provided graphics for every segment of the ongoing story. The Akron community was energized and did not intend to allow such an unfriendly takeover. In Washington, D.C., U.S. Rep. John Seiberling introduced anti-takeover legislation and interrogated Goldsmith before a congressional committee with lots of Akron supporters in the gallery. And after Goldsmith withdrew his offer, most of us spent all-nighters working to present the story, including an eight-page section produced in a week. To pay Goldsmith to go away, Goodyear had to sell off a lot of assets. I remember doing graphic timelines and an illus-tration showing the Goodyear world headquarters being split in half. The newspaper's coverage of this event earned the Akron Beacon Journal its third Pulitzer Prize.

Seven years later, the paper won another Pulitzer, and the art department contributed heavily.

A think tank of newsroom editors and reporters decided to undertake the colossal assignment of looking at race relations in Akron. The package was planned to encompass five major topics presented over one year. We used charting software that we could overlay on a census tract of Akron to dimensionally show how different numbers could be represented. The software was still in beta testing and thus had no users guide. Yikes! But somehow Bob Paynter, one of the editors directing the project, and I figured it out.

Mango was the project's art director and determined we needed a keystone image to kick off the series. The whole department was tasked with coming up with an image emotionally as powerful as the topic.

I knew a drawing would be a tall order to represent the project, A Question of Color. I mulled it over and realized we needed an image that could represent us — ALL of us as human beings. I began to sort through the Beacon's image library, when I spotted the image of an angry young Black man. I knew immediately that I had the start for my illustration — a photo collage of all races and colors. I looked at hundreds of photos, Soap Box Derby crowd shots, pictures of racial unrest and movie stars. All would be a part of the face of this package. Zeroing in I took a piece of each of the photos I selected and, using Adobe Photoshop, I assembled the pieces: a nose or a chin, part of a cheek and ear. I re-sized the photos to proportionate sizes and swapped pieces in and out. I used famous actors' features such as one of Elizabeth Taylor's eyes. But mostly, the montage was everyday people.

Ultimately, the editor, Dale Allen, felt this image was strong enough to carry through the series. Graphics and illustrations by nearly all the members of the art department added immensely over the year. The series began to appear in 1993, all powerful stories about the people of Akron, where they lived, education levels and incomes. Accompanying the stories were dozens of dimensional maps and illustrations showing the numbers from the 1990 census. The package, together with the creation of an ongoing community Coming Together project, was awarded the Pulitzer Gold Medal for Public Service in 1994.

After A Question of Color concluded and the celebrations over the Pulitzer were finished, there was another project with revolutionary consequences: PAGINATION — the digital conversion of type and photos that were assembled on a computer screen and designed like the pages for the next day's paper.

Over the next few months, Bruce Winges, Phil White and I, working with the production department and especially the IT department, wrestled with the complex problem of producing the paper with a digital system. Composing room workers no longer had to cut and paste the day's stories.

Pages were produced as a whole, and eventually, went directly from the news-room computers to the printing presses, eliminating the compositor jobs.

In 2000, technology had become so important in the newsroom that the Beacon created a department, Newsroom Technology, to help usher it in. I was named the director.

However, my career at the Beacon Journal ended sooner than I had planned.

In early 2001, Knight Ridder Newspapers was under pressure from stock-holders to reduce costs even though the profit margins at the paper were around 20 percent or more. The paper had its first-ever round of layoffs and it was painful. Later, when more cuts were needed, the editors fashioned a package to entice people to retire.

I'll never forget the meeting when it was announced that people who chose to leave or retire could qualify for a generous financial buyout. As I left the room, I announced: "Retired man walking."

On the day after my retirement that summer, I awakened and remem-bered why I had loved the nearly 35 years I had spent in the art department. Every day I went to work felt like Christmas morning, even with a tree made of rolled-up Beacons.

# Chapter 21
## Getting the Picture

Michael Good

In addition to being known as an outstanding newspaper for reporting, the Akron Beacon Journal is equally recognized for its quality photojournalism and was once considered by many to be the best paper in the state in that regard. To work on the Beacon photo staff was coveted and we were looked up to by other photo staffs in Ohio.

For years, photographs were considered accompaniments to the written story at newspapers. Photographers were more often than not asked or required to take pictures that echoed the story, or shoot what the reporter said to shoot on their "assignment" sheet.

That changed as photographers became photojournalists. At the Beacon we went from a system of photographers leaving "proof sheets" so the news desk could select which picture(s) to run, to being equal partners with reporters — each of us telling the story through our own unique set of eyes. A reporter with words, a photographer with images. The photo department established its own picture editors and those assignment sheets became photo requests.

Since photographers are *sometimes* known for having VERY strong opinions, our picture editors became the go-between for communicating with the news desk and other editors. Susan Kirkman Zake and Michael Chritton both performed admirably in those roles.

One of the best showcases for photojournalism was Beacon Magazine, and a few select photographers were chosen to rotate into the magazine schedule, as were various reporters. We did some serious journalism but also had great fun doing lighter lifestyle pieces.

I could write a well-deserved paragraph on each photographer at the Beacon, but I don't have that kind of space (or the best writing skills). I do however want to single out one person: Paul Tople. In a world of egos, Paul was everyone's friend. He bent over backwards to help someone whenever possible. He truly had a generous, kind heart that showed in his work. His photos were key parts of three Pulitzer Prize-winning projects, Kent State in 1971, the attempted takeover of the Goodyear Tire and Rubber Co. in 1987 and a Question of Color in 1994. He was the only staffer to work on all three. Rest in peace, Paul.

During my tenure we still shot film — digital came later. But while digital makes the mechanical part of photography easier, it doesn't change the mission of telling stories. Great photographs make you feel and elicit an emotional reaction, and Beacon photographers excelled at that. We won more than our fair share of awards, not only for the big stuff like the Pulitzers, but also for the small daily stories of ordinary people, like the photos on display in this chapter from the award-winning book "Wheels of Fortune," edited by Zake. As Edward Steichen said, "The mission of photography is to explain man to man and each man to himself. And that is the most complicated thing on earth."

Beacon photographers did that with excellence.

The Airdock, an engineering marvel, is shown in a rare opening to the public that drew 300,000 people to a United Way campaign event in 1986. No blimp had been in the Airdock for 25 years. (Akron Beacon Journal/Paul Tople)

Goodyear Chairman Robert E. Mercer greets well-wishers at a Goodyear victory rally held at the University of Akron's Rhodes Arena two days after Sir James Goldsmith ended his takeover attempt. (Akron Beacon Journal/ Ed Suba, Jr.)

John Pettiford, left, and Walt Norman, coworkers from Firestone's Barberton plant, greet each other outside the Grandview Grill after the plant's closing was announced in 1980. (Akron Beacon Journal/Bill Wade)

John S. Knight golfs at the Portage Country Club with Vice President Richard M. Nixon in 1959. (Akron Beacon Journal/Julius Greenfield)

# Chapter 22
## Taking a Position Without Being Bland

Michael Douglas

It felt like a chapel.

At least, that was my early impression of the John S. Knight Room on the third floor of the Akron Beacon Journal building at High and Exchange streets in downtown Akron. It sat off the newsroom and played host to meetings momentous and less so. It wasn't so much a place for reflection — no pews, let alone confessionals. Yet in attending gatherings there, I sensed emanations of civic religion, drawing inspiration from photos of Knight with presidents and other notables, his typewriter encased in glass, his memorable words etched on the walls.

A map captured all he built, most notably the many Knight Ridder newspapers across the country, the Beacon Journal the first, inherited from his father in the 1930s. Above a photograph of Knight at his typewriter, the words read: "There is no higher or better title than Editor."

Our newspaper work carried larger importance. The room urged: Do your part.

Knight famously said in 1977, four years before his death at age 86: "I don't care who runs Akron. Just so somebody runs it. It's too important to be left alone." Yet there was a related quotation also featured in the room that invariably caught my attention: "I cling to the old-fashioned view that editors are supposed to have opinions. So I express them."

I spent most of my 36 years at the Beacon Journal expressing the opinions of the paper, first as an editorial writer, then as chief editorial writer and finally, the past two decades, as the editorial page editor. The work happened at the intersection of those two Knight quotes.

If it mattered that somebody runs Akron, then expect the paper to have views about how all of that is going.

The late Vermont Royster, a legendary editorial writer at the Wall Street Journal, described his job as "a peculiar occupation." He had in mind its "professional amateur" quality, "rarely an expert on anything but...forced to learn a little about many things — economics, law, science, government, sociology, and so forth." The step too far for some readers comes in shaping that collection of information into opinions. They ask: Why not let us think for ourselves?

Stick to the facts, they advise.

Yet part of the mission of becoming well informed involves making sense of the facts. If the people rule, it follows they have the task of choosing or deciding the direction of a city, county, state or country. The editorial writer helps out, assembling facts into coherent arguments, putting an opinion out there for others to find holes in the thinking.

A good editorial page has no illusions about somehow riding herd on readers. Look no further than the many candidates recommended by the Beacon Journal who have fallen short at the polls. Or Summit County voters rejecting the idea of an appointed engineer, long backed by the newspaper. The purpose is to invite productive discussion.

In a 1978 interview, Knight spoke about how to succeed in opinion-making. Asked whether newspaper editorials, especially in local newspapers, are less controversial today, he responded: "Well, as a generalization, and it's only a generalization, I'd say yes, I think they're too bland. I don't think they always cope with situations as forthrightly as they should." They aren't "gutsy enough," he summed up.

So not only does the editor have opinions. Expect the editorial page to express them with a strong and passionate voice.

As the interviewer suggested, that becomes harder as the newspaper industry experiences flux, and later the full disruption of its profit model. A financial cushion aids such independence. Still, the chapel words serve well, and of the publishers under whom I directly worked, John Dotson and Jim Crutchfield stood out. Both from the Knight mold, skilled journalists who knew the business, they wanted to avoid bland. They sided with forthright.

Firm, clearly stated views increase the likelihood of reader response, in particular, the contrary variety. That is just what an editorial page seeks — a debate, in short, with letters to the editor and commentaries opposite of the editorial page part of the package. At times, some readers puzzle over the anonymity of the editorials. The critique comes in a question: Why are letter writers required to provide a name while the opinions of the paper are unsigned?

My answer usually pointed to the masthead on the editorial page, the names of the paper leadership in plain sight. As the editorial page editor, I was responsible for the paper's views.

The Beacon Journal hardly broke from the pack. This is how newspapers across the country have operated, the more conservative and the more liberal, in the era of John Knight and today. The institution takes a stand, reflecting its considerable stake in a community or the country.

A longer exchange with a reader would get into how the editorial page functions. The New York Times now attaches a brief explainer to its editorials: "The editorial board is a group of opinion journalists whose views are informed by expertise, research, debate and certain longstanding values. It is separate from the newsroom." That last thought often brings raised eyebrows. Separate, really? The separation may be fudged as papers cope with declining resources. During my time at the Beacon Journal, the line was bright.

Editorial writers react to what is in the paper, for instance, when the newsroom reports comprehensively on race relations in Akron, ultimately winning a Pulitzer Prize in 1994, or exposes the corrupting pay-to-play culture at the Statehouse, or the waste and abuse in charter schools managed by for-profit businesses. Most of the time, editorial writers add another dimension, their own reporting generating new information as part of building an argument.

I watched the size of our editorial page staff shrink, under financial pressures, from roughly eight members to one, me alone, with assists from the newsroom, after Steve Hoffman retired in April 2017. Hoffman brought an expertise fueled by years as the politics reporter and earlier the labor writer for the paper. Laura Ofobike elevated the page through her previous academic work, her journey from Ghana and judgment from 25 years on the editorial board. Sarah Vradenburg connected us more closely to the community. Steve Love brought the broad knowledge and sharp eye gained from covering just about everything in his career.

Chip Bok, our editorial cartoonist, injected valuable skepticism, challenging views and making our work better as a result.

All this points to the collective effort, including regular meetings to raise ideas, share information and hone views, in the context of where the Beacon

Journal long stood in its editorials, the principles and values held close over the decades, from public education to a woman's right to choose, from the health of the city's core to improving race relations.

That means managing the editorial voice, starting with editorial writers recognizing they are not expressing their own opinions but the views of the paper. That can be a tricky voice to locate. Among the lessons I learned is the power of repetition. One editorial may appear to say it all. Yet a crucial aspect of persuasion is saying it again, and again, using the slight opening of altered circumstances, the number of editorials making clear: This matters!

We did as much in pressing for the addition of two judges to the Summit County Common Pleas Court, something favored by the local bar and approved by the Ohio Supreme Court yet opposed by the local Republican Party chairman. A series of editorials asked two resistant state lawmakers: "Who's your daddy?" It may be easy to push aside a single editorial. A daily offering for two weeks poses a larger challenge.

The Legislature soon gave its approval.

Voice management includes serving as the referee in election campaigns, calling out those who play unfairly in their television spots, direct mail or social media. Sounding four alarms won't work on a daily basis. The tone and approach must be built to endure. Solid management advances reason in a polarized time and sees a path to worthy compromise. It makes the case for the whole, or what serves the entire city, region, state or country. It requires saying necessary and uncomfortable things.

It covers election endorsements. Some readers are offended at the paper "telling" them how to vote. That isn't the purpose. Endorsements heighten the profile of races that receive less attention, in particular those for judicial positions. They provide readers with information, and, most important, seek to help by performing the task voters face — making a choice.

More than anything, a good editorial page crafts a shared narrative. A personality emerges from the voice, no small benefit when personality trumps ideas in so much of the civic conversation. So those editorials aren't anonymous, after all. In taking strong positions, an editorial page projects a character readers will follow.

All of this may sound quaint, or out of touch, in today's fractured media sector, newspapers hardly commanding the stage the way they did in the Knight era, or when I landed at the Beacon Journal. Yet the concept of an editorial page still has merit. Facebook and Google not only pocket a huge share of all new online advertising dollars — primarily at the expense of newspapers. The Facebook platform, especially, has become a vehicle for weaponizing Big Data in election campaigns, leaving many readers desperate for clarity amid the gusher of information, good and bad, true and false.

The past three decades or more, Akron and the rest of Ohio have engaged in a hard discussion of trade and globalization. This conversation has been at the center of how the state adapts to change and recovers economic ground, its median income falling further behind the national number. Tom Sawyer anguished over supporting the North American Free Trade Agreement. Barack Obama and Hillary Clinton talked tough about the accord, though each understood the benefits outpaced the costs. Donald Trump sounded like he would do more than talk.

The casualties of globalization are real. They are present in the opiate epidemic. The Beacon Journal editorial page argued there are better ways to help than resisting the inevitable global economy and in the process creating new victims. (See the Trump tariffs harming Ohio farmers.) That starts with addressing the entire problem: Automation, no less reversible, is wiping out many more jobs than trade agreements. Constructing alternative paths to new work, or what falls under the label "workforce development," is something often identified yet the state, and country, still are without an effective answer.

Part of that answer involves investing in higher education, an area of prolonged neglect. The objective isn't to see all Ohioans, or even half, with a four-year college degree. Rather, workers increasingly need skills beyond high school. The workforce problem becomes easier with a program of investment in public works, clean energy and research.

In 2004, Eric Fingerhut unsuccessfully campaigned statewide on such a platform, his slogan, "Make Ohio Great Again." Soon, the Statehouse cut taxes instead, the result skewing heavily to the wealthy.

The editorial page frequently applauded Don Plusquellic because whatever his shortcomings in temperament, fueling his bizarre resignation in 2015 after 28 years as Akron mayor, he was innovative and energetic, practical and strategic, eager to try and thus much accomplished in leading Akron to a better place. He laid the cornerstones for the current and more inclusive approach of Dan Horrigan.

That isn't to overlook recent debacles, such as the implosions of both the Austen BioInnovation Institute and the University Park Alliance, two ambitious projects, backed by big sums from the John S. and James L. Knight Foundation. Civic and corporate leaders who boasted about their capacity to collaborate failed to work together. They also squandered an opportunity outlined by expert advisers from Battelle Memorial Institute to develop a niche in the expanding biomedical sector — in "biomaterials," led by the polymer science and engineering departments at The University of Akron.

Soon, the university fell into trouble, aggravated by the missteps of its politically appointed trustees, and poor leadership accompanied by declining enrollment and sagging morale.

To getting globalization right, advancing the central city and elevating higher education, add finding a fix for school funding. The problem dates to the early 1990s, when a poor rural district challenged the adequacy and equity of the state school-funding formula. In 1997, the Ohio Supreme Court issued the first of multiple rulings ordering repairs. Today, the required overhaul still hasn't been devised.

The primary challenge involves responding well to the trauma of poverty and its effect on learning. For Akron, that matters in view of the city poverty rate the past two decades climbing from 17 percent to 27 percent. It follows that data show the city's Black population largely has been excluded from economic opportunity. So this is about race, too. The city's schools have embarked on an effort to upgrade their performance, including an assist from the LeBron James I Promise School. What they could use is a sustained commitment from the state to the evidence: It takes more resources to educate a child burdened by poverty.

Pay attention to poverty, race and education, and you end up speaking for those who struggle to be heard. That explains aggressive editorial support for such things as the Medicaid expansion. In the same way, the editorial page has highlighted the folly of the death penalty. The state is now without access to the appropriate drugs for its lethal injection. The dilemma plays out in the shadow of Ohio witnessing since 1973 eight inmates released from death row, new evidence showing each was wrongly convicted. A ninth still sits in prison, the case against Tyrone Noling for the 1990 murders of an elderly couple in Atwater Township having collapsed long ago.

Did I veer into rearguing editorial positions? The idea is to sketch how an editorial page gains personality by defining the stakes, including the pres-ervation and enhancement of public spaces, such as the Metro Parks and the Cuyahoga Valley National Park. It's no surprise the exercise draws on the past. For me, it was personal.

During my high school years, I regularly read the Detroit Free Press, a Knight paper, its editorial page as often as the sports section. Recall the moment — the Vietnam War and its mounting toll, racial strife and escalating culture clashes. John S. Knight appeared on Sundays through his Editor's Notebook, a weekly column. He won a Pulitzer Prize for his commentaries in opposition to the war.

Most intriguing were the Free Press editorials, a daily narrative about the city, state and country, accessible, thoughtful, ardent. They helped me understand and think about the rush of news. Several years later, as a graduate student aspiring to write editorials one day, I connected with Joe Stroud, the editor in charge of the Free Press editorial page. He opened his door and provided guidance, leading eventually to David Cooper, the associate editor of the Beacon Journal who previously worked as Stroud's deputy at the Free Press.

Cooper offered me a job on his staff, and another chapter in my schooling began, my primary teacher one of those responsible for the Free Press editorial page I had read and admired. I faced a steep learning curve, and Cooper supplied timely prods and pushes to get better. I understood quickly the Knight legacy mattered.

I was struck then, and still am, by the 1979 work of the late Ron Clark, then the chief editorial writer and later the editorial page editor at the St. Paul Pioneer Press in Minnesota, detailing the wasteful spending and lack of accountability in county government. He examined "government by surprise." Scandal accelerated the change from three commissioners to a charter, and more accountable, form of government with an executive and council. The editorial page made the argument.

Summit County was the first in Ohio to make the change, followed by Cuyahoga County more than three decades later, after a mammoth corruption scandal.

This is the legacy my colleagues and I tried to maintain as resources diminished, staffing declined and media fragmented. I was the last of the cohort to depart the Beacon Journal, exiting in September 2019. Now the paper, owned by a new Gannett company built from the merger of Gannett and Gatehouse Media, lacks an editorial page editor and often publishes the voices of other newspapers instead of its own.

That may not seem so troubling, a newspaper doing what it must to weather hard realities. The Beacon Journal has company, others having taken similar routes. More, our civic conversation can appear overwhelmed by opinions. Yet there is value today in devoting a team to conceiving and crafting reasoned, informed and strongly expressed views, especially as contributions to the direction of a city, region or state, adding independent and considered thinking.

This democracy thing is about making decisions. Good the editor has opinions.

# The Competition

# Chapter 23
## The Golden Days of Radio WHLO News

James Carney

It was a beautiful April morning in Akron in 1976 and about 11,000 members of the United Rubber Workers were on strike in the city.

The union had called a strike against the Goodyear Tire and Rubber Co., the B.F. Goodrich Co., Firestone Tire and Rubber Co. and Uniroyal Inc.

I was a reporter for AM radio station WHLO at the time and had my pockets full of quarters to call the station with descriptions of the labor unrest from outside the Goodyear complex in East Akron. I needed the quarters to make pay phone calls because there were no cell phones then and we had no two-way radios.

Other reporters were at plant and corporate offices at Goodrich and Firestone that morning.

It was the best morning of radio news in which I participated because of the importance of the strike to the local economy.

The night before I was with the union and company negotiators at a Cleveland hotel as the deadline came and the nationwide strike was called. Then I drove back to the station after 3 a.m. to record a few versions of the story for the morning news program and to cut up what we called "actualities," or sound bites of union and company officials. After finishing that work, I drove to the picket line at Goodyear with other WHLO reporters as the strike began.

It lasted about four months and I covered every aspect of it as the labor strife rippled through the region.

Three years later, I left the broadcasting world to begin a 35-year career as a newspaper reporter at the Akron Beacon Journal.

This is what I left at WHLO, 640-AM:

We were a double-knit-pants-wearing band of young radio reporters.

The tools of our trade were manual typewriters, razor blades, pay phones, reel-to-reel tape recorders, small cassette recorders and a desire to tell the stories of Akron.

We came of age in the months and years after Watergate, before the rise of National Public Radio and long before the Internet changed everything in the news business.

Back then, there were as many as 30 radio reporters in the city at WHLO, WAKR and the other local stations. At WHLO, we monitored the newscasts of the other AM stations in town, but in truth, we considered the Akron Beacon Journal to be our main competition and vice versa.

A headline on a column by the Beacon's James Ricci on December 12, 1975, confirmed that:

"Our best competition is WHLO radio news."

I was proud to be a part of that team.

It was through WHLO news director Dave Lieberth that I found myself in the narrow newsroom in the radio station that was then located in a building on West Market Street in Fairlawn next to a Big Boy restaurant.

I discovered radio around the time of the Kent State University shootings in 1970 when, as a junior at the University of Akron, I asked to volunteer at the campus radio station, WAUP-FM. I was a psychology major at the time looking for something new.

From the moment I walked into the studios of WAUP in Kolbe Hall, I realized I found something I wanted to do.

I had discovered my people.

My senior year I took a few journalism classes, including a broadcast newswriting class taught by Lieberth and one by legendary Beacon Journal editorial writer Hal Fry.

After graduating with a degree in psychology and working at radio stations in Ironton and Toledo, I landed at WHLO in August 1974.

At the time, it was adding staff to its newsroom as a result of the vision of both Lieberth and its general manager, Allen Saunders, who a decade later would become the first voice of the brand-new entity CNN — The Cable News Network.

The station began broadcasting a news block that fall called All News in the Morning.

The program aired from 6 to 9 a.m. during the summer and from signing on at 7:45 to 9 a.m. in the shorter winter hours.

Eventually, an hour of news was added at noon and the All News Hour at 5 p.m.

From 1976 to 1981, the station programmed talk shows between news blocks and called itself NewsTalk 64.

It was a glorious time to have been part of the broadcast team at the station, which was then owned by Susquehanna Radio Corp., which in turn was owned by Susquehanna Pfaltzgraff, the kitchen dishware company. The station now is part of the iHeart Radio chain and operates 24 hours a day.

When I was there, WHLO had a beat system, with reporters covering Akron City Hall, Summit County government, courts and justice, Akron public schools, crime, business, labor and local sports.

"It was a matter of personal pride that we could even compete with such limited resources," said Lieberth, who attended the University of Akron Law School while he worked as news director.

"We hustled, we worked long hours, we did good journalism. It was a rush on many days."

The staff included many people who went on to long careers elsewhere:

- Lieberth, an Akron attorney, one-time deputy mayor and chief of staff for Mayor Don Plusquellic, a historian, author, video-and-lecture presenter and community leader.
- Bill Jasso, news reporter at WHLO who left broadcasting for a long career in media relations and community affairs with the City of Akron, as a spokesman for Plusquellic, as a top executive with Time Warner Inc. and as a professor at Syracuse University.
- Larry States, a local legend who left WHLO to spend more than 30 years as an anchor, reporter and editor at WAKR.
- Tony Agnesi (radio name Nick Anthony), program director and talk show host at WHLO from 1976 to1980. He worked as a national radio consultant and programmer for many years and became an executive with Akron's Rubber City Radio Group. He also is the author of inspirational books.
- Steve "Boom Boom" Cannon, a popular talk show host at WHLO as well as in the Columbus area for many years.
- Steve Fullerton, long-time radio newsman, commentator and talk show host who worked in the Cleveland and Akron area. He also worked under the name of Bob Fuller.

- Rich Barnett, a reporter at WHLO who worked many years in radio and television in Cleveland, then moved on to teaching at Wadsworth High School.
- Marilyn Miller Paulk, a reporter who worked at both WHLO and WSLR before spending 31 years as a reporter at the Beacon Journal.
- Allen Saunders (Alvin Steinwedel), a long-time radio executive who was the general manager at WHLO in the 1970s.
- Dick Russ, who worked in the WHLO newsroom for two years in the mid-1970s and had a long career in radio and television news in Akron and Cleveland as a reporter and anchor. He went on to become an executive at a non-profit that serves those with disabilities.
- Dave Osterland, who went by Scott Thomas on the air. He worked for many years as an executive at Ohio Edison/FirstEnergy and later as an associate vice president and adjunct professor at the University of Akron.
- Robert Winer, a long-time salesman and sales manager and later station manager. He left to pursue a career as an entrepreneur and inventor and worked in the real estate business in Akron.
- Tom Krisher, who left WHLO to spend 24 years in reporting and editing jobs at newspapers. He has been with the Associated Press for more than a decade.
- Lee Hamilton, who hosted a popular evening sports talk show on WHLO, then spent decades doing sports broadcasting in the San Diego area.
- Phil Ferguson, a board operator at WHLO who later worked for the Pro Bowlers Association and then became news director at WNIR.
- Ron Verb, a board operator at WHLO in the 70s who then worked radio in Canton and has been at WKBN in Youngstown for about 35 years.
- Bill Younkin, a long-time Cleveland television reporter and anchor.

Agnesi has fond memories of his time at WHLO.

"WHLO was a special radio station," he said. "We had a dozen people in the newsroom, many went on to do television and radio news elsewhere, many to the newspaper business and some to do public relations and advertising. In my humble opinion, no station has even come close to what we accomplished."

Agnesi said what happened at WHLO was remarkable.

"We took a station that was losing money when I arrived to a profitable voice for the Akron area that doesn't exist in 2019," he said. "Just like the newspaper business, radio has downsized away the community involvement, journalism and personality that existed in the late 1970s and will never return."

Cannon said the newsroom at the station at the time was second to none in the region.

"In-depth reporting, commentary, being on top of a story and the newsworthy items that had to be covered, there was none better," said Cannon, whose career took him to 13 radio stations in numerous states over a 45-year career. He now lives in Scranton, Pa. "WHLO had a family feeling to it," he added.

States, who worked at WHLO for eight years until joining WAKR, focused on sports some of the time he was at the radio station and had a once-in-a-career one-on-one interview with Muhammad Ali.

The Akron newsman said he waited at the now demolished Coliseum in Richfield all day for an interview before Ali's fight against Chuck Wepner.

More than 100 reporters were waiting to talk to Ali, but as the day wore on and Ali didn't show up, more and more reporters left the interview room.

But States remained patient and finally was the only reporter left when the champ walked into the room still wearing his boxing trunks.

"You're the winner," States recalled Ali said to him.

"He then gave me a great interview, commenting at length on the lifestyle sacrifice he had to make to train for a fight. Heady stuff for a young reporter."

That fight also became the inspiration for a little movie called "Rocky" and its many sequels.

Jasso was a student at the University of Akron when he began working at WHLO.

"Back in the early '70s, radio was still dominated by one-and-done spot news," he said.

"Thirty seconds or less on each story and then move on."

But Jasso said the newsroom was encouraged by Lieberth, Fullerton and others to pursue a different philosophy.

"They wanted to go beyond spot news and provide expanded coverage of local news, going in great detail for several days on stories that warranted the attention."

What was wanted out of reporters, Jasso said, was storytelling.

"Not just laying down the facts, but telling a story with a beginning, a middle, and an ending with the various characters involved, and the challenges they faced," he said.

Jasso recalls doing a story about a legendary spot in downtown Akron called the Walsh Brothers Cigar Store.

"I fought Carney for weeks on his stupid idea to do a story on the Walsh Brothers Cigar Store," said Jasso, who worked as a professor of practice in public relations in the Newhouse School of Public Communication at Syracuse University for several years. "I relented and it became one of the best stories I did as a reporter."

Jasso said he believes WHLO competed with the Beacon Journal at the time.

"That's who we thought of as our competition for news, because the other radio and TV outlets were still focused on quick, spot news coverage," Jasso said.

Barnett said he felt like he was part of a great team.

"We were all young and energetic," said Barnett, who has taught media communications at Wadsworth High school for nearly two decades.

"I remember the clatter of the teletype machine and how cool it was when the bells rang for bulletins.... I always felt we had each other's back. I was later to learn not all newsrooms were like that."

Osterland, who was at WHLO for more than five years before working as a speech writer at FirstEnergy Corp. and the University of Akron, said the radio station had the advantage of immediacy in its reporting.

"I always thought we had a great news team and for the most part checked our egos at the door," he said. "Every day was a learning experience."

Russ, who was later elected to the Cleveland Journalism Hall of Fame, said the news team at WHLO "was equal to anyone in terms of news ability, judgment, leadership, on-air talent."

Paulk said she learned much during her days at the station, before joining me at the Beacon.

"We were able to get the story out to the public faster and update people throughout the day," she said. "We went head-to-head with the Beacon."

Winer was selling typewriters, adding machines and calculators when he joined WHLO as a salesman. He climbed through the ranks, eventually becoming station manager in the late 1970s.

"We competed with them in a lot of areas," he said of the competition with the city's daily paper. "Our news coverage was terrific. The Beacon Journal felt the pressure."

Krisher said his time at WHLO was a huge influence on the rest of his career.

"It was radio that was ahead of its time, doing long-form reporting that now is a staple on NPR," he said.

Lieberth not only managed the newsroom but also was an award-winning reporter.

He won the Silver Gavel Award from the American Bar Association for a series called Inside the Grand Jury and later a national Associated Press award for a documentary looking at the case of convicted killer Carl Lamont Bayless.

And when Elvis Presley died in 1977, Lieberth flew to Memphis to cover the Akron angle of the story — the Rev. Rex Humbard of the Cathedral of Tomorrow performed the funeral service.

"We were the only alternative to the Beacon Journal, doing serious stories and even some investigative reporting that they chose not to do," he said.

My memories of the station are vivid.

We were well aware of our broadcast competitors as well as what the Beacon Journal was reporting every day.

When Firestone closed its 60-year-old bias-ply tire Plant 2 in 1978 and laid off 1,000 workers, I produced a 30-minute documentary about the plant and its history.

We learned to use a razor blade to cut audio tape and then splice it onto another reel.

It was like a fast-food restaurant that cooked and served news stories.

Most of the time, getting a story on the air first was the most important thing.

But we all had time to produce in-depth enterprise stories that could be aired over several days.

It was fun and hectic and always exciting.

Some of the work done when I was at WHLO has been preserved by the University of Akron Archival Services, where there is a collection of 310 reel-to-reel tapes that include sound bites and some stories from 1962 to 1977.

I became news director in 1978 after Lieberth left and continued to have fun as the newsroom of about a dozen reporters covered the region. But several Beacon reporters lived in my neighborhood in Akron and I became friends with them and developed a desire to work for the newspaper.

On April 2, 1979, I worked my first day at the paper as a reporter covering Barberton and southern Summit County.

I had never been happier.

I missed my radio friends and the excitement of the business but when I arrived in the third-floor newsroom at 44 E. Exchange St., I felt like I did when I first walked into WAUP in 1970.

I had found a new home.

I again was with my people, including Ricci, whose 1975 column about WHLO praised the work of Lieberth and the reporters at the radio station:

"Under Lieberth's leadership, WHLO newsmen have tried to devote as much time as possible to the kind of stories that are not part of day-to-day breaking news — the kind of enterprise stories that usually have been left to the Beacon Journal.... For my money, the best of the Akron broadcast news lot is WHLO."

# Chapter 24
## Caught in a Catch 23 — The End of Local TV News

Mark Williamson

Its end was ignominious. Just a passing comment to a young reporter and that was that. Local television news in Akron was dead.

Lowell "Bud" Paxson, the Florida-based founder of the Home Shopping Network, took ownership of WAKC Television, Channel 23, at midnight February 26, 1996.

By 10 the next morning, as news crews headed out to cover their stories for the early newscast at 6 p.m., Paxson had ordered his management team occupying TV 23's studios at 853 Copley Road to terminate nearly the entire staff.

They came accompanied by armed guards, firing nearly a hundred people by word of mouth. Ironic, perhaps, that a communications company would merely tell a young reporter named Steve Litz, passing in a hallway on his way to an editing suite, "We're firing you and your co-workers. Go around the place and pass the word to your friends that we won't be needing you people anymore."

It is important to note here that Paxson made a personal appeal six months before the takeover. The staff had been notified to attend a meeting in the studio to meet and greet him. Paxson, the staff was told, was coming to talk to everyone about his plans for WAKC once he assumed ownership. He promised to take the news product to a "whole new level." It would be "competitive" with Cleveland. He was going to "sink more money" into the set design, the news product, the people doing the news. And there would be raises, higher starting pay and "more promotion of the product" out in the community.

Reporters are suspicious by nature but most stayed on to see it through. That would turn out to be regrettable for most.

Paxson made verbal commitments to plans he never intended to keep. His intent, as it turns out, was to keep everyone he could on the payroll to maintain the value of the operation until he officially owned it and then turn it into another portal for syndicated TV shows and home shopping.

Nothing local, save for the occasional and obligatory public affairs program, would ever appear again on the "Akron" station. It no longer looked like Akron on TV 23. That broadcast could have been coming from anywhere: Amarillo, Texas; Gallup, New Mexico; Flagstaff, Arizona; Winona; Kingman; Barstow or San Bernardino (with apologies to Bobby Troup). The AK, the Akron in WAKC, was gone forever. So was Bud Paxson 19 years later, when he died in Montana. But he certainly left a mark on Akron.

After Paxson chose the nuclear option, Akron tried to fight back. Mayor Don Plusquellic went to West Palm Beach, Fla., in 1997 to express to Paxson, in person, how he felt about what he had done to his city. Plusquellic wanted to work with Paxson to see about funding for just a pared-down newscast once per day on the station. Paxson refused.

You have to give Plusquellic credit. Plenty of government leaders would be happy to have one less gaggle of reporters following them around with cameras and audio recorders. But the mayor had a good story to tell about Akron and understood the value of what a local television news operation could bring to promoting that story to his community every day.

"It's a two-edged sword," he would say. "A love-hate relationship we have with the media. We need them. They need us. But sometimes, there's a helluva price for people in my business to pay for those relationships. They never pay."

Another amusing aside about the mayor's view of the media was that he felt the good people in government who were doing their jobs and doing them well received no coverage to speak of. "They only cover two kinds of people in my business," he said. "Crooks and clowns. That's it."

As the mayor's communications director and media relations person for many years after leaving WAKC, I'd have to say that when it came to television news, that was pretty much right on the money.

But back to Copley Road and TV 23.

A mere 18 hours after taking ownership of WAKC, Bud Paxson removed a news broadcast that had been a part of the TV landscape and people's daily habits since the early 1970s, and replaced it with an episode of "The Love Boat." The switchboard lit up at the old theater building that had housed WAKR Radio and Television since the 1940s, and for the very first time in more than 50 years, calls were answered at the station by automated voice mail. Not by Hazel Botzum or Isabelle Summerville. Both women had been part of the station and their community for many years. They typified the style of ownership of founder Bernard Berk, son Roger Berk Sr., and grandsons Roger Berk Jr., and Robert Berk. They hired local people, for the most part. Nice people. Friendly people who cared about Akron. The Berks are from Akron and it mattered to them that they served the community in which they lived.

But now, that personal touch was gone. The news went dark. The commitment to community was jerked out from under the city that had watched a mix of young college students and wily veterans work their tails off to capture the day's events on camera and present them on the air.

The relatively small station had its struggles competing with four bigger-market TV news operations in Cleveland, 30 miles to the north. Our challenge each day to compete for viewers was akin to putting a mom-and-pop grocery store next to a massive chain store and telling it to go out there and make some money.

The people on the air at WAKC had endeared themselves in many ways to Akronites and viewers around Northeast and North Central Ohio. (Its over-the-air signal was strong to the south, even beyond Canton, which is 20 miles south of Akron). It was the little engine that could of TV news. Viewers got to know the staff, reporters, anchor people and the videographers (mobile cameramen and camerawomen). Mark Johnson, from Ashtabula, and Mark Nolan, from Stark County, both did the weather at TV 23 and moved on to do the same in Cleveland television. Phil Ferguson, our Copley-Fairlawn born-and-bred sports anchor, has been a fixture in local radio ever since TV 23. Tim Daugherty, who grew up in the Cleveland area, also did the weather at WAKC while working on the air at 97.5 WONE. He remains at WONE today.

Our viewers may also remember from the last couple of years on the air: Lauren Glassberg is with WABC in New York City as a reporter; Steve Litz is a reporter at NBC 6 in Miami; and Dawn Gigi (Gigi Hinton) is a producer at TV ONE in Washington, D.C. Carole Sullivan, who was Carole Chandler on the air, went to work at Channel 3 (WKYC) in Cleveland after leaving TV 23 and then to hosting "Today in Nashville" on WSMV. Co-anchor Jim Kambrich went on to anchor the news in Albany, N.Y. And, of course, Carol Costello was at CNN, then Headline News until the fall of 2018.

A host of talented off-camera people who got their start in Akron are still working in Cleveland television as editors, producers and videographers. They were mere rookies when we hired them at TV 23. Now many of them are closing in on retirement.

The Cleveland on-air presentation was more polished, with more money to invest in every aspect of the broadcast. But the no-nonsense approach at WAKC (and, before it, WAKR-TV) had a loyal following from viewers who regularly lauded the station for just delivering the news. No comedy. No contrived cross chatter on the news set. Nothing fancy. Just the facts, as Jack Webb would say.

The job was to cover what happened each day while the viewers were otherwise occupied. So the team would hit the streets and bring back a product every day that folks came to rely upon. The sudden ending was truly a shock to many. Even those folks who might have poked fun at the station's sometimes less-than-polished look (compared to bigger city news) realized what they were losing.

The irony of what was about to occur wasn't lost on me. After spending nearly 20 years at TV 23 as a reporter, news anchor and news director, I was intimately aware of the difficulties of covering news in our town — a town that was losing jobs, population, businesses, nightlife and its downtown. In fact, our downtown had been made famous in a song by native daughter Chrissie Hynde and it wasn't for anything positive.

Akron's population was falling from its peak of around 290,351 in 1960 to 217,613 in 1996, when Bud Paxson pulled the plug on local news. A city that once boasted five Fortune 500 corporate headquarters, was the tire and rubber capital of the world, and was once the trucking capital, too, now was struggling with unemployment, the pivotal companies that made it great looking to move out of town. Many did. Akron no longer employed 40,000 in the rubber industry. There may have been 5,000 or fewer by the early 1980s.

One of the many phrases coined about the TV news business is that it doesn't cover planes that land. Or, if there's a second coming of Christ and we don't have video, then we're not leading with it. There's no shortage of crassness, that's for certain. But there is a point to be made in that TV news relies on conflict, negative emotion and the kinds of seedy things people just might not see every day. Murder. Mayhem. Fire. Chemical leaks.

And scandals.

A spate of high-profile scandals that thrust Akron into the national news more than once served to energize viewership in local news in the late 1970s and early '80s. Perhaps the most notorious was a public corruption scandal within Summit County government that took down a few public officials and gave news reporters more than a year's worth of follow-up stories that led directly to the indictment and conviction of a local probate judge.

The story received coverage by a new reporter on the national scene named Geraldo Rivera, who was on a relatively new format of news program on a show called "20/20" on ABC with Hugh Downs and Barbara Walters. Its ratings were strong. That didn't bode well for Akron's reputation in the Rivera-created, theatrically produced segment titled "Injustice for All."

I have argued in the last 20 years that even murders, for the most part, capture much less attention than before because they have become more commonplace. We needed stories about the city itself and where it was going. What was it doing to attract business, jobs, people?

There wasn't much to say at that time. But a city's image, the face it shows to the region and the rest of the world, as it were, comes often from the high gloss of chamber of commerce-type commercials, fun promotional spots for the local stations, and the kinds of news stories that promote a lifestyle that might retain and attract young people and families.

In Akron, a town that endured decades without much of a good story about its image, a town that had more news about layoffs and business closures (especially in the vital rubber industry) than anything else, except crime, something was about to change.

*But there would now be no television station left to cover it, to tell the stories, and most importantly, to show nightly images of the evolving city.*

The irony — especially for the mayor and the investors sticking their necks out to make Akron catch up after about 50 years of neglect — was that this all began to change almost immediately *after* the demise of local television news. Not long after Capt. Merrill Stubing began to pilot the 6 o'clock hour on TV 23, downtown Akron began to demonstrate it had a pulse. It was coming alive. With $100 million in investments, Mayor Plusquellic was able to deliver three high-profile projects that would draw people back downtown: the John S. Knight Center, Inventure Place (National Inventors Hall of Fame) and Canal Park, home to the AA baseball affiliate for the Cleveland Indians.

"A city's downtown is like the front room of a home. It's the first and last thing people see when they visit, and it better leave a good impression," Deputy Mayor for Economic Development James Phelps once said.

Within 10 years, by the early 2000s, downtown Akron was out-producing all other areas of the city combined when it came to the taxes generated. The investment was working and sending tax dollars to the city treasury in amounts stout enough to keep as many as 100 of Akron's police force on the payroll. Close to 25,000 people were working downtown, another huge leap even from the early 1990s.

But without local television to assist in telling this story — with images of crowds of people and traffic coming back to downtown for baseball and nightlife — how would Akron get its story out to even its own citizens?

Not through Cleveland media. Cleveland television news has never done a thorough job covering Akron. How can it? But as long as there is no one else doing it in our city, Cleveland can get away with reporting on news here as if we were a mere suburb. That's why for years, much of the time, newsrooms in Cleveland have merely opened the morning Akron Beacon Journal, scanned it, and pulled out the stories they wanted to cover that day. Most of the work was already done by a print reporter, so there really wasn't much to it, and let's face it, 70 percent of their audiences lived in the Cleveland area and had no idea it was old news. It was, as we at TV 23 used to say, news to THEM.

I'm going to share with you a secret Cleveland doesn't want you to know. When the Nielsen Corp. does ratings surveys to determine how many folks are watching television news in Cleveland, it includes the population of Akron. Akron was and is considered part of the Cleveland TV market. That helps Cleveland because the larger the population, the more advertisers pay the stations to run commercials.

In New York, Los Angeles and Chicago, they charge more than in Lincoln, Neb., or Daytona Beach, Fla. Cleveland's stature in the world of TV markets is inflated by Akron residents who make up 30 percent of Cleveland's TV population.

Have you ever seen a successful business that could ignore a third of its customers? If I owned a men's clothing store and refused to sell the white dress shirts that one in three of my customers demanded, and those customers quit coming to my store, I'd be out of business. Not in Cleveland television. It makes money from Akron merely because we exist. We are a number that serves them well whether we watch or don't watch and whether they cover news here or not.

At WAKC, we called this phenomenon a Catch 23. Akron advertisers were not crazy about paying Cleveland ad rates to buy time on a local news program that didn't have Cleveland's larger population watching. Nielsen did not want us selling advertising without using its numbers. But, if we used them, it appeared we had no audience because 70 percent of the people it was looking at as potential viewers lived in Greater Cleveland and couldn't pick us up and, quite frankly, did not want to. Why would they?

We had some loyal advertisers who sustained us for years, but I'm fairly certain we continued to lose money year after year. When we went on the market to purchase syndicated programs to air whenever there was no network programming, Akron television had to pay the much higher Cleveland rate for those shows. But, again, we could not get the size of audience to justify or even pay for the shows we had to buy. Hence, Catch 23.

Former WAKC weatherman Tim Daugherty knew the value of those images of the Akron area. His nightly weather always featured video shot that day of something interesting going on around the region. "We actually would receive comments from viewers asking about the weather video... where it was taken and even what we might have been looking at in the shots we used. It was an effective way of showing off something new, a development, a natural resource such as the river or parks or an event that was drawing crowds," Daugherty said.

Half an hour of local television time twice each day could be a powerful vehicle for getting the good that was going on into homes around the city. The Akron Beacon Journal did a good job of those days of downtown growth, though Plusquellic would disagree, but a newspaper is a poor substitute for video when it comes to showing off a city's best elements day or night.

Missing were the cameras at the opening of a brand-new park for professional baseball. Or at the opening ceremony for the National Inventors Hall of Fame. There was coverage of the christening of the John S. Knight Center downtown in 1994, but as the new convention center started to come into its own, attracting convention business and new visitors to the city, television news was gone.

We missed the opening of the remodeled and redesigned O'Neil's Department Store building into a beautiful home for a local law firm overlooking center field at Canal Park.

We missed restaurant openings and the creation and completion of the Towpath Trail. Akron Children's Hospital has expanded about 10 times since

TV 23 went under, but not one image of this beautiful transformation has been broadcast on local television news.

The East End development, the new Goodyear headquarters, the new Bridgestone headquarters, GOJO's move into downtown and so many more big stories all came about after the signal from TV 23 was cut off for local news.

There's a new hotel downtown near Luigi's restaurant. Heck, Luigi's is now just a small part of what has transformed the north end of downtown, including high-rise condos, cool new apartments, businesses, galleries, a fencing school and the rebirth of America's first and oldest public housing complex, once known as Elizabeth Park.

Lock 3, an outdoor entertainment venue along the banks of the historic Ohio & Erie Canal, the waterway that made Akron grow in its infancy, is again a resource. The entire downtown area has the canal in view.

New office buildings went up downtown. Old ones were saved and restored by Tony Troppe, a loquacious developer who was a lot more than just talk as he brought new life to historic buildings that Akron had long since written off as useless.

But you will hardly see any of that.

Much of what I've written is within an almost archaic model in the first quarter of the 21st century. Fewer and fewer people are watching traditionally delivered television (over the air, or cable). Of those who still do, the numbers watching television news are dropping. Younger generations are finding it obsolete, not part of their culture, too linear to view in their on-demand world.

Newspapers, sadly, are in decline as well. So I'm not sure the idea of resurrecting TV news for this community (as many continue to suggest today) is at all worthwhile. In Akron, even during its very best days, it was a struggle to make it work commercially with dedicated owners (the Berk family) and enthusiastic employees because of the forces of the Cleveland market.

With today's declining viewership nationwide, it's unlikely we'll ever see true, local television news in that form again. It was local theater, live in your living room every night, done by young people you may have known. It gave many a good start to a long career. But the strangely configured market it was trapped in made it vulnerable to out-of-town owners who truly cared not about Akron or news. They stalked it, killed it, made a bundle and took off.

That, my friends, is a Catch 23.

# Dealing with Change

# Chapter 25
## Screwing the Pooch: Switch to A.M. Paper Was Rocky

Dale Allen

Less than a month after we in the Akron Beacon Journal newsroom were patting ourselves on the back for winning the 1987 Pulitzer Prize for coverage of the attempted takeover of Goodyear Tire and Rubber Co., Publisher John McMillion sprang a surprise on us. He had decided, as he had suggested the previous summer, that we would switch the newspaper from afternoon to morning publication. This time, he gave us a firm date. We would become a morning newspaper on July 13, just three months after his bombshell announcement.

"If the Beacon Journal is to be successful in attracting new readers and advertisers," he said, "it must meet the changing needs of society. Publishing in the morning is just a part of that change."

I agreed with the decision. I had watched through the past three decades as morning newspapers became dominant in the nation. Several afternoon newspapers were on the brink of extinction; others had made the switch to morning publication to stave off the death rattles. Still others were contemplating the move. Moreover, in cities where morning and afternoon papers were being published by a single publisher, consolidation was taking place, with afternoon publications being folded into their morning partners. Knight Ridder's newspapers followed in line with that trend.

The corporation had closed or was preparing to close its afternoon newspapers in Charlotte, N.C.; Lexington, Ky.; Columbus, Ga.; Columbia, S.C.; Saint Paul, Minn.; Wichita, Kan.; San Jose, Calif., and Long Beach, Calif., among others. The closings certainly created issues for the folks running those papers, trying to figure out how to merge staffs and make the transition for their readers and advertisers as smooth as possible. But those papers already had mechanisms in place to print and distribute papers in the morning market. That was not the case in Akron, where the Beacon Journal had been the only newspaper in town since 1938, when John S. Knight purchased the Times-Press from the Scripps-Howard corporation. Sure, we had always published a paper on Sunday mornings, and we had only four years earlier switched the Saturday paper to morning distribution. But we knew converting to morning publication seven days a week would require major changes in the way we did business.

It was the most difficult job I had taken on since becoming a newspaperman back in 1957.

McMillion asked me to supervise preparations for the switch — not just in the newsroom but in all departments at the paper. I accepted the job, knowing it would be difficult but also knowing I would benefit by gaining the knowledge offered by the process. Moreover, I felt confident the Beacon Journal could pull it off, so long as we had the cooperation of managers and employees throughout the building.

Editor Dale Allen (left) and Managing Editor Larry Williams examine the first weekday morning edition of the Beacon Journal as it comes off the press on July 13, 1987. (Beacon Journal file photo)

The announcement came as a shock to some of the old-timers at the newspaper, despite McMillion's advance warning. Many of our editors had never worked the morning cycle every day of the week, so they could only imagine what effect the change might have on their lives. Those of us who had migrated to the Beacon Journal from morning publications understood their workday assignments — and ours — would be irrevocably changed.

While I had grown accustomed to the afternoon cycle in the seven years I had been in Akron, I knew morning publication offered a lot more pluses than minuses, particularly as it related to the newsroom. Foremost, the switch would permit us to truncate the staffing cycle, giving us more concentrated firepower within fewer hours.

Here is how: As an afternoon newspaper the Beacon Journal had newsroom staff working 24 hours a day, six days a week. Only on Sunday mornings — from about 1 a.m. until noon — was the newsroom not staffed. On morning newspapers, the newsroom was usually staffed only from 9 a.m. until 1 or 2 a.m. the next day. So, there was a seven-hour period each day when the newsroom was bereft of staff. Yes, morning publication concentrated our work into a shorter time period, but it also concentrated the number of people we had available to do it. Plus, it gave editors more opportunity to work the same shifts as their reporters and their assistant editors and, thus, a lot more time to work one-on-one on stories. I knew that the newsroom would become an easier place to manage, precisely because we were able to eliminate the overnight shifts.

I also understood we would need more firepower on our copy desks, where the crunch of deadline work would be more demanding. McMillion understood that, too. He agreed to let us add three copy editors: two on the news copy desk and one in sports.

The crunch of copy on deadline was particularly acute for the sports department of a morning newspaper. On an afternoon newspaper, the copy editing could be done overnight, long after the games typically were completed. On a morning newspaper, the editing had to be done in quick, 30-minute bursts from the time the games ended — usually between 10 and 11 p.m. — to the first edition deadline, which we figured would be around 11:30 p.m. to ensure a press start of midnight.

Games originating on the West Coast presented big problems because they usually did not end until between 1 and 2 a.m. in the Eastern time zone.

We figured, even with later home-delivery editions for Akron and Summit County, we still would be unable to get all West Coast results in the paper. To compensate, we created a new, final edition, which we labeled the Sports Final, to be distributed in racks on street corners and other single-copy sales outlets.

### For some, not that much change

In some departments of the paper, the move from afternoon to morning publication required very little change. Advertising executives and sales personnel would still work day shifts, keeping their schedules consistent with the optimal hours for selling advertisements. The folks in accounting would continue to count their beans on the same schedules as in the past. In other departments, such as research and promotion and human resources, the switch to a morning cycle required only minor scheduling changes.

The same could not be said in the production and circulation departments, where schedules of many employees would literally be turned upside down. The bulk of pages handled by the composing room would be put together in late afternoon and into the evening, instead of during the early morning shifts required by afternoon publication. The same was true in the engraving department, which handled photos and artwork for news stories and advertisements, and which had become the platemaking department, creating plastic plates for use on the presses to print the pages.

Schedules for folks working in the final two production departments — the pressroom and the mailroom — also required big changes. Employees in the pressroom, obviously, would be working different schedules to print the paper from midnight to five in the morning instead of nine in the morning until one in the afternoon. The same was true in the mailroom, where advertising inserts were stuffed into the papers and where the newspapers were bundled for distribution.

Of all the changes required, however, none loomed greater than in circulation, which had to distribute the papers to our home-delivery customers and to single-copy sales outlets, such as the multitude of street-corner newspaper racks, newsstands, drugstores, supermarkets, business offices, and restaurants. The potential for problems was enormous because, in large part, the Beacon Journal's home-delivery apparatus depended on the kids — we called them "little merchants" — who delivered the afternoon paper after school or after baseball or softball practices in the summer. The kids and the few adults who delivered the paper for us were not employees. They were independent contractors. We could not order them to make the change. We had to coax them to continue carrying their routes after the switch. Here was the nexus of the issue: Could we persuade roughly 2,000 kids to get up at 5 a.m. and deliver their papers instead of delivering them at 4 or 5 p.m.? Some of us were skeptical. We had worked in other morning markets and realized the vast majority of our carriers there were adults, not kids.

The switch would also radically alter the schedules of our district managers, the men and women who worked in the field, making sure the kids delivered their papers and seeing to it that complaints about delivery were handled expeditiously.

Soon after McMillion announced the intention to switch, managers from throughout the building began meeting once a week — and sometimes more frequently — to get things started and then to monitor our progress. Initially, we discussed the changes each of us knew would be required within our departments. As the overseer of the project, I took copious notes, as managers in each department explained the actions necessary to get the job done. I also encouraged the department heads to pick the brains of their counterparts in Knight Ridder papers where the switch had already been undertaken. It made sense to compare their steps with those we planned and to hear about the unanticipated pitfalls they discovered as they made the conversion.

Within a couple of weeks I began assembling a master checklist of all the changes required. The list described each change in detail and named the person charged with seeing the task to completion. The list also included start dates and end dates for each task, and one last column, indicating whether the project had been completed or was still outstanding. The list was dozens of pages long. Here are some of the items charged to the newsroom:

- Establishing new deadlines for each section, including all news, features, and sports pages, and getting the production department to agree to them.
- Creating new schedules for reporters, editors, photographers, and artists to conform with the demands of new deadlines.
- Checking all wire service contracts, particularly the Associated Press, to see whether the switch would cost us more in monthly assessments.

- Checking syndicated features contracts (comics and columnists) to ensure their continued use.
- Interviewing and hiring the new copy editors.

The master list contained even the remotest items to ensure that the jobs were assigned to someone and that they were completed. Example: We decided to order all-new sales racks, to be placed on street corners throughout the region. The individual tasks related to the new racks included designing their appearance (assigned to the research and promotion department), then ordering the racks, making a list of all locations, then delivering the racks when they arrived from the manufacturer (all tasks assigned to circulation).

The weekly progress meetings were grueling sessions, often lasting hours. We went through each incomplete item on the list, seeking an explanation. I became a pox on some of the folks who fell behind in their assignments. Tough questions had to be asked, and I was a somewhat unmerciful taskmaster, even though I believe it's fair to say that I was an equal-opportunity scourge. I picked on supervisors from every department in the building.

The reason was simple: There was no give in our scheduling. We had already announced to the outside world, our readers and advertisers, our intention to convert to morning publication on July 13. So all of the tasks on that master list had to be completed in time for a conversion by then.

To ensure that our "little merchants" would stay with us during the conversion, the circulation department distributed contracts to every carrier, asking them to sign a pledge to continue carrying the paper. Those who did not sign were replaced immediately. But, to our great relief, the vast majority of carriers indicated a willingness to continue delivering the papers after July 13.

In the newsroom, we began work on our conversion plans, distributing assignments to editors in every department. While we got approval to hire the three new copy editors, we also decided to create a universal copy desk, combining the features copy desk with the news copy desk. All content except sports stories would be filtered through the single desk.

We also got approval to add significant space to the business section to accommodate vastly expanded stocks, bonds, and mutual fund quotations, working on the theory that stock quotations are fresher in a morning paper and more meaningful to our readers. As an afternoon newspaper, the

Beacon Journal offered less than a full page of quotations each day because our deadlines precluded the publication of closing numbers. We did offer a more nearly complete report on Sundays.

Larry Williams, our managing editor who had been business editor of The Philadelphia Inquirer, was the perfect manager to oversee the new markets content, working with the business editor, Doug Oplinger. On the master checklist the expansion of stocks pages occupied several lines, beginning with an identification of the quotations we wanted to add, a notification to the Associated Press that we wanted those quotes added to the daily feed, a design of the pages containing the information, and a test of each new listing in advance of the conversion to see that it worked.

We also decided to join a national trend by implementing an innovative approach of running the Metro desk, assigning reporters to teams based on topics. The move was led by John Greenman, the assistant managing editor in charge of local news, with advice from Williams. Several editors became team leaders, each supervising the work of eight to 10 reporters.

Steve Hoffman, who had been a metro reporter then editor of the new Stark County Bureau, became the leader of the team covering the state and region.

Maureen Brown, who had joined us two years earlier as a reporter, became leader of a team concentrating on major topics, including science, medicine, religion, education, and higher education.

Deb Van Tassel led the team focusing on city and suburban coverage in Summit County.

Jim Quinn, hired as a reporter from the Knight Ridder newspaper in Fort Wayne, Ind., moved to North Canton to lead the Stark County bureau, and Kathy Fraze became chief administrative officer of the metro desk.

But we faced an even greater task beyond the newsroom: We had to convince customers of our reasons for making the move to morning publication in the first place. In one of the columns I wrote in advance of the conversion, I tried to explain our reasons for doing so: "There are lessons to be learned from history, of course. We think one of the important lessons is that nothing can stand still, for change is a part of the fabric of our society."

Not all of our readers bought the argument. In fact most of them did not. We heard loud and clear from our customers something we already knew in our hearts: Newspaper readers do not like change. As most any editor can attest, even the slightest shift of a comic strip from one place on a page to another can set off protests from untold numbers of readers. Locate the crossword puzzle any place but an outside corner of a page and the howls of protest will echo through the building. Kill off a favorite comic, even one that readership surveys show is popular among only 10 percent of the readers, and thunderbolts of agony will descend upon you for days.

### What would John S. Knight do?

In Akron, the protests usually ended with a common note of dissent: "This wouldn't have happened if John S. Knight were still alive." Or a variation on a theme: "John S. Knight must be rolling over in his grave."

John S. Knight's feelings about shifting to morning publication will remain a point of conjecture. He had been dead for six years. But my suspicion is he would have seen merit in the move, as long as he did not have to listen to the protestations. Certainly, the folks running Knight Ridder Newspapers in Miami felt the conversion made sense, if only because it moved the Beacon Journal into more familiar territory for most of them.

Throughout the three months leading up to the conversion, the corporate bigwigs wanted frequent updates on our progress. But, typical of Knight Ridder's corporate *zeitgeist* at the time, decisions about the conversion were left to those of us in Akron. The corporation had not yet become the Big Brother it would become within a few years, when peering over our shoulders and engineering change at the local level became *de rigueur*. Larry Jinks, the senior vice president for news and my boss in Miami, wanted reassurance that our plans were going smoothly, but he did not insist on a day-to-day report. On the business side, the concerns were obvious. The corporate bigwigs did not want us to lose subscribers or advertising dollars. In fact, they wanted to see gains in both those numbers.

As July 13 approached, the meetings to assess our progress became more arduous and more contentious. Among other assignments that were slow in developing, we had not made much progress in negotiating new language in labor contracts, chiefly with the Teamsters, who represented the district managers and drivers in circulation and the employees who worked in the mailroom. The Teamsters wanted more money for their members, arguing that their assignments would require them to work early morning shifts to produce and deliver the papers.

Finally, with the union issues resolved, the big day arrived. An aura of excitement could be sensed throughout the building on Sunday evening, as we prepared to produce our first Monday morning newspaper. John McMillion was there to push the button, firing up the first presses at midnight.

While there were a few hiccups involving carriers missing their assignments, the consensus was all of our planning had paid off. In a follow-up meeting that first afternoon, we assessed our efforts and decided we had done a good job. That lasted about one month. Then, disaster struck.

As the fall term began in area school districts, carriers began to drop off like flakes in a winter snowstorm; not just one flake here and there. They came down in clusters. We began noting the trend in mid-August. By the first of September it was an avalanche.

At one point, we had almost 100 routes "uncovered," as the circulation folks labeled routes where no carrier was assigned. Facing the pressures of school, those pesky "little merchants" who had signed a pledge to remain on their routes, decided getting up at four or five in the morning was more commitment than they wished to make.

The folks in circulation — in fact folks in every department — were pulling their hair out, trying to get all the newspapers delivered. It soon became clear it was an impossibility. The district managers, who were supposed to take over when a route went uncovered, simply could not keep up with the unprecedented demands put upon them.

Meanwhile, in accounting and in Miami, folks charged with counting the beans and the newspapers we sold were seeing a concomitant drop in our circulation numbers. Instead of the rise we had predicted, we were watching as the numbers plummeted; not just a few subscribers but thousands over the course of the next two months.

In none of those hours of planning sessions leading up to the conversion had we contemplated the reality we were now facing. It was time for action.

Within days, the circulation department was running big advertisements in the classified section of the paper, seeking adults who wanted to make some extra bucks delivering morning newspapers. We needed to deliver ourselves of the school kids and replace them with reliable adults, who would see that subscribers got their papers on time.

In all of our advance notices to subscribers, we promised them we would get their paper to their home by no later than 6:30 a.m. on weekdays and 7 a.m. on weekends. Clearly, it was a promise broken. And we paid the price for that oversight for the next full year, which is the time it took us to get our act together and to begin recouping our losses.

### Many Teamsters opposed the conversion

So, who was responsible for the *faux pas*?

I'm positive no one at the Beacon Journal foresaw the development. In looking back at our planning, none of us realized the carriers would break their promise within a one-month period. Moreover, we had not heard of that problem from folks at the other newspapers we consulted before making the conversion. But, boy, there it was in black and white in all those reports the bean counters were sending off to Miami.

We had, to use the coarse idiom of the day, "screwed the pooch." There was not much consolation in realizing that we were, in fact, producing a better and more timely newspaper than we had been providing as an afternoon newspaper. It didn't much matter to the folks whose papers never arrived.

In retrospect, there was one other factor at play. Many of the Teamsters — the drivers and district managers — did not like the fact that we had made the conversion. Some of them felt, if the switch to morning publication failed, the newspaper would ultimately be forced to return to afternoon delivery. So, they set up little roadblocks here and there to see if they could influence that decision.

I learned that years later, when a retired driver and I were discussing our days at the Beacon Journal. It should not have come as a surprise. Generally, the Teamsters looked askance at most anything we did if it involved change.

What they did not understand was that the conversion to morning publication was one of the smartest moves the Beacon Journal ever made. We could only look down the path toward the future and hope brighter days were ahead for us after the convulsions we felt when we switched to morning publication.

We had to wait for a few years to pass before the genius of that move became apparent. It surfaced in many ways, but became absolute when The Plain Dealer of Cleveland launched an aggressive campaign to attract new readers in Akron's suburbs, including areas within our prime circulation market. If we had remained an afternoon newspaper at that time, there's no telling how much circulation the Cleveland paper could have siphoned from us.

(This chapter was reprinted from Dale Allen's unpublished memoir, with permission of his family. Allen died on Sept. 28, 2019.)

# Chapter 26
## Managing Through Changing Times

Bruce Winges

It started slowly, with hints of things to come.

An early round of layoffs and buyouts in 2001 was dramatic and painful. That reduction was tame compared to what the future held.

Everything was changing.

By the end of 2005, Knight Ridder was for sale.

In 2006, McClatchy Co. bought the Knight Ridder papers. There was a catch: McClatchy did not want John S. Knight's paper. McClatchy only wanted newspapers in growing markets. The Beacon was one of many that McClatchy did not want.

Black Press of Canada bought the Beacon Journal and Ohio.com that June.

Reorganization and more drastic staff cuts followed quickly.

Everything had changed.

In May 2007, I became editor of the Akron Beacon Journal.

It was a job I held for the next 12 years as the Beacon Journal continued to cover Akron and be a voice in the community while going through more change. How well the newsroom adapted to the challenges and opportunities it faced would determine how well the Beacon Journal would tell the story of Akron and Summit County.

### Becoming editor

My world sure changed in 2005 when the publisher sent me to work on the business side of the company. Although I did not realize it then, that time became an education in how other departments functioned, how revenue was generated and how it felt at the Beacon Journal outside the newsroom.

The most valuable lesson: Numbers matter. They matter a lot. With numbers on your side, you can effectively manage change.

The knowledge I gained during this time served the newsroom well as we navigated digital storytelling and budget challenges. I also learned how other departments affected the newsroom and were affected by the newsroom. This knowledge helped break down barriers between Beacon Journal divisions as we all tried to manage change.

I was back in the newsroom by the end of 2006.

Managing Editor Mizell Stewart led the newsroom in the months after the sale following the departure of Editor Debra Adams Simmons. He was ready to leave in the spring of 2007.

Under Knight Ridder, there would have been an extensive search for a new editor.

Not anymore. No national search. No long process.

Within a week of being offered the job, I was the editor.

Within two weeks of my being named editor, the publisher who hired me left town.

### Economic reality

In June 2007 the Cavs, led by LeBron James, faced the Spurs in the NBA Finals. In the old days, the Beacon would have sent a platoon of journalists to San Antonio to find local connections in the city of the team the Cavs were going to play.

Looking at the numbers, that was not going to happen. A smaller group — reporter, sports columnist and one photographer — would cover the finals. Journalists in the newsroom groused, but they began to learn. (The Cavs lost in four games.) Over the next years, the newsroom would realize a budget was something put together at the beginning of the fiscal year. But expense decisions were made month-to-month, depending on how much money was coming in from advertising and circulation.

Dealing with monthly expenses was relatively easy compared to reducing the size of the newsroom.

Revenue declined.

Newsrooms shrunk.

That was painful.

Again, it came down to the numbers — less revenue meant a smaller newsroom. From August 2006 to 2019, 117 people left the Beacon Journal newsroom. There were 24 hires, so 93 people were not replaced.

Newsrooms across the country became smaller because there simply was not enough money to support the staff. From 2008 to 2017, newspapers lost 45 percent of their journalists, according to the Pew Research Center.

The Beacon Journal staff moved out of its historic building on 44 E. Exchange St., in Akron, on Nov. 1, 2019. (Beacon Journal file photo)

There was no easy way to reduce the size of the newsroom. Through no fault of their own, people were forced to leave jobs they loved. But we were able to reduce staff through a series of buyouts — as opposed to layoffs — in 2008, 2014 and 2017.

There were layoffs elsewhere in the building.

There were hires, but they were few and strategic.

Steps were taken to save money or bring in revenue.

The presses that Knight Ridder installed in the 1990s used technology that was expensive — the printing plates alone cost about five times more than plates to conventional offset presses. Printing moved first to the Canton Repository and later to The Plain Dealer in Cleveland. There were no buyers for the Beacon Journal's presses. They were sold for scrap. Money was saved.

To generate revenue, the circulation department delivered not only the Beacon Journal but also took on The Plain Dealer, New York Times, USA Today and others.

A paywall eventually was put up on Ohio.com.

The newsroom created revenue by selling its content to book publishers and others. The library became a consistent source of income, with historical photos being of particular value. The Beacon Journal had been the only publication to cover LeBron James through high school. Now that he was in the NBA, editorial use of those photos in books and other publications brought money to the bottom line.

### Working together

As the newsroom became smaller, the space became too big. So we moved everybody closer together toward the north wall, which faces Exchange Street. (Eventually, all departments at the Beacon Journal would fit on the third floor.)

This meant we got to know each other a little better.

The editor's office has windows that look out into the newsroom. Assigning editors were on the other side of those windows. Looking through the windows, the editors became expert at reading how my day was going (and how that may affect their day). The redder my forehead, the more difficult the day.

We also got to hear each other's phone calls. Even by hearing just one side of a conversation we could tell when there was a difficult caller on the other end. There would be applause after an editor ended a particularly exasperating call.

There were other times when the caller was not satisfied talking with reporters or assigning editors. So they would transfer the call to me. If I saw people frantically waving their arms at me as the phone started to ring, I knew to let that call go to voicemail.

### Understanding audience

The newsroom slowly adjusted to the new economic reality. We reset expectations as beats changed to deal with a smaller staff. We had to make sure the stories we told were meaningful to our readers.

The margin for error was thin.

Sometime along the way I came up with the tagline Informing, Engaging, Essential. Those words appeared throughout the newspaper (and still do). They helped keep the newsroom focused while reminding the readers why they bought the Beacon Journal or went to Ohio.com.

Fortunately, we were getting digital tools to help close the gap between the newsroom and the readers. It came back to the numbers.

Online analytics allowed the newsroom to see how people were reacting to our stories. Sophisticated software could tell not only which stories were being read the most, but also the average time a reader engaged with a story and even how far someone read a story before quitting.

I had a 60-inch monitor put in the middle of the newsroom that displayed in real time what readers were viewing on Ohio.com. It also showed how the audience was coming to the website (social media, Google searches, etc.) and where the audience was (Akron, Summit County, Ohio and beyond).

At first members of our newsroom were reluctant to accept this change. They were skeptical of being judged "by the numbers." It took some effort to convince the them that these numbers were another tool by which to judge their stories. Their experience as professional journalists and expertise in their beats still mattered. But unlike the newspaper, the online analytics gave us the ability to see what was being read by whom for how long. That was good information.

Eventually, more and more reporters spent time looking at the big screen, seeing which stories were being read and even betting with each other whose story would climb to the top first. They put apps with this data on their smartphones.

One reporter constantly seemed frustrated when he would look at monthly Ohio.com numbers I posted outside my office. At first, I thought he did not like the idea of having the numbers posted. It turned out, he was ticked off because he thought his blog was better than another reporter's blog, but the other reporter was getting more page views.

Another time, a reporter had what he thought would make a good anecdote for a notes column. Others in the newsroom thought different — the item was good enough to be a story on its own. The two sides went back and forth for a while until they came up with a solution: They would post the item on its own on Ohio.com; if the audience reacted well, it would be a stand-alone item.

They posted it.

They watched.

The item rose to the top of the big screen.

We had a clear winner.

This change also brought the realization that there is an audience beyond print that was growing.

Social media offered more ways to reach the digital audience. Once the newsroom embraced the numbers on the big screen, editors, photographers and reporters used Twitter and Facebook to reach wider audiences and bring them to Ohio.com.

There were two other changes that the digital space offered.

Storytelling tools expanded. Video added voices and motion to stories. Maps and graphics could be interactive with pop-up information. Photo galleries offered space for more images. At one point, we brought a Google News Lab trainer to the John S. Knight Room for a day-long session on digital storytelling tools. (It did take a minute to get past the Cubs logo facing us on his laptop — Cleveland had just lost to Chicago in the World Series.)

Our digital audience grew as the print readers shrank. That meant flipping the traditional way of doing journalism that put print above everything else. Putting digital above print was a slow process for the newsroom. Some departments — particularly sports — were early adopters. Sports reporters liked the immediacy of online and the ability to tell deeper stories without the space limitations of print. Updating to technology designed for digital platforms also helped.

### Hearing audience

Those outside the four walls on Exchange Street — our audience — made their voices heard. Email had been around for more than 10 years in 2007;

voicemail existed even longer. Social media offered another way to reach the newsroom.

But it was not so much how people reached the newsroom as it was what they had to say and how they said it. Civility waned as political divisions hardened. The calls and emails at times turned ugly with racism, hate and insults. When we encountered loud, argumentative calls, a favorite response in the newsroom became, "The productive part of this conversation is over." Then we hung up.

Story commenting could be a cesspool of hate, particularly on crime stories or those involving minorities. A feature to turn off comments on a story was used a lot. The comments became more civil when we started using Facebook as a platform for comments.

Not everything was negative.

Some readers had wanted civil dialogue, wanted to know how or why a story was reported, and offered story ideas. There were expressions of deep-felt appreciation for the stories told by the Beacon Journal. Others got to know those of us who worked in the newsroom by calling on a regular basis.

One reader would bring me a pumpkin pie every Christmas. I would give her tickets to First Night or something else from the Beacon Journal. Another reader called to sing "Happy Birthday" to the Beacon Journal one April 15. (The Beacon traces its first publication day to April 15, 1839.)

*Collaboration*

In December 2007 the editors of Ohio's eight largest newspapers — Cleveland, Columbus, Cincinnati, Dayton, Akron, Toledo, Canton and Youngstown — met at the Columbus Dispatch. Our publishers thought it would be a good idea if we got together to talk about our common interests and challenges. The publishers are our bosses, so we thought that was a great idea.

Out of that meeting, six months into my tenure as editor, came the Ohio News Organization. Susan Goldberg, then editor of The Plain Dealer in Cleveland, came up with the acronym OHNO.

Initially, we decided to share our content. The feeling was we all would benefit by sharing stories and that we could do a better job of sharing directly with each other rather than depending on The Associated Press. This was an acknowledgment by the editors that as our newsrooms were shrinking, we all could benefit by sharing resources. We set some rules of engagement (stories would be shared in print, but linked to originating websites for online), created a site to share content and got it going.

The Beacon Journal newsroom was skeptical. Why should we share OUR stories with our longtime competitors? There even was a union challenge. Having good stories kept us relevant. Having stories from across the state — no matter the origin — helped that effort. It did not matter as much who produced the stories; it mattered that we had the stories. With that realization, the newsroom changed, even getting used to seeing their bylines in other papers and those of others in the Beacon Journal.

Eventually the OHNO collaboration brought cooperation among the newsrooms.

OHNO did statewide election polling. The polling became possible when the expense was shared among the eight papers, with each paying a percentage based on circulation. OHNO sponsored gubernatorial and U.S. Senate debates.

Sharing stories evolved further when GateHouse bought the Beacon Journal and Ohio.com in 2018. The Beacon Journal no longer was alone in Northeast Ohio. Stories not only were shared, but coverage was coordinated to take advantage of newsrooms from Wooster to Kent and including Columbus and Canton. The numbers in the newsrooms were smaller, but the coverage was wide. After I left, the reach expanded again as GateHouse and Gannett merged, adding nine more papers from Cincinnati to Port Clinton. The new company took the Gannett name.

### The journalism

One thing that did not change was — and is — the commitment to quality journalism. The Beacon Journal continued to fight above its weight class in Ohio despite the distractions of being sold twice and losing staff, and the challenges of adapting to the digital world.

From 2007 to 2018, the Beacon Journal newsroom won 265 first-place awards from The Associated Press, Press Club of Cleveland and Ohio Society of Professional Journalists, among others. These awards included recognition for best reporter, photographer, headline writer, page designer, columnist and editorial writer in Ohio. The Beacon Journal was named the best newspaper in the state by the Ohio SPJ and the Press Club of Cleveland (twice).

There was a national Casey Medal for Meritorious Journalism. The National Association of Black Journalists recognized the Beacon Journal for reporting on Akron's African American population. Projects brought public service awards. Ohio.com was named the state's best website.

Getting these awards felt good. The recognition also spoke to the Beacon Journal's commitment to tell stories that made a difference to its readers and its city.

### The "good" old days

Those who had gone before us had no idea what we went through because they did not live through it. They didn't understand how much the disruption of the business model affected the newsroom. They also did not realize how many more tools we had to tell our stories as we adapted to the internet. But those who went through the changes learned, adapted and kept telling the story of Akron.

At the end of the day, managing change came down to this: It was not as important how many people we had in the Beacon Journal newsroom as the stories we chose to tell.

Shrinking newsrooms were a fact. We had to concentrate on the stories we were going to tell and make sure those stories would touch the community we served. Making those decisions was difficult, but doing so kept the Beacon Journal and Ohio.com relevant.

The margin for error was thin, but the journalism kept going.

### Time to go

Newsrooms have traditions. While those traditions may evolve or even change over time, the traditions are followed.

At the Beacon, you are given a Goodyear blowup blimp and a farewell card created by a staff artist when you leave. During my time as editor, that tradition expanded to include a T-shirt from Rubber City Clothing (selected to fit the person in size and personality) and a small sun or moon face from Don Drumm Studio with "Thank you for telling the story of Akron" engraved on the back.

After 37 years in the Beacon Journal newsroom — nearly 12 of those years spent as editor — it was my turn for a blimp, card, T-shirt and sun/moon face.

After all, everything changes, and that includes editors.

I had a good run. I got to work with a lot of good journalists, be part of a lot of good journalism and meet a lot of the good people of Akron and Summit County who care about their Beacon Journal. Done right, journalism is hard work, but getting a story right and making a difference is nothing short of rewarding.

This was engraved on the back of my Don Drumm piece: "Thank you for leading us in telling the story of Akron."

# Chapter 27
## The Last Day at 44 E. Exchange St.

Katie Byard

The newsroom was hot. It felt like it was a sweltering summer day outside, instead of a nice fall one.

It was as if the old Akron Beacon Journal newspaper building was punishing us for our imminent departure.

In a little more than a week, Nov. 1, 2019, we would mark our last day at 44 E. Exchange St., home of the newspaper for more than eight decades. I looked up and saw those large columns that were painted orange a few years back — someone's misguided (at least I think so) attempt to brighten the place.

The day before, a couple of the younger reporters went over to see the new offices, on the seventh floor of a redone building in the former B.F. Goodrich complex. It's about two blocks southwest of the old Beacon home.

Listening to these reporters was a wee bit like listening to stories of Shangri-La.

"There's natural light" (from the skylight and the windows running along one side), one of them said.

"It's not dark and dreary," another said. "It's clean," added another.

It's not as if 44 E. Exchange St. was a cave.

But the place seemed awfully dreary nonetheless.

Maybe it was the yucky dark carpeting installed some two decades ago, and the years of dust, in hard-to-reach places, ignored by cleaning crews and staffers. And the weird smells. Food burned in the microwave by a staff member too busy or absentminded to keep watch was one thing. Those smells wouldn't linger too long. The more baked-in odors — i.e. dank carpeting? — were another.

Maybe the place had long been too big for us, and as the move approached it was especially bleak, what with all the boxes around, open spaces where there used to be desks, and big trash receptacles on wheels filled with paper tossed from one desk or another.

It was quiet — as it often was in recent years. Fewer people, less noise.

These days, roughly 30 people are members of the Newspaper Guild, working as reporters, copy editors and photographers in the newsroom. That's less than a fifth of the peak of 170 unionized staffers reached before a big staff cut in 2001.

One of the latest cuts took out the remaining artists/paginators. Gate-House Media moved those jobs to a hub in Austin, Texas, after it bought the paper in 2018.

As the final day grew closer, the building grew even emptier as old furniture was disassembled and moved out. We were getting new desks and chairs at the new place. It was to be a "fresh start," a manager said.

"It's not even our original building," a 20-year veteran of the paper said a couple of days before the final day.

He was bewildered at some former staffers' and community members' dismay — expressed on social media — about the move.

I thought the same thing — partly in an effort to explain to myself why I just wasn't feeling all torn up about our exodus.

The hulking building at 44 E. Exchange St. is a gray limestone structure that opened in 1930 as the home of the Akron-Times Press, a Scripps-Howard Co. newspaper.

It was constructed on the former site of the German-American Music Hall.

But in 1938, the Times-Press ceased publication, bought by the rival Akron Beacon Journal, then led by legendary John S. Knight.

Eighty years later, GateHouse Media purchased the newspaper from Black Press Group Ltd. of Canada in a fire sale reflective of the declining newspaper industry.

GateHouse paid $16.5 million for the paper — a tenth of the $165 million that Black Press paid for it 12 years earlier. GateHouse did not buy the building — it's still owned by Black Press, which has been looking for a new tenant. With an addition and parking lot, the complex fills a downtown block.

Long before GateHouse's purchase of the paper, the building had become way too big.

The paper had moved printing off site; the paste-up people were gone, as well as many other jobs. The Beacon employed more than 600 people in 2001, the year of the first big newsroom staff reduction (and cuts in other parts of the building). Today, there are about 140 employees.

Essentially, only the third floor of the place was being used.

"Wow, this place is depressing," my husband, retired Beacon Journal reporter Jim Carney, said when he stopped by the newsroom on the last day.

Jim left five years earlier, before even more newsroom cuts, before the installation in the newsroom of the giant flat TV screen where we could see how many people were clicking on which stories at any given time of the day.

"There was emptiness everywhere," he said later, echoing many of us still at the paper.

It was a far cry from the often smoky, busy place it was when I moved to Akron in 1983 as a new Ohio State University grad.

Before I went for interviews and a weeklong "tryout" (a hiring practice later deemed too costly), I had never been to the city, even though I worked in the paper's Columbus bureau as a journalism student.

I knew of the Beacon Journal's reputation as a quality paper, and that it had won a Pulitzer Prize for its coverage of the Ohio National Guard's fatal shootings of four students at Kent State University.

I grew up in Columbus and Toledo, and I knew little of Akron. I think I first learned about its legacy of tire manufacturing in fourth grade when we had to make a shoe box float representing a city. A fellow student topped his Akron float with a toy truck tire.

I might have never known much more about Akron if not for Bill Hershey, who headed the Columbus bureau and recommended me for the tryout.

I first saw the Beacon building the day before that tryout began in the spring of 1983.

I checked in at the Red Roof Inn in a suburb, and drove downtown to get a peek. The slight rise up Exchange Street seemed like a hill to someone who had lived in flat, flat Ohio places.

The building, with its revolving clock tower with the giant red BJ letters that lit up, looked imposing in the twilight. I wanted to work there.

I was hired a few weeks later, the day I graduated, and I was elated.

I thought I'd work in Akron for a few years and move on. But I stayed and became the person with the longest tenure at 44 E. Exchange St. when we left.

I spent 36 years there, arriving years before the internet began to take its toll and the paper launched its first website (in 1995).

When I started, there were still people working as printers "out back," in the area off the newsroom where cold-type stories were actually cut and pasted to build a page — before pagination.

The trek to the "printers pot," a huge coffee maker tucked behind drafting tables, was an opportune time to hash over stories or gripe with colleagues.

One of the friends I made on the coffee trek became my husband, Jim.

The newsroom is a place of moments both personal and historic.

In 1986, space shuttle launches had become routine. But we in the newsroom were paying close attention, watching the three televisions on one wall.

Akron native and astronaut Judy Resnick was among the crew. Seventy-three seconds after takeoff, the shuttle exploded and the crew perished.

The newsroom quickly swung into action, as it did for 9/11, stock market crashes, mass shootings, serial killers like another local native, Jeffrey Dahmer, and more, such as local plane crashes, strikes and plant layoffs.

We joked we were all in each other's laundry, knowing perhaps too much about each other's lives. Newsrooms were open workspaces long before the concept was fashionable.

I was at my desk 19 years ago when my sister called me with news of her pregnancy. I was there several years later when she called to tell me of the cancer that would take our mother's life.

I was there about three years ago when the doctor's office called with results of a biopsy: I had breast cancer.

I was there when the tension was high amid multiple contract talks, when there were whispers and anxiety about impending layoffs, and when workplace disagreements involved shouting and tears, often followed by commiseration and camaraderie in the bathroom.

I was also there for celebrations, such as when the staff won a Pulitzer in 1987 for coverage of the attempted takeover of Goodyear Tire and Rubber Co. I was proud to be a member of the business news team at the time.

In 1984, the newsroom staff raised hundreds of dollars to send longtime staffer and D-Day veteran Tom Ryan to France for the 40th anniversary of the Allied invasion of Normandy. Ryan died less than a year after his trip.

The newsroom came together time and time again to collect money for food and flowers for sick staffers, presents for new babies and parting gifts for those retiring, being laid off or moving to a job elsewhere.

The departure of newsroom legend Fran Murphey was bittersweet, but worth celebrating nonetheless. Her old-school "Good Afternoon" and "Good Morning" columns about area happenings ran for decades, granting countless area residents their moment in the spotlight.

We were happy to send her off to retirement and we were witnessing the end of an era. Her small glassed-in office was a hoarder's delight, filled to the ceiling with stacks of files, paper and photos.

I can't remember the origin of the "clap out" tradition, in which everyone in the newsroom applauds as someone leaves the Beacon. I have clapped many a dear friend out.

It's not that I don't have some sadness about leaving the old building. But I carry its legacy with me — in my memory and my stories — published and personal. Over 37 years, I've had so many reporting beats, it would be tedious to list them. But here are a couple of lessons.

A few years after I joined the paper, I covered a 12-week strike by United Auto Workers against Loral Corp., a defense contractor. I was 26 years old and, well, I was out of my element. I will forever be grateful to fellow Beacon Journal reporter Terry Oblander, who died in 2011 after working at the Plain Dealer in Cleveland for several years. He advised me on the fine art of schmoozing with folks on the line to get information. "Ask to bum a cigarette," he said. I was an infrequent smoker and I'm not sure I ever did bum one from a striker. Nevertheless, I schmoozed — and I learned.

Getting to know someone beyond their role in a story paid off many times. In 1992, I was among the few journalists who talked to the parents of Steven Hicks, serial killer Jeffrey Dahmer's first victim. Hicks' father, Steven Hicks, told me — as well as other news media — this was because he had dealt with me on another story. That story was about another strike, and I had spent time talking with Hicks about family, though he hadn't told me then of his missing son.

Perhaps I would feel more grief about leaving 44 E. Exchange St. had the old building been maintained better, if there hadn't been so many newsroom cuts, if there weren't so many ghosts and if it hadn't been emptied of so much of its vibrancy.

The new building has a tremendous legacy of its own. It's downtown and is not in a sterile office park in some 'burb. (It is weird sharing a building with other companies — oddly makes me feel more adult.)

A month after we moved into the new place, I'm just relieved we are not returning daily to a stark reminder of the industry's decline. The purchase of Gannett by GateHouse parent New Media Investment Group has led to layoffs at the combined company, but so far no one at the Beacon Journal has been let go. (We've heard the newsroom might be immune because it already is so small.)

A few days after we began settling into the new offices, we learned the Pulitzer Prize Gold Medal — awarded for the Beacon's 1994 A Question of Color series about race in Akron — had been stolen from the old newsroom.

It was one of three Pulitzer Prize displays in the former newsroom, and was enclosed in a display case, which was broken by the thief as the building was still being emptied out. The display was to be moved to the new offices. The other displays celebrated the Pulitzer Prizes won for the attempted take-over of Goodyear and the Kent State shootings.

John S. Knight, who won a Pulitzer Prize for a selection of his columns in 1968, had a whole room celebrating him at 44 E. Exchange St. — complete with his typewriter enclosed in a display case.

The theft is your coda for this piece, a former staffer suggested.

Our move made news in a way we didn't want it to. A symbol of the newspaper's heady days of the 1990s was gone. The staff was big those days. We had brown bag lunches, where we'd give tips to each other, talk about our mistakes, our successes.

Not only did the paper snag a Pulitzer that decade, it published a 52-week series on the history of the rubber industry in Akron. I am proud to say I did work on this project; its main writers were David Giffels and Steve Love. One of my contributions was locating the quintessential West Virginia town — Spencer— that saw many of its residents leave over the years to find work in the Rubber City.

But I'm gonna end this another way.

Not quite three weeks after we moved to the new place, a fellow reporter put a bag of Arby's food in the new microwave in our break room, not knowing foil ketchup packets were inside the bag.

A fire burned inside the microwave.

The new place was starting to feel — and smell — like home.

# Afterword
## The Empire Is Gone but the Knight Spirit Lives On

Jim Crutchfield

In 1989, Editor Dale Allen called, asking if I would be interested in the managing editor job at the Akron Beacon Journal. At the time, I was the deputy managing editor for news at the Detroit Free Press, a warrior in the newspaper fight between the Free Press and the Detroit News and not much interested in going anywhere. Always willing to talk to anybody about anything, however, I agreed to discuss the job. Dale and I also agreed I would fly to Washington, D.C., to meet Larry Williams, the managing editor who resigned that year to become a Knight Ridder Washington Bureau editor.

Over dinner, wanting to be gracious, I told Larry I understood the Beacon Journal was the best newspaper in Ohio. He gave me a disdainful stare. "I would hope we aimed higher than that," he finally said. We finished the evening with Larry asking me to give his former newspaper a chance.

I was ready to listen. It would be a challenge I would enjoy.

What I learned over time was the medium-sized Akron Beacon Journal, like the medium-sized city where it lived, competed on a higher level than its weight class. Akron was home to some of America's largest corporations and of fine institutions.

Incidentally, Larry said one of his smartest moves as managing editor was making columnist Stuart Warner — the co-editor of this book with his wife, Deb Warner — the lead writer reconstructing the attempted takeover of Goodyear Tire and Rubber Co. in 1986, which was the centerpiece of the paper's Pulitzer Prize-winning coverage.

Six years later, Stuart, by then a ranking editor, brought David Hertz, a night assistant metro editor, to my office in Akron. Los Angeles had just exploded in racial violence after a jury failed to convict anyone in the notorious police beating of Rodney King. David proposed a project on race. We pulled together a brainstorming group, including Bob Paynter, the leader of our award-winning investigative team. This would be a hard-hitting series on race in Akron, not touchy-feely.

The Beacon Journal was a traditional place, and I thought I pushed the team as far as we could go when I took the idea to Dale Allen. Detroit valued change. It once created a job called risk editor. Dale hired me from Detroit as a change agent, a pretty relentless one at that. As I saw my job, it was to push change within the best traditions of journalism. Dale approved of the race project. Next, I approached our new publisher, John Dotson, with some trepidation. I knew John before he became our publisher, but not well. To my shock and delight, John questioned only whether the project was big enough.

I left the paper for a top editor job in Southern California before the first installment of A Question of Color published in early 1993, and the project got bigger and bigger after I left, expanding beyond the newsroom to a community-wide effort called Coming Together. It would win the Beacon Journal's fourth Pulitzer, the Gold Medal for Public Service.

I saw a very pleased Jim Batten, Knight Ridder's revered chief executive officer, in California after the prize was awarded. Causing controversy within and outside of Knight Ridder, Batten had plunged the company into customer obsession and community connection. It was what A Question of Color/Coming Together was all about.

And though I was a couple of thousand miles from Akron then, I would be back.

## The Knight era began in 1903

On their own, the men and women of the Akron Beacon Journal deserve credit for the journalism in Akron, from C. L. Knight's purchase of the newspaper in 1903 and on through his son Jack's inheriting it in 1933 and navigating it through the Great Depression, to Jack and his brother Jim's building of the national Knight Newspapers company and continuing through the merger with the Ridder newspapers to become Knight Ridder. It really was a sale, Knight buying Ridder.

The original Knight newspaper, the Beacon Journal and Akron benefited from Knight Ridder's commitment to quality journalism, community leadership and innovation. Knight Ridder's experiments with the Internet went back to the early '80s. Long before that, Jack Knight, the great editor, tried out new writing styles and color photos in places like Chicago and Detroit. Staving off a printers' strike, KR's Miami Herald developed advanced printing methods. Yet, Knight Ridder valued local editorial autonomy, reasoning a newspaper reflecting its community was valuable to the community.

I came to work for Knight Ridder in Detroit in 1976. Except for a two-year adventure early on as a press secretary for a U.S. senator, I stayed with Knight Ridder until the end. After four years as managing editor in Akron, I went to Long Beach, Calif., as executive editor and then to Philadelphia as assistant to the publisher and as director of the newspapers' non-subscription circulation. From Philly, I returned to Akron as general manager in 2000 and was named president and publisher in 2001. Knight Ridder was a quality organization with quality people.

I remember deciding twice I wanted to keep working for Jim Batten. Jim, who came up from the journalism side, died in 1995. His successor, Tony Ridder, came from the business side.

Tony often said he could not remember disagreeing with Jim over anything significant. He also would say he did not want to be at the head of the financial pack of newspaper companies, but he did not want to be at the back, either. Still, Tony would be vilified during and after his time as CEO. From my perspective, in Jack Knight's old office, there was not a whole lot of difference between Jim and Tony. I considered them both leaders in the tradition of Knight.

In 1956, the Beacon hired Al Fitzpatrick, its first African American reporter. At the time, there could not have been many more African American reporters in the country outside of the African American press. Al would become the Beacon Journal's executive editor and a KR executive. As publisher, I succeeded John Dotson, Akron's first African American publisher. Akron got its second African American publisher when I followed him. When Editor Jan Leach resigned in 2003, probably a dozen outstanding candidates applied from across the country and Canada. Jan's managing editor, Debra Adams Simmons, was promoted to editor. After Debra's managing editor was promoted to another Knight Ridder paper, I was encouraged by Knight Ridder to consider a former midlevel Beacon editor, Mizell Stewart, to fill the again vacant managing editor job. Mizell had just helped lead KR's Biloxi Sun Herald to a Pulitzer Prize for Hurricane Katrina coverage. We hired Mizell.

So the Beacon had an African American publisher, an African American editor and an African American managing editor, probably unheard of before or since. It developed organically out of the Knight Ridder culture. It happened for the same reason Knight Ridder received the 1996 Catalyst Award for advancement of women.

The publisher job was the most difficult I ever had. In the newspaper industry, we were fighting for survival. It also was the best job I ever had. It was exhilarating.

When I took the publisher job, I said I would wear a WWJD bracelet to remind myself to ask What Would John Do. It also would make me ask What Would Jack Do. I was only half joking. John Dotson presided over perhaps the most prosperous period in the Beacon Journal's history, expanding the news staff and coverage. When Jack Knight's advertisers could not pay their bills in the Depression, Knight accepted IOUs, with which he paid employees so they could buy from the advertisers. It was a good business decision and a caring one.

The Beacon Journal in Rust Belt Akron was a canary in the coal mine of American Journalism. Our business was slipping in the early 2000s, foreshadowing what would happen across the industry. We had to reduce staff. As a new publisher, I knew my standing with the company would never be higher. I told corporate we would not get the staff cut we needed without an attractive buyout offer. I asked for and got four weeks of pay for every year of an employee's service, with no cap on the amount of each buyout.

On top of their pensions, some employees got more than $100,000 to accept their buyouts. It reduced the Beacon Journal's bottom line by $9 million. At $12 million, only KR's Philadelphia Newspapers, five times our size, spent more on staff reductions in 2001. I imagined Jack Knight would have approved. We hired a consultant group, telling the consultants we wanted to find fresh ideas and efficiencies across the Beacon Journal, not layoffs. The consultants did meet resistance. It's not always tradition getting in the way of progress. Change is difficult. Sometimes it's fear, disbelief or just discomfort.

To the end, the Akron Beacon Journal and Akron, Ohio, benefited from the spirit of Jack Knight and the invisible force of Knight Ridder's commitment to quality journalism, creativity, change, research, innovation, community leadership and connection, responsiveness to readers and appreciation of people no matter their color or gender. The Akron Beacon

Journal and Knight Ridder had employee testing and training, company psychologists and scientific surveys long before analytics took over sports and most newsrooms. The company knew early on trouble was coming to the industry because it saw the downward trends in newspaper readership and circulation decades before.

The company also saw trouble on the horizon for classified advertising, those unglamorous want ads that were 40 percent of newspapers' revenue — double the value of newspaper circulation revenue. I remember an expert on real estate advertising telling us that real estate companies bought newspaper advertising only to placate their customers. Both houses and cars were really being sold online. Speaking to Knight Ridder publishers, Amazon's Jeff Bezos said his relatively new company could turn a profit when it wanted, but he was focusing on revenue growth. He was confident and, more importantly, his investors were confident, the profits would come.

It was not like we weren't paying attention. In the '80s and '90s, as the company transitioned from veteran company leadership into Jim Batten-Tony Ridder leadership, Knight Ridder and AT&T started Viewtron, offering news and financial services on home computers. Viewtron closed after losing $50 million. Five years after shutting down Viewtron, Knight Ridder and Tribune Co. formed Dialog to deliver business news to personal computers. In 1993, the San Jose Mercury News partnered with America Online to make the Mercury News the first newspaper also published online. Knight Ridder created Knight Ridder Digital, a parallel online news and advertising company, and KR's local newspapers developed their own online news-advertising operations that also reported to KRD. The Beacon Journal's was Ohio.com. It was called Ohio.com because Dale Allen thought to buy the domain name for the whole state before anybody else did.

Around the country, we had national and local KR task forces and projects. Knight Ridder invested in Careerbuilder, a jobs site, and Cars.com, for selling cars. Cars.com was particularly important for Akron. With no television stations in Akron, the Beacon Journal dominated the key auto advertising market. I remember my chief financial officer telling me, as any good CFO might, we needed to shut down our special projects for news and advertising publications on paper and online because they were killing our profitability. No, I said, we wanted to grow revenue. Our thinking was the same as Jeff Bezos', the onetime KR Miami Herald newspaper carrier who would go on to become the world's richest person and buy The Washington Post out of his own pocket.

In the end, however, all of it was not enough.

Ironically, it was a form of corporate raiding that took down Knight Ridder and the Beacon Journal, not unlike financier Sir James Goldsmith's attempted raid on Goodyear. A major Knight Ridder investor forced Tony Ridder's sale of the company in 2006. Tony's critics, who said he personally made a lot of money on the deal, some of them business reporters, apparently did not understand stock options.

The buyer, McClatchy, in turn, announced it would sell 12 of Knight Ridder's 32 newspapers, including the Beacon Journal. Up for sale were mostly newspapers not located in the more prosperous Sun Belt. As the KR publisher representative on the John S. and James L. Knight Foundation board, I floated the idea of the Knight Foundation buying the Beacon Journal to make it a laboratory to create a 21st century news company. The board split on the idea, and I was disappointed when it did not happen. Looking back, I realize I had no idea how quickly and how much the news business would change.

Assured by the newspaper's broker the Beacon Journal's sale was not likely to occur before the end of June 2006, I went to France on vacation. I was in Paris when the broker warned me the paper's sale might move faster than expected. Within a few days, I walked to the top of the iconic Montmartre neighborhood, where cellphone reception was best, to be told I needed to cut my vacation short. The buyer was Black Press of Victoria, British Columbia, Canada.

David Black, the chief executive officer, would not be there. He wanted me to make the announcement. It was the end of an era. I was the last Knight Ridder publisher.

Black Press paid $165 million for the Beacon Journal in 2006. In 2018, GateHouse Media bought the Beacon Journal for $16 million, not including its real estate. Both sales included Ohio.com, the ABJ's not insignificant Internet investment. The figures reflect the demise of the news business model across the country, particularly for local and regional news media and including radio and television. The New York Times Co. bought the Boston Globe for $1.1 billion in 1993 and sold it for $70 million in 2013. At 6 percent, it was a bigger price drop than the Beacon Journal's.

The entire Knight Ridder group, America's second largest newspaper company, sold to smaller McClatchy for $6.1 billion in cash, stock and debt, paying $60.70 a share. Thirteen years later, history would repeat. The Beacon Journal's new owner, GateHouse, which the decade before would not have been mentioned among major media companies, announced the purchase of Gannett, the country's largest newspaper and online company, for less than $1.2 billion at $6.64 a share. In the meantime, McClatchy, in the midst of a debt crisis it blamed on pension obligations, including payments to former Knight Ridder employees, was selling below 50 cents a share at the end of 2019. In 2020, McClatchy declared bankruptcy.

### An indomitable legacy

I believe we always will need credible news and information, particularly for democracy, local, national and international, but the power of economic forces and technology is formidable and maybe, like the rising waters of oceans, will not be denied. Thankfully, concerned individuals and organizations are exploring alternative approaches, including nonprofit models beholden to the masses of consumers of news instead of stockholders.

At the forefront, spending hundreds of millions of dollars, is the John S. and James L. Knight Foundation. Since 2007, the foundation has conducted a Knight News Challenge, a competition for foundation grants to support the best new ideas for journalism. As a news challenge judge in the early years, I learned from and enjoyed the debates about the hundreds of projects seeking grants. For example, one proposal was for a fund to encourage people to contribute toward coverage of news stories they wanted to get reported. I loved it. Some of my more traditional fellow judges did not. The foundation funded the idea. Nobody today gives much of a second thought about what some thought then was an outrageous and simple idea. Other ideas have been more technologically oriented. "It was the Challenge that opened up the foundation to the innovation, technology, startup culture," Knight President Alberto Ibarguen said. Among the proposals rejected was something called WikiLeaks. There was something about it that did not feel right, Alberto said later.

The foundation has supported ProPublica, the Texas Tribune, Vermont's VTDigger, the Voice of San Diego and other successful online journalism nonprofits across the country. Barred by federal law from giving money to profit-making enterprises and from self-dealing — putting tax-exempt money back into the entities from which its money has come — the foundation offered money for journalism innovation from community foundations, including Akron's and others in former Knight Ridder cities.

Knight brought leaders of community foundations to Miami in 2007 for a first annual Media Learning Seminar to explain journalism and solicit proposals for local journalism projects. Among grantees three years later was The Pittsburgh Foundation, which got $253,000 toward the start of a public service online journalism project in Pittsburgh. I am no longer a Knight board member, having concluded my limit of two six-year terms in 2016, but I serve as the board president of the nonprofit website, PublicSource.org, in my hometown Pittsburgh.

The Knight Foundation instigated NewsMatch, a collaboration of foundations annually matching contributions to nonprofit newsrooms and encouraging American giving to journalism. In 2019, the foundation announced a $300 million commitment to strengthening and rebuilding local news coverage over the next five years. Among the first-year grants were $5 million to the national investigative journalism nonprofit ProPublica for the creation of partnerships with local newsrooms, $10 million to the Reporters Committee for Freedom of the Press to help local newsrooms defend reporting and $1.5 million more to NewsMatch.

The Knights' indomitable spirit lives through the Knight Foundation.

# About Our Authors

**Dale Allen** directed the Akron Beacon Journal to two Pulitzer Prizes during his 17 years as the paper's executive editor and editor. He started his journalism career in Newport, Ark., after graduating from the University of Missouri in 1961. He joined the Charlotte Observer in 1962 as a copy editor, working his way up to national editor by 1970, when he was hired by the Philadelphia Inquirer. In Philadelphia, he helped Editor Gene Roberts build one of the nation's best newsrooms. Allen was named executive editor in Akron in 1980 and replaced Paul Poorman as editor in 1986, leading the newspaper to its third Pulitzer with its coverage of the attempted takeover of Goodyear Tire and Rubber Co. that fall. In 1994, the paper won the Pulitzer Gold Medal for Public Service after reporting for 14 months on race relations in Akron to produce a 16-part series, A Question of Color. When the reporters and editors working on the series reached an impasse on whether there should be more engagement to bring about change, Allen settled it by inviting people in the community for advice, which led to a separate phase of the project, Coming Together. Allen left the paper in 1997, teaching at Kent State University for several years. He died Sept. 28, 2019.

**Chuck Ayers** was born and raised in Akron. He received his BA in graphic design from Kent State University in 1971. From 1967 to 1994 he was an artist at the Beacon Journal, serving as the paper's editorial cartoonist from 1973 to 1986. With reporter Russ Musarra, Ayers created the monthly feature Walks Around Akron. He was co-creator and illustrator of the comic strip Crankshaft with KSU classmate Tom Batiuk from 1987 until 2017. He currently is working with Batiuk on the comic strip Funky Winkerbean. Chuck also has contributed to more than a dozen books as an illustrator or art director. He taught cartooning at the University of Akron and KSU from 1976 to 1987.

**Regina Brett** is the New York Times bestselling author of "God Never Blinks: 50 Lessons for Life's Little Detours," which has been translated into 20 languages. She is also the author of "Be the Miracle: 50 Lessons for Making the Impossible Possible" and "God Is Always Hiring: 50 Lessons for Finding Fulfilling Work." Brett earned a Bachelor of Science degree in journalism from Kent State University and a Master of Arts degree in Religious Studies from John Carroll University in Cleveland. She joined the Beacon Journal as a reporter in 1986, leaving in 2000 for The Plain Dealer, Ohio's largest newspaper, and was twice named a Pulitzer Prize finalist for columns she wrote there. She also won a Silver Gavel for columns on the Cuyahoga County justice system's refusal to hand over information to defense lawyers. She is a columnist for the Cleveland Jewish News. Her website is www.reginabrett.com.

**Katie Byard** joined the Akron Beacon Journal after graduating with a degree in journalism from Ohio State University. She grew up in Columbus and Toledo, Ohio. As a business writer, she helped with daily coverage of the attempted takeover of Goodyear Tire and Rubber Co., which won a Pulitzer Prize in 1986. She also covered labor, downtown Akron development and more. Most of her career has been spent on the metro desk, where she has covered K-12 education, higher education, suburban communities and has served as a general assignment writer. She retired in 2020 but continues to write a column on the local food scene, which she has covered since 2014. She has won awards for feature and enterprise stories, as well as breaking news. She is married to retired Beacon Journal reporter James Carney and has three stepsons, four grandchildren and one miniature schnauzer.

**James Carney** is a retired reporter and former broadcast journalist. He grew up in Akron, graduating from Firestone High School and the University of Akron. He worked at radio stations in Ironton and Toledo before joining the news staff at WHLO AM 640 in 1974. He left there as news director in 1979 to join the Beacon Journal. He covered a variety of topics while at the Beacon Journal, including environment, religion, non-profits, Summit County government, suburban communities, features and local military issues and retired in 2014. He conducted interviews for the award-winning yearlong series Wheels of Fortune, was part of the news staff covering the community impact of the attempted takeover of Goodyear and won a statewide award for feature writing. He is the father of three adult sons, Will, Patrick and Michael Carney and is married to longtime Beacon reporter Katie Byard.

**Jim Crutchfield** was the Akron Beacon Journal and Ohio.com president and publisher from 2001 to 2006. He started in journalism as a reporter for The Pittsburgh Press in 1968. After three years, he worked as public information officer for the Pittsburgh Model Cities Program briefly before joining the Pittsburgh Post-Gazette as a reporter for four years. In 1976-79, he was a Detroit Free Press reporter. He was press secretary for U.S. Sen. Carl Levin of Michigan in 1979-81, returning to the Free Press as state capital bureau chief in 1981-83. For the next six years, he worked in a series of editing positions at the Free Press. In 1989-93, he was the Beacon Journal managing editor. He went to Long Beach, Calif., in 1993 as senior vice president and executive editor of the Press-Telegram. In 1998-99, he was assistant to the publisher and single copy sales director for Philadelphia Newspapers Inc., returning to Akron as general manager and promoted to publisher the following year. Crutchfield was the inaugural visiting professor in journalism ethics at Arizona State University's Walter Cronkite School of Journalism and Mass Communication and then ASU's student media director in 2007-08. He was on the Duquesne University journalism faculty from 2008 to 2012.

**Michael Douglas**, a Seattle native, came to Akron in late 1983 to work as an editorial writer for the Akron Beacon Journal. He moved to the newsroom in 1989, covering Portage County, and then returned to the editorial page two years later to work as the chief editorial writer. He became the editorial page editor in 1999 until his retirement in September 2019. He has served on the board of Akron Roundtable, Leadership Akron, the Sir Thomas More Award committee and the First Tee of Akron. He also was a member of the Akron Children's Hospital Community Benefits Advisory Committee. He is a graduate of Georgetown University. He resides in Akron with his wife. They have one daughter.

**Bob Downing** was widely known as one of the best and most experienced environmental reporters in Ohio, a beat he covered from 1990 to 2016. His beat coverage included parks, transportation, science, public health and shale drilling. He started full time at the Beacon Journal in 1972, holding several posts before taking over the environmental beat. Downing won several Best Environmental Coverage awards from the Ohio Society for Professional Journalists. He and reporter Margaret Newkirk were runners-up in 2001 for the national John B. Oakes Award for Distinguished Environmental Coverage for a four-part series on Ohio's coal-burning power plants. He wrote "Whale Rock: The New and the Gauley" and a chapter with Russ Musarra in "Canal Fever: The Ohio and Erie Canal from Waterway to Canalway." In retirement, Bob is working part time covering North America energy including shale drilling for Kallanish Energy, a London-based media company.

**Bob Dyer** has served as a feature writer, radio/TV writer, investigative reporter and general-interest columnist since joining the Beacon Journal in 1984. Dyer's stories and columns have won 81 regional and national awards. In 2008, the National Society of Professional Journalists voted him Best Columnist in the Nation. In 2013, the National Society of Newspaper Columnists named him Best Humor Columnist in the Nation. The College of Wooster graduate has been named Best Columnist in Ohio 11 times. The Cleveland native also was one of the lead writers for *A Question of Color*, a yearlong examination of racial attitudes in Akron that won a Pulitzer Prize in 1994. In addition, he has written three books. One of them, "Omar! My Life On and Off the Field," an autobiography co-written with Cleveland Indians baseball star Omar Vizquel, spent four weeks on the New York Times bestseller list in 2002. In 2015, Dyer was inducted into the Cleveland Journalism Hall of Fame.

**Mary Ethridge** is a freelance writer living in Akron. After graduating from Princeton University with a degree in English literature, Ethridge began her career at the University of Akron where she served as director of editorial projects. She joined the Beacon Journal as an environmental reporter in 1988. That year, she was one of four reporters who worked on a series on climate change that won a journalism prize from the United Nations. She went on to report for the business section and wrote a weekly column on retail that remained a reader favorite for years. Her series on the expansion of Walmart and other big-box retailers won awards from the Cleveland Chapter of the Society of Professional Journalists and the Associated Press of Ohio. A series written by Ethridge and food writer Jane Snow on mad cow disease won an award for best science reporting from the Ohio SPJ. After leaving the Beacon Journal, Ethridge went on to write for trade publications, web sites and community magazines. She is currently writing a novel.

**Bob Fernandez** has won numerous awards covering economic enterprise and general assignment on the business news desk at The Philadelphia Inquirer. As a national telecom and media reporter, Fernandez covered Comcast Corp., NBC, sports media, the Federal Communications Commission and broadband. Fernandez has published two investigations into financial abuse and the systemic lack of accountability at the $16 billion Milton Hershey School and Trust for impoverished children — one of the world's richest charities that controls the Hershey Co. candy giant and owns Hersheypark. In 2015, Fernandez published a book on the scandalized institution, "The Chocolate Trust." In 2019, The Inquirer and the Reporters Committee for Freedom of the Press in Washington jointly filed to unseal court records in federal lawsuits claiming negligent child care at the free, vastly under-enrolled, 2,000-student boarding school. Fernandez started at the Beacon Journal as an intern out of Ohio Wesleyan University in 1987 and remained as a business reporter until leaving for Philadelphia in 1993. Bob lives in Yardley, Pa., with his wife, Mae, who was raised in Doylestown, Ohio. He has three sons, Zack, Luke and Seth.

**Kathy Fraze**, a graduate of Bowling Green State University, joined the Beacon Journal as a reporter in 1973. Over the next 39 years, she held many writing and editing positions, including metro editor and assistant managing editor for features. She retired in 2012 after her second tour as copy desk chief. In between her job at the Beacon and many semesters as a copy editing instructor at Kent State University, she began writing police detective novels. Her ninth, "Final Fling," was published in 2018. Since retirement, she has been a volunteer in the Cuyahoga Valley National Park and a copy editor for local attorneys. In 2018, she went back to school and was certified through the University of Akron as a paralegal. She and fellow Beacon retiree Mike Needs live in Akron, where Lottie, the German shepherd, keeps them in line.

**Glenn Gamboa** is an award-winning journalist based in Brooklyn, N.Y. A native of Cleveland, he led the Newsday project about the impact of hip-hop on America that was a finalist for the Pulitzer Prize in explanatory reporting. As Newsday's music critic for nearly two decades, Gamboa interviewed everyone from Beyoncé and Jay-Z to Barbra Streisand and Billy Joel and covered numerous Rock and Roll Hall of Fame inductions and music festivals from London to Austin, Texas. His pop culture coverage has also appeared in Wired, Spin and CNN, as well as Alternative Press and Cleveland Scene in Northeast Ohio. As an industry expert, he has appeared on the BBC, NPR and several TV and radio stations, and is quoted in USA Today and other publications. Gamboa worked at the Beacon Journal from 1993 to 2000, covering health care reform, the tire industry and technology, as well as pop music. He launched the Beacon Journal's Net Rider column, which was one of the nation's first weekly columns on Internet culture.

**Michael Good** was director of photography at the Beacon Journal from 1990 to 1998 and supervised the editing of the photos for A Question of Color/Coming Together, which won the Pulitzer Gold Medal for Public Service in 1998. The jurors specifically cited photos and graphics as playing a key role in the success of the series. Previously Michael worked as a special assignment photographer at the Beacon and director of photography at the Rocky Mountain News in Denver, the Washington (D.C) Times and the Journal-American in Bellevue, Wash., where he also served as photo editor of the book "Volcano, the Eruption of Mount St. Helens," which sold 300,000 copies. Michael was selected Ohio Photographer of the Year in 1973, when he worked for The Journal in Lorain. After leaving Akron, he and his wife, Sally, moved to the Pacific Northwest, where he ran Michael Good Photography LLC for 18 years.

**Art Krummel** spent nearly 40 years at the Beacon Journal as an illustrator, graphic designer, art director and technology guru. After working as a copyboy and later in purchasing and billing at Portage Newspaper Supply, Krummel was hired as an artist in 1967. He is a graduate of the University of Akron with a degree in fine and applied arts. During his years as art director, he designed the faces of two packages awarded Pulitzers to the Beacon Journal. Krummel's interest in the computer and its potential as a tool to produce the newspaper pulled him deeper into digital technology in later years. He represented the newsroom as the newspaper transitioned to digital and full-color reproduction. The Beacon was the first Knight Ridder newspaper to be fully digitized. He retired in 2001 and later worked with young reporters at the University of Akron's student paper, the Buchtelite. Krummel and his wife, retired journalist Charlene Nevada, raised their family in Tallmadge and still live there.

**Steve Love** changed newspapers almost as often as underwear before he arrived at his third Knight Ridder newspaper, the Beacon Journal, in 1981 and learned a neat trick: He could change jobs at the same paper, provided he whined enough. This benefited all concerned. He won numerous local, state, and national writing awards, including contributions to two Pulitzer Prizes, one for a segment of A Question of Color, the other for a small story and a large important contact (Gaylon White) who offered a unique inside view of The Goodyear War. Love also wrote or co-wrote five nonfiction books: "The Golden Dream" about football coach Gerry Faust, "Wheels of Fortune: The Story of Rubber in Akron," "Stan Hywet Hall & Gardens," "The Holden Arboretum" and the biography of a larger-than-life Akron institution "The Indomitable Don Plusquellic: How A Controversial Mayor Quarterbacked Akron's Comeback." He finished his sixth book, "Football, Fast Friends, and Small Towns," personal essays about friends and football in Oklahoma.

**Ann Sheldon Mezger** joined the Beacon Journal in 1972 as a reporter and three years later moved to the copy desk. In 1978 she became lifestyle editor, followed by stints as suburban editor, Beacon magazine editor, deputy features editor, features editor, deputy metro editor and metro editor. She was the project editor for "Of Loss and Learning," which marked the 20th anniversary of the Kent State shootings and was named Ohio newspapers' Best Special Section for 2000 by the state's chapters of the Society of Professional Journalists. She accepted a buyout offer in 2008, one of 18 newsroom employees to do so that year. She and her husband, Roger, live in Akron and have two sons.

**Roger Mezger** was a reporter and an editor at the Akron Beacon Journal from 1972 to 2000 and at the Plain Dealer in Cleveland from 2000 to 2010, earning awards from the Society of Professional Journalists, the Press Club of Cleveland, the Association of Black Journalists, the Society of American Business Editors and Writers, and the Society for News Design. He served as secretary and executive board member of The Newspaper Guild Local 7 in Akron. A graduate of Ohio State and Kent State universities, he wrote a 1981 master's thesis titled, "The American Newspaper Guild in Ohio, 1933-1938: Forefront of a National Movement."

**Charlene Nevada** always wanted to work for a tabloid newspaper but wound up making the Akron Beacon Journal her home. Her goal was always to write stories that people WANTED to read, as opposed to what they felt they HAD to read. She was born in Wheeling, W. Va., and raised on the Ohio side of the Ohio River in Bridgeport. She is a graduate of Ohio University and joined the Beacon Journal's Action Line staff in 1970. She retired as the deputy metro/city editor in 2005. In between she handled various reporting assignments including county government, City Hall, the courthouse and the labor beat. She spent two years as the paper's food writer. She currently spends part of the year explaining and signing up seniors for Medicare insurance plans and volunteers as a grant writer for an Akron food pantry. She and her husband, retired Beacon Journal artist and graphic designer Art Krummel, live in Tallmadge.

**Bill O'Connor** was born in Philadelphia in 1941, the son of a Philadelphia fireman and a full-time homemaker. He graduated from St. Francis Preparatory School in 1959, and St. Francis University in 1964 with a Bachelor of Arts in Philosophy and English. In 1965-66, he was a part-time instructor of writing at Bowling Green State University, where he earned a Master of Arts in English. He was an assistant professor at Northern Montana College from 1966 to 1969, and its dean of students from 1969 to 1973. He was a reporter and columnist for The Steubenville Herald Star from 1976 to 1979. He joined the Akron Beacon Journal in 1979 and held various positions including general assignment reporter, movie and theater critic, and Side Roads/Side Streets columnist before retiring in 1998. He is the author of four novels: "Bums and Hershey Bars," "The Legend of Horn Mountain," "The Era of Long Thoughts," and "St. Leo." In 1965 he married Jacquelyne Tarr. They are the parents of four children and six grandchildren. In 2002 he married Elsbeth Stuber Fritz. He and Elsbeth live in Bath.

**Laura Ofobike** joined the editorial department of the Akron Beacon Journal as commentary editor in 1989 from the Wichita (Kansas) Eagle-Beacon. She retired from the Beacon Journal as chief editorial writer in 2014. As an editorial writer, Ofobike's primary interests were K-12 education, health care and social issues. Ofobike holds a Ph.D. in telecommunications and film from the University of Oregon and master's degrees in theater arts and English literature from the University of Leeds, England, and the University of Ghana. Before relocating to the United States, Ofobike taught at the University of Cape Coast and the University of Nigeria, Nsukka. She was also a principal research officer at the Nigerian Television Authority in Enugu, Nigeria. Ofobike lives in Akron with her husband and volunteers with a number of local nonprofit organizations.

**Marla Ridenour** became a professional sportswriter on Dec. 26, 1976, when her first boss at the Lexington Herald-Leader told her of course she could have Christmas off. A Louisville, Ky., native and a 1978 graduate of Eastern Kentucky University with degrees in journalism and marketing, Ridenour was inducted into the Kentucky Journalism Hall of Fame in 2013 and received the professional achievement award from the EKU Alumni Association in 2019. She was also the first woman sports editor of the Eastern Progress. While with the Dayton Daily News, Ridenour became the first woman to cover the Cleveland Browns in 1981, before the NFL mandated teams must open their locker rooms to females, and that remained her primary beat. Ridenour also worked for the Columbus Dispatch and Akron Beacon Journal, including serving as its sports columnist. Ridenour received writing awards from the Associated Press Sports Editors, the Pro Football Writers, the Golf Writers Association of America, the Ohio AP Sports Editors, the Ohio Society of Professional Journalists and the Press Club of Cleveland.

**Tim Smith** is a mostly retired criminal defense lawyer, living with his wife of 53 years on a private lake outside Kent State University, where he taught reporting and media law classes for 30 years. Before that, he worked at the Beacon Journal for nearly 20 years, leaving as managing editor in 1986 to join the School of Journalism and Mass Communication faculty. He has bachelor's and master's degrees in journalism from THE Ohio State University and a law degree from the University of Akron. In 1991 he took a leave to clerk for Ohio Supreme Court Justice Craig Wright. Later that year, he was named acting director of the journalism school, a post he held until June 1994, when he returned to teaching. In the fall of 2003, Smith took a sabbatical to work in the Portage County Public Defender's office, representing indigent clients in municipal and common pleas courts. He enjoyed that so much that, after retiring from KSU, he was appointed the Public Defender in 2017-2018.

**Jane Snow** was the food writer and restaurant critic of the Beacon Journal for more than two decades until her retirement in 2006. During her career she won many national and state writing awards including two James Beard Awards and a Penney-Missouri Award, and her Food section was named best in the country in its circulation division twice. She is past president of the Association of Food Journalists, an organization for food writers and editors across North America. In her parallel life, Snow was president of Local 7 of The Newspaper Guild (now The NewsGuild) for six years, leading contract negotiations for her fellow reporters and editors, and served on the union's national board of directors. In retirement she writes a weekly Internet food newsletter, See Jane Cook, and is author of a cookbook, "Jane Snow Cooks." She lives in Copley with her husband, Tony Kawaguchi, a sushi chef.

**Thrity Umrigar**, a recipient of the Nieman fellowship to Harvard, has written for the New York Times, the Washington Post and the Boston Globe. She was named a Distinguished University Professor of English at Case Western Reserve University. Her novels, including "The Space Between Us," The World We Found," "The Weight of Heaven" and "The Story Hour" have received international critical acclaim. She joined the Beacon Journal in 1987 after graduating from Ohio State University and working at the Lorain Morning Journal. She left for a teaching post at Case Western in 2002. She also has won the Cleveland Arts Prize.

**Deb Van Tassel Warner** enrolled in a pre-law program at Seton Hall University but after working her freshman summer at the local newspaper in Woodbridge, N.J., made an abrupt U-turn to journalism studies. She joined the Beacon Journal in 1982 and held various editing positions, including supervising local coverage of the attempted takeover of Goodyear Tire and Rubber Co. and as news editor for A Question of Color, two of the paper's Pulitzer Prize winning initiatives. As business editor of the Seattle Times from 1993 to 1995, her staff won awards from the Society of Business Editors and Writers. She returned to the Beacon in 1995 as an enterprise editor directing the award-winning series and book, "Wheels of Fortune," about Akron's rubber industry, and relaunched the newspaper's popular Sunday Beacon Magazine. She joined The Plain Dealer in 1999 and oversaw award-winning coverage of the collapse and rebirth of Cleveland's steel industry and edited the acclaimed special report "Beyond Rape" by Joanna Connors. In 2013 she left Northeast Ohio for the Valley of the Sun to be features editor at the Arizona Republic, retiring in 2017. She and her husband, Stuart Warner, couldn't talk "Baby Corner" out of a journalism career. Denise Warner Schaefer has written and edited for aol.com, Hollywood Life, Entertainment Weekly and billboard.com. She and Stuart live in Brooklyn, N.Y., with their rescue dog Panther.

**Stuart Warner** is best known in Akron for writing a local column called Warner's Corner and for his solos at TubaChristmas. At the Beacon, he also served as executive sports editor, religion writer, assistant managing editor/features, assistant managing editor/region, deputy managing editor/news, deputy managing editor/operations, associate managing editor and interim managing editor. He was part of the teams that won Pulitzers for covering the attempted takeover of Goodyear and race relations in Akron. As writing coach at The Plain Dealer in Cleveland he edited four Pulitzer finalists, including Connie Schultz's columns that won the Pulitzer for commentary. He also worked at numerous news organizations that have closed, including the Lexington Leader, the Rocky Mountain News, the Seattle Post-Intelligencer, AOL News and The Daily. We are assigning no blame. He retired in 2019 as editor in chief of Phoenix New Times, where for the first time he wrote the f-word in a headline.

**Mark Williamson** was unceremoniously dismissed as news director and anchor at WAKC-TV Channel 23 in 1996, which might have been a blessing in disguise. Now, 23 years later — oddly enough — he has invested as much time working for government and public schools as he had in broadcasting. When Williamson worked as City Hall communications director for Mayor Don Plusquellic, he had a front-row seat to some of the most exciting developments to come to Akron in decades as Plusquellic invested aggressively in its future. Working for Akron Public Schools now in a similar capacity gave Williamson another chance to use his journalism skills in communicating the important news about our children, education, teachers and more. While he sees colleagues from his three careers retiring at a younger age than his, Williamson still enjoys the hectic world of news and information. He mourns, however, the escalation of the purposely misleading publishing and broadcasting of words masquerading as news.

**Bruce Winges** held a number of management position during his 37 years at the Beacon Journal, which included almost 12 years as the paper's editor. He retired on March 1, 2019, almost a year after the paper was purchased by GateHouse Media. The University of Kentucky graduate joined the Beacon in 1982 after working at the Huntington (W.Va.) Herald-Dispatch. Before becoming vice president and editor of the Beacon in 2007, Winges was deputy managing editor, executive news editor, assistant manager for technology and night managing editor. As executive news editor, he supervised the design of The Goodyear War, which was a key part of the newspaper's Pulitzer Prize-winning package in 1987. Winges led the newsroom through several rounds of downsizing, but managed to keep quality high despite the reduced staff. From 2007 to 2017, the Beacon Journal won more than 250 first-place awards from the Associated Press, Press Club of Cleveland and Ohio Society of Professional Journalists, among others. "We have told the story of Akron well and will continue to do so in the future," Winges said on his retirement.